# Digital Developments

A volume in
*Unifying Science, Culture, and Society*
Dominik Stefan Mihalits, Brady Wagoner, and Jaan Valsiner, *Series Editors*

**Unifying Science, Culture, and Society**

Dominik Stefan Mihalits, Brady Wagoner,
and Jaan Valsiner, *Series Editors*

*University in the 21st Century* (2023)
Lisa-Marie Geberth and Lisa-Teresa Woller

*Farewell to Variables* (2023)
Jaan Valsiner

# Digital Developments

## Perspectives in Psychology

*edited by*

**Dominik Stefan Mihalits**
*Sigmund Freud University*

**Greta Riboli**
*Sigmund Freud University*

**Regina Gregori Grgič**
*Sigmund Freud University*

IAP

INFORMATION AGE PUBLISHING, INC.
Charlotte, NC • www.infoagepub.com

**Library of Congress Cataloging-in-Publication Data**

A CIP record for this book is available from the Library of Congress
http://www.loc.gov

ISBN: 979-8-88730-592-9 (Paperback)
979-8-88730-593-6 (Hardcover)
979-8-88730-594-3 (E-Book)



Printed in the United States of America

# CONTENTS

# SECTION III

## VIRTUAL REALITY



# SECTION IV

## ROBOTICS AND ARTIFICIAL INTELLIGENCE



# SECTION V

## SOCIAL MEDIA

# PREFACE

The new technological developments and the quick evolution of the digital world have an impact on each aspect of our lives. All the professional activities, psychology included, are facing a continuous transformation and technological update. This book represents an overview on the intersection between psychology and the digital world. Digital psychology, also known as cyberpsychology, is a discipline that studies the way and to what extent our behaviors and our psychological conditions are influenced by the new media, considering the impact of new technologies on users, from the latest mobile devices and gaming systems to high-end virtual reality equipment. Furthermore, digital psychology analyzes the way technologies can be utilized to complete and integrate the humans' potentials and weaknesses.

Why is it necessary that today's psychologists, not only the future ones, become familiar with new technologies and their effects? The first reason is that it's important to deal properly with new generations and to catch the new types of psychological distress related to the use of technologies. Moreover, many digital tools can be useful in order to treat the distress in a more efficient way (by increasing the patient's compliance and engagement). Finally, integrating technologies in clinical practice—providing evidence-based therapies—allows them to stand out inside a competitive market. Digital psychology is therefore an essential area of expertise for anyone who wishes to make the most of online technologies for clinical, educational, organizational or other purposes.

Digital and technological development open a new series of cultural changes and issues to explore in the field of clinical and applied psychology.

*Digital Developments*, pages vii–ix

Firstly, society is increasingly influenced by the overcoming of space–time limits: involving new ways of generating groups, conflicts, and personal psychological structuring. Secondly, the advent of new forms of communication and new tools has generated an increase in new forms of addiction, which in addition to being studied in clinical psychology, also became a focus of psychotherapeutic treatments. Thirdly, people who come to the attention of psychologists today, shape their functioning and their identity through the social media; therapy itself, remains abreast, offering a social and digital solution to the clinical problems reported. Finally, the aim of psychology is, therefore, to make the new media and tools serious and educational, supporting theoretical foundations and appropriate research-based lines of development for the shift from analogical to digital worlds. To address these issues the international authors in this book provide a multitude of possible scenarios for the future development of a digital and technological society.

This volume addresses how state of the art digital technologies can interact with psychological science. Research, education, teaching, training, diagnosis, rehabilitation and therapy is facing a series of changes dictated by the establishment of the digital and technological world in everyday life. Different types of instruments modify psychological practice and, on a larger scale, may have an impact on the cultural framework that defines and conceptualizes psychological phenomena and how to deal with them.

The book is divided into five major thematic areas: (a) the world of e-therapy and mental health digital applications, (b) the role of video games in clinical psychology, (c) virtual reality, (d) robotics and artificial intelligence, and (e) social media. Each area is explored through chapters produced from a team of researchers that met in Milan in 2021 for a conference about digital developments in the field of psychology (i.e., the first European Conference on Digital Psychology, organized by the Sigmund Freud University branch in Milan).

Each chapter comprises a main subchapter dealing with the clinical implication of the specific technology addressed in the section. Since many digital tools illustrated can be new to the reader and/or their use in such a different context from daily life can be hard to visualize, some chapters offer an additional subchapter presenting which technologies exist and how they can be utilized proficiently in clinical practice. The section dealing with robotics also provides a supplementary subchapter highlighting how this technology can, and should, be used with children, since the noteworthy developmental implications on the social skills of this growing population when interacting with human-like robots since their first years of life.

Every subchapter presents the state of the art, potential benefits, potential risks and future directions of the use of each technology in the field of psychology.

This book offers new insights and knowledge to students of psychology and to those psychologists who want to embrace technologies and exploit new technological tools in clinical and/or educational practice, being aware of the behavioral and psychological consequences of the use of technologies in treatment, but also in everyday life. Indeed, this volume examines the digital world and its impact on human behavior such as potential new developments for applied clinical psychology that could include applications of computer sciences, virtual reality, and artificial intelligence.

**—Regina Gregori Grgič**
**Gabriele Caselli**

# SECTION I

## E-THERAPY

CHAPTER 1

# THE WORLD OF E-THERAPY AND MENTAL HEALTH DIGITAL APPLICATIONS

**Enrica Gaetano**
*Sigmund Freud University, Milan*

## THE STATE OF THE ART IN E-THERAPY: FROM COMPUTER AND ONLINE-BASED INTERVENTIONS IN COGNITIVE BEHAVIORAL THERAPY TO MOBILE THERAPY AND SMARTPHONE MENTAL HEALTH APPLICATION

In 2020, the COVID-19 pandemic forced the mental healthcare community to connect with clients online and psychologists and psychotherapists to quickly adapt to the circumstances transforming their clinical practice. However, the phenomenon of *e-therapy* or *e-health* is not recent because it has grown over the past 2 decades, and its technology and infrastructure have been available since the mid-1990s.

Speaking about e-therapy or e-health, we referred to all clinical telehealth activities delivered through the Internet (McLendon, 2000) between mental health professionals and clients. This term is included in the more general nomenclature of *online clinical practice,* which refers to the use

*Digital Developments,* pages 3–16

of *psychotechnologies* to deliver therapeutic dialogue or interventions at a distance (Maheu et al., 2004). The adoption of technology or psychotechnology within the field of mental health care has grown to provide a bridge for continuity of care when the client or the practitioner is unavailable for an in-person consultation, and it uses many different kinds of digital devices such as laptop computers, mobile phones and videoconferencing, or web-based platforms.

Psychotechnology or digital mental health interventions (DMHI) are typically based on psychological treatments that have demonstrated efficacy and effectiveness in traditional and face-to-face mental health care and flexibility in online settings such as cognitive behavioral therapy (CBT) and psychodynamic therapy (PDT). Compared to other types of psychological interventions, PDT and CBT delivered online or by computer demonstrated better adaptability in untraditional and remote settings because they have some similar characteristics during sessions such as weekly psycho-educational modules, homework assignments and e-mail support from therapists. These specific characteristics of the interventions made them more suitable and appropriate for a digital context than others and more suitable to study as rationales for developing DMHIs (Lattie et al., 2022). However, compared to other iPDT programs, CBT delivered through computers (cCBT) or Internet (iCBT) has been demonstrated to be as effective as face-to-face CBT for depression and anxiety. In line with abundant evidence from randomized control trials, they showed more substantial effect sizes than those found in a meta-analysis of iPDT programs (Olthuis et al., 2016). These findings in the disparity between cCBT–iCBT and iPDT effectiveness and the small number of studies on iPDT contribute to selecting CBT as the principal framework used in developing DMHI (Lattie et al., 2022).

Before the spread of Internet and online programs, the first example of how psychotechnology started to be included in clinical practices was cCBT. This kind of online psychological treatment program was initially provided to manage depressive symptoms, stress, or anxiety using CBT modules in which clients, at their places, interact with computer software—either on a PC or sometimes via a voice-activated phone service—instead of face-to-face interactions with the therapist (Maheu et al., 2004). Initially, cCBT consisted in delivering some modules to clients with audio or video information about mental health symptoms and practice strategies to tackle unhelpful thoughts, behaviors, and physical feelings associated with difficult emotions. Furthermore, these computerized modules provided different types of self-help homework to increase awareness and monitor their moods and dysfunctional thoughts or behaviors over time. Through CD-ROM and other systems such as the *interactive voice response* (IVT)—an automated telephonic technology that allowed clients to report symptoms, quality of life, and their general functioning—people received help and feedback.

Given these advantages, cCBT was focused initially on the treatment of anxiety and depression because it was able to provide self-help and guided self-help interventions that included general educational information and skills for preventing dysfunctional health-related behaviors or promoting positive health. These interventions consist of cognitive and behavioral activities and strategies that clients could learn and use in their everyday life to deal with and prevent their difficulties (i.e., relaxation training, systematic desensitization, and restructuring negative thoughts; Maheu et al., 2004). This type of intervention that specifically selected elements of the CBT therapeutic process (psychoeducation about the disease and cognitive techniques and behaviors and thoughts modification strategies) provided enormous benefits because it offered accessibility, affordability, acceptability, adaptability, and in some cases, even anonymity (Maheu et al., 2004).

With cCBT, psychotechnology started to show its benefits (a) in reaching people with severe social or emotional problems who received no treatment at all and (b) in reducing the burdens associated with geographic distances and economic costs (Mohr et al., 2006). Moreover, the computerization of CBT therapy offered not only enhanced accessibility but also improved cost-effectiveness because it reduced clients' travel and increased access to quality specialist care. It also improved public knowledge about mental health, reducing the stigmatization or the embarrassment of mental or psychiatric problems and fostering the adaptation of flexibility to the unique needs of groups worldwide. There were significant improvements in clients' health outcomes thanks to self-management care. However, computerized-based programs did not provide the presence of a therapist on the other side; therefore, to reduce these limitations and with the widespread availability of the Internet, in the nineties, an iCBT was delivered (Olthuis et al., 2016). This approach is similar to cCBT because it involves the client following a written treatment program, but, in this case, it is available on the Internet and provided in conjunction with the therapist's support, either via texts or email (Andersson & Cuijpers, 2009). iCBT provided a valid option for patients who usually would be reluctant to seek mental health services or have economic problems or geographic difficulties in accessing therapy. Therefore, the internet communication formats provided additional availability in receiving guided help, especially in cases where therapists were not always available (Olthuis et al., 2016).

Although iCBT showed more advantages, such as guided interventions and human support within DHMIs, compared to cCBT, iCBT requires significant resources and time (Lattie et al., 2022), and for this reason, there has been growing attention to design and study conversational agents, or chatbots, to simulate human support (Miner et al., 2017). More specifically, chatbots can reduce costs because they reduce reliance on humans and increase the opportunity to provide immediate support by responding to users at any time and immediately after users' messages (Lattie et al., 2022).

The first and most famous example of computerized therapy was ELIZA, a program that responded to a natural written language and simulated a client-centred therapist. ELIZA was developed by Joseph Weizenbaum, a researcher at the Massachusetts Institute of Technology, in 1966 (Weizenbaum, 1966) and simplistically emulated a Rogersian therapist. It responded to clients' words by merely forming questions and affirmations from words used by clients. Find below a typical ELIZA dialogue adapted by Maheu et al. (2004):

**ELIZA:** How do you do? Please state your problem.
**Patient:** Men are all alike.
**ELIZA:** Would you like it if they were not all alike?
**Patient:** No, I guess not. But my husband is a real nerd.
**ELIZA:** Your husband is a real nerd?
**Patient:** Yes, he's constantly sitting at his computer and doesn't seem to care about me anymore.
**ELIZA:** Do computers worry you?
**Patient:** No, but my husband should pay more attention to me.
**ELIZA:** Your husband should pay more attention to you?
**Patient:** Well, I'd like to go out with him more.
**ELIZA:** Please go on.
**Patient:** At the time we married, we were always doing a lot of great stuff together, and now things have changed.
**ELIZA:** Can you think of a specific example?
**Patient:** For example, we used to go hiking together almost every weekend.
**ELIZA:** What does that suggest to you?
**Patient:** Maybe my husband doesn't love me anymore.
**ELIZA:** You don't seem quite certain.
**Patient:** Well, he sometimes tells me he loves me, but I think he's lying.
**ELIZA:** Please go on.

Although ELIZA facilitated the opening of some users counteracting their perceived sense of judgment, Weinbaum's attempt to simulate an actual face-to-face session and a nondirective therapist had raised questions about ELIZA's capacities to face the ambiguity, complexity, idiosyncrasy, emotional connotation, and social context of natural language occurring in the psychotherapeutic process (Maheu et al., 2004). Although ELIZA offered some benefits in enhancing accessibility to health care and reducing social stigma, geographical distance and clients' financial limitations, it failed to develop personalized suggestions for dealing with problems the user raises and to recreate clients' active involvement in sessions. Indeed, many subsequent studies underlined the passivity of this type of computerized program and the risk of client alienation without specific therapeutic support and synchronous communications between the client and the therapist (Maheu et al., 2004). The adoption of conversational agents like ELIZA in mental health care has been upgraded over time to popular smartphone-based digital assistants (e.g., Siri on iPhone). However, the risks of ineffective care and patient harm are still real because, in some cases, their responses might be unrelated, inconsistent, and inappropriate, especially when people disclose high-risk behaviors, such as nonsuicidal self-injury or suicidality (Miner et al., 2017).

In the last 2 decades, mobile technologies and text messaging services were developed to improve health system efficiency and mental health problems to overcome interventions based on computerized asynchronous communication and reduced therapist availability. These programs improve access to and the use of care services and also provide the opportunity to connect patients and therapists in real time through live chats or digital applications (Dülsen et al., 2020).

The first mobile software applications were downloaded on a mobile device in 2008. Since then, an estimated 1,520,000 apps have been developed for mobile devices; nowadays, around 6 % targeted mental health outcomes such as depression and anxiety, substance abuse, sleep disturbances, suicidal behavior, self-harm, gambling, and psychotic symptoms (Donker et al., 2013). As opposed to computer-based programs, they have considerable advantages for clinicians as well as for clients thanks to (a) their convenience (treatment programs and activities can take place anywhere and anytime), (b) their anonymity (clients can seek treatment options without involving other people), and (c) their lower cost (some apps are free or cost less than traditional care).

In addition, they can represent a good starting point and an introduction to therapy for those who are reluctant or have avoided it because they might appear more appealing and focused on their care needs (Dülsen et al., 2020). Thanks to their technology, innovation, cost-effectiveness, and more friendly user experience, they might encourage clients to start or be more involved in continuing the treatment process. From a clinical point of view, possible implementations of mobile applications are extended to support specific steps of the clinical process from access, assessment, monitoring progress or relapses to follow-up, increasing the understanding of the intensity of symptomatology's course over time and patients' mental well-being (Castelnuovo et al., 2003). Moreover, these tools can support clinicians in collecting information about the therapeutical programs' effectiveness allowing patients' therapy monitoring during treatment. However, over 10,000 apps target mental health conditions and offer a massive range of possibilities (e.g., clients' symptoms monitoring, therapy-inspired homework, psychoeducation) in multiple formats. The most popular areas of apps for mental health include (a) self-management apps, (b) apps for improving thinking skills, skill-training apps, (c) apps for illness management with supported care, and finally, (d) apps for passive symptom tracking with sensors built into smartphones (National Institute of Mental Health, 2023). For these reasons, it could be challenging for clients to stay updated and select those applications that might be more useful and effective for their care demands without specific professional information about apps' appropriateness, usefulness, and usability.

## THE POTENTIAL BENEFITS OF E-THERAPY AND DIGITAL MENTAL HEALTH INTERVENTIONS: THE BLENDED CARE SOLUTION

Although there are many advantages of online treatment and interventions provided, a qualitative study by Johansson and colleagues (2015) highlighted that CBT interventions or applications exclusively proposed through the Internet failed to promote patients' adherence to treatment. The authors showed that these interventions fail to investigate the patient's perceptions and prior expectations about the treatment process, providing standardized and insufficient information without answering the patients' unique needs. Furthermore, they were considered excessively inflexible and demanding regarding reading and writing skills. The value of the study results is in stressing the significance of providing patients with detailed information about Internet-delivered treatment to generate more accurate expectations and greater adherence. Indeed, most of the study's participants reported a lack of information about the rationale behind the application of technology during the treatment processes and the rigidity of these digital tools that do not offer face-to-face contact with therapists. Indeed, some participants perceived that the therapists did not care about their issues and, in some cases, the therapist is considered only a person who checks participants' text modules and exercises (Johansson et al., 2015). These new tools and apps can offer resources which make therapeutic techniques accessible, portable and cost-effective for clients, but their application might have unsuccessful outcomes if people are not instructed to use them correctly or without a therapist's guide or presence. Therefore, a new way of integrating technologies and face-to-face contact with therapists is needed (Wentzel et al., 2016).

*Blended* care digital solutions have the promising opportunity to be guided by clinicians, therapists, or care providers and integrate the advantages of online and offline clinical interventions (Wentzel et al., 2016). In particular, blended treatments or care are described as "technology-supported care" that offers synchronous or asynchronous guidance, support via online guidance or self-help modules, and personal or automated feedback. Moreover, it provides support to patients from therapists because they are actively involved and can consistently guide the two modalities (Wentzel et al., 2016). Blended treatments integrate the benefits of both online and offline components because they allow effective use of technology within the treatment and are suitable for patients' difficulties and needs. By integrating both approaches, patients and clinicians have the best of both dimensions, offering (a) low-cost web-based interventions that also allow better clients' organization of sessions; (b) more supportive clinical online activities that extend in-person agenda sessions, and clients can use that in times of sudden need; and (c) more increased patient's sense of ownership and a more potent therapeutic alliance of in-person treatment (Kip et al., 2020). However, there is still no consensus about which face-to-face components or online modules can be replaced by the other modality or what specific population of patients might benefit from blended interventions. Questions like "What works for whom, and in what blend?" need to be answered.

Furthermore, among therapists, there is still a lack of knowledge and training that might create barriers to DMHI use and its implementation. Indeed, many mental health providers use these interventions sporadically to support treatment without a "real" integration (van der Vaart et al., 2016). For these reasons, Wentzel and colleagues (2016) proposed five postulates for applying blended intervention to provide a specific rationale for e-therapy application, offering information that helps therapists fulfill blended treatment goals. Based on scientific evidence (van der Vaart et al., 2016), Wentzel and colleagues (2016) described how integration between online and offline components in a treatment process could be possible, highlighting the treatment efficacy from the interconnection of the two and not from the standalone treatment pathways. Online modalities contribute equally to the therapy as face-to-face components do only if these are carefully selected and adjusted to the treatment process. Their efficacy is also guaranteed if technology is appropriately selected to motivate and support patients to follow the treatment process and adjust to therapy protocols and patients' characteristics and capabilities to receive and participate in online treatment. From a therapeutic point of view, these indications are crucial as they contain all the suggestions therapists or clinicians should consider in e-therapy applications: integration between technological tools, traditional clinical techniques and protocols and clients' characteristics. Following van der Vaart's postulates, the application of technology within the clinical process has advantages because it has become more flexible to the rapid expansion of online practices and the therapeutic priorities decided by therapists and clients throughout treatment. Therefore, clinicians should consider blended interventions' potentials, limitations, and rationale. They must provide patients with detailed information to increase blended interventions' effectiveness and favor clients' engagement and technology familiarity.

## VIDEOCONFERENCING TECHNOLOGIES: A POSITIVE IMPLEMENTATION OF BLENDED CARE POSTULATES

The description and explanation of postulates of blended care that should be used in the e-therapy application allow understanding of another way of providing psychological services: videoconferencing technologies (Capner, 2000). Videoconferencing consists of the use of live, two-way interactive, video and audio communication between therapists and clients or between therapists themselves in supervision groups or meetings, using specific digital platforms such as Skype, ZOOM, Meet, Polycom, Cisco, Microsoft Lync, and many others (Capner, 2000). In particular, videoconferencing allows one to provide and share information from a distance as if individuals are sitting in the same room. Different clinical practices can be provided through videoconferencing, from initial assessment in terms of initial clinical interviews and the administration of scales for rating symptoms of mental state dysfunctions, medication management, therapy sessions, group and family sessions up to sessions in training and supervision (Dülsen et al., 2020). Although evidence suggests the effectiveness and comparability of interventions delivered through videoconferences to in-person care in diagnosis and treatment (Fletcher et al., 2018), psychologists and clinicians express dissatisfaction and concerns about their experiences using videoconferencing. In particular, a study by Capner (2000) about clinicians' satisfaction levels reported resistance and negative opinions about replacing person-to-person contact when conducting psychotherapy through videoconferencing. Indeed, they reported a general scepticism and some criticisms in establishing a good alliance with clients because of the reduced nonverbal feedback, lack of contact and general anxiety regarding equipment difficulties such as connection problems, muffled audio, and slight desynchrony between audio and video during sessions. Moreover, some clinicians are concerned that home-based care would reinforce patients' avoidance in certain circumstances (Interian et al., 2018).

Despite clinicians' concerns, patient surveys indicate a better sense of being in control and better retention of information shared within online sessions, increased adherence to treatment associated with a reduced number of missed mental health appointments and more satisfaction with the quality of sessions perceived as more task-oriented and structured (Fletcher et al., 2018).

Beyond these results, it is important to stress that the major obstacle to videoconference implementation in sessions resides in the culture and the clinicians' competencies. Indeed, the sense of the inadequacy of videoconferencing for clinical interventions is experienced more by therapists than by clients (Capner, 2000); then, it becomes crucial to educate therapists to be more familiar with psychotechnology and to understand how telehealth might provide benefits to their clients and how they can keep the effectiveness of their clinical interventions. Moreover, from the therapists' perspective, an initial focus on conveying the use and the purpose of psychotechnology to patients within the clinical process has to be made to enhance patients' involvement and motivation for treatment, as suggested by blended care postulates (Wentzel et al., 2016). Topics such as safety, ethics, and legal issues continue to be essential considerations even for videoconference and smartphone applications (Barnett & Kolmes, 2016). However, Morland and colleagues (2015) suggested evaluating their appropriateness when considering the patients' characteristics before using them because patient safety is always the most critical consideration for effective clinical care delivery.

## POTENTIAL RISKS OF E-THERAPY: MANY PROS BUT ALSO MANY CONS

As already described in the chapter, the use of psychotechnology in clinical settings has several benefits that are advantageous both for the social community and for clinicians or mental health providers. In particular, as already described, these benefits include: (a) an improvement of public knowledge about mental health and more direct access to cost savings mental health cares, (b) more flexibility to address the unique needs of indigent people or risk groups worldwide, (c) the opportunity to make treatments more available, transparent and manageable (Dülsen et al., 2020). For clinicians, psychotechnology can help monitor and document clients' symptoms, progress or relapses, provide professional psychoeducation and support practice management; moreover, they can make more convenient, less expansive, faster, and more accurate the phases of the different interventions from administration and assessment through psychological tests, to discharges and follow-up (Maheu et al., 2004). Computerized and online-based interventions, smartphone applications and other videoconferencing tools also allow helping people in novel ways in the context of mild to moderate severity mental disorders such as depression, anxiety disorders, obsessive-compulsive disorders, sleep problems, risky behaviors, alcohol and substance abuse, and post-traumatic stress disorder (Fletcher et al., 2018). These interventions can be purely self-help, guided self-help, or a combination of face-to-face and Internet-based sessions (i.e., blended care interventions) and can be delivered at both low or high intensity within stepped-care models (Bower & Gilbody, 2005). However, clinicians who have included psychotechnology in their practice should be fully aware of its implications and potential risks because they might negatively impact the effectiveness of clinical interventions and the clients' adherence and motivation to treatment. In particular, there could be potential downsides to using psychotechnology (i.e., mental health applications, videoconference) if clinicians do not have digital mental health competencies, experiences, or access to scientifically rigorous studies that could help them to understand what works and for whom (Batastini et al., 2021) and support their ethical decision-making (Lattie et al., 2022). For example, a study by Kumar and colleagues (2013) highlighted that adopting an ineffective app could discourage people from seeking therapy or disrupt a treatment plan or protocol, interrupting it or providing information inconsistent with established clinical practice. There are concerns and discussions about videoconferencing potential risks (Lattie et al., 2022): in particular, some are about protecting clients' data, privacy, and security. Clinicians need to be aware of the possibility of data breaches and ensure that the platforms used are complied with national privacy rules and laws to help clients make informed decisions about the potential risks and how they would be managed. The informed consent provided by competent clinicians should also communicate what clients can do to minimize risks in their environment (i.e., finding private space where they will not be overheard; Batastini et al., 2021).

## FUTURE DIRECTIONS. THE NEW CHALLENGES IN THE FIELD OF E-THERAPY: THE DEVELOPMENT OF DIGITAL SKILLS OF DIGITAL PSYCHOLOGISTS

As just said, the potential roles of e-therapy and psychotechnology in supporting mental health and wellness are numerous and significant, but their exploration and implementation in the clinical practice require addressing some gaps. The rapidly evolving nature of technology, the more widespread of DMHIs and the lack of evidence-based digital therapy packages for their users identify "new" responsibilities for mental health providers and clinicians and an urgent need for further education and training regarding ethics, privacy, safety, efficacy, usability, and technology use (Pote et al., 2021). Indeed, there is a significant gap in the scholarly literature on the knowledge-based and current use of psychotechnology. Indeed, only recently, there has been a growing interest in providing flexible and evidence-based frameworks, guidelines or checklists to assess technological tools and support clinicians in decision-making in this field (Nebeker et al., 2020).

For example, it has been shown that an inaccurate knowledge of different types of DMHI and technological opportunities, as well as poor information about their strengths and weaknesses, is potentially risky and harmful both for users and for DMHI effectiveness because it contributes to the widespread of incorrect or misleading information to patients who might not understand or perceive the DMHI useful. Moreover, the reduced patient involvement in the intervention might negatively influence its success and make users themselves refractory to any future treatment (Borghouts et al., 2021). Therefore, new challenges are emerging in the field of e-therapy concerning the development of *digital competencies* and the new characterization of the role of digital mental health providers as "gatekeepers" of DMHI use.

According to this affirmation, a survey by Pote and colleagues (2021) reveals that specific training is needed to develop digital skills and ensure successful digital delivery. Furthermore, a study by Cowan and colleagues (2019) from Mayo Clinic found that clinicians' lack of knowledge about how and when to adopt guided digital interventions negatively affects DMHIs' effectiveness in improving patients' anxiety and depressive symptoms because patients were not sufficiently informed about the treatment and, then, they did not integrate the actual use of the intervention into their everyday routine. In turn, clinicians' unfamiliarity with technology or how to overcome technical difficulties in sessions and limited evidence-based information about the potential benefits of DMHIs reduced their satisfaction and increased their reluctance to DMHI implementation. These findings are significant because they highlight how DMHI effectiveness seems to be highly affected by clinicians' perspective, discomfort, scepticism, and acceptance of DMHI rather than that of patients (Cowan et al., 2019). The survey by Pote and colleagues (2021) also shows that, among professional respondents, the most critical barriers to integrating digital interventions within UK healthcare services were the lack of specialized skills, knowledge, and concerns about patients' data protection. Therefore, the authors suggest the necessity to build training programs, curricula, and opportunities for DMHI experience and practice. More specifically, from the authors' analysis emerges that psychologists need (a) guidelines in the form of teaching manuals or a consensus-based and well-informed digital competence framework and (b) the opportunity to practice digital competencies across teaching and placements experiences to strengthen what was already learned, to explore all possibilities, and to change their negative attitudes or fears (Pote et al. 2021).

## REFERENCES

Andersson, G., & Cuijpers, P. (2009). Internet-based and other computerized psychological treatments for adult depression: A meta-analysis. *Cognitive Behaviour Therapy, 38*(4), 196–205. https://doi.org/10.1080/16506070903318960

Barnett, J. E., & Kolmes, K. (2016). The practice of tele-mental health: Ethical, legal, and clinical issues for practitioners. *Practice Innovations, 1*(1), 53–66. https://doi.org/10.1037/pri0000014

Batastini, A. B., Paprzycki, P., Jones, A. C., & MacLean, N. (2021). Are videoconferenced mental and behavioral health services just as good as in-person? A meta-analysis of a fast-growing practice. *Clinical Psychology Review, 83,* 101944. https://doi.org/10.1016/j.cpr.2020.101944

Borghouts, J. E., Eikey, E., Mark, G., De Leon, C., Schueller, S. M., Schneider, M., Stadnick, N., Zheng, K., Mukamel, D., & Sorkin, D. H. (2021). Barriers to and facilitators of user engagement with digital mental health interventions: Systematic review. *Journal of Medical Internet Research, 23*(3), e24387. https://doi.org/10.2196/24387

Bower, P., & Gilbody, S. (2005). Stepped care in psychological therapies: Access, effectiveness and efficiency: Narrative literature review. *The British Journal of Psychiatry, 186*(1), 11–17.

Capner, M. (2000). Videoconferencing in the provision of psychological services at a distance. *Journal of Telemedicine and Telecare 6*(6), 311–319. https://doi.org/10.1258/1357633001935969

Castelnuovo, G., Gaggioli, A., Mantovani, F., & Riva, G. (2003). From psychotherapy to e-therapy: The integration of traditional techniques and new communication tools in clinical settings. *CyberPsychology & Behavior, 6*(4), 375–382. https://doi.org/10.1089/109493103322278754

Cowan, K. E., McKean, A. J., Gentry, M. T., & Hilty, D. M. (2019). Barriers to use of telepsychiatry: Clinicians as gatekeepers. *Mayo Clinic Proceedings, 94*(12), 2510–2523. https://doi.org/10.1016/j.mayocp.2019.04.018

Donker, T. P., Petrie, K., Proudfoot, J., Clarke, J., Birch, M.-R., & Christensen, H. (2013). Smartphones for smarter delivery of mental health programs: A systematic review. *Journal of Medical Internet Research 15*(11), e2791. https://doi.org/10.2196/jmir.2791

Dülsen, P. B., Bendig, E., Küchler, A.-M., Christensen, H., & Baumeister, H. (2020). Digital interventions in adult mental healthcare settings: Recent evidence and future directions. *Current Opinion in Psychiatry, 33*(4), 422–431. https://doi.org/10.1097/YCO.0000000000000614

Fletcher, T. L., Hogan, J. B., Keegan, F., Davis, M. L., Wassef, M., Day, S., & Lindsay, J. A. (2018). Recent advances in delivering mental health treatment via video to home. *Current Psychiatry Reports, 20*(8), 1–9. https:/doi.org/10.1007/s11920-018-0922-y

Interian, A. K., King, A. R., St. Hill, L. M., Robinson, C. H., & Damschroder, L. J. (2018). Evaluating the implementation of home-based videoconferencing. *Psychiatric Services 69*(1), 69–75. https://doi.org/10.1176/appi.ps.201700004

Johansson, O. T., Michel, T., Andersson, G., & Paxling, B. (2015). Experiences of non-adherence to Internet-delivered cognitive behavior therapy: A qualitative study. *Internet Interventions 2*(2), 137–142. https://doi.org/10.1016/j.invent.2015.02.006

Kip, H. W., Wentzel, J., & Kelders, S. M. (2020). Shaping blended care: Adapting an instrument to support therapists in using emental health. *JMIR Mental Health, 7*(11), e24245. https://doi.org/10.2196/24245

Kumar, S., Nilsen, W. J., Abernethy, A., Atienza, A., Patrick, K., Pavel, M., Riley, W. T., Shar, A., Spring, B., Spruijt-Metz, D., Hedeker, D., Honavar, V., Kravitz, R., Lefebvre, R. C., Mohr, D. C., Murphy, S. A., Quinn, C., Shusterman, V., & Swendeman, D. (2013). Mobile health technology evaluation: The mHealth evidence workshop. *American Journal of Preventive Medicine, 45*(2), 228–236. https://doi.org/10.1016/j.amepre.2013.03.017

Lattie, E. G.-S., Stiles-Shields, C., & Graham, A. K. (2022). An overview of and recommendations for more accessible digital mental health services. *Nature Reviews Psychology,* 1, 87–100. https://doi.org/10.1038/s44159-021-00003-1

Maheu, M. M.-C., Pulier, M. L., Wilhelm, F. H., McMenamin, J. P., & Brown-Connolly, N. E. (2004). *The mental health professional and the new technologies: A handbook for practice today.* Taylor & Francis.

McLendon, K. (2000). E-commerce and HIM: Ready or not, here it comes. *Journal of the American Health Information Management Association, 71*(1), 22–23. https://pubmed.ncbi.nlm.nih.gov/11009645/

Miner, A. S., Milstein, A., & Hancock, J. T. (2017). Talking to machines about personal mental health problems. *JAMA, 318*(13), 1217–1218. https://doi.org/10.1001/jama.2017.14151

Mohr, D. C., Hart, S. L., Howard, I., Julian, L., Vella, L., Catledge, C., & Feldman, M. D. (2006). Barriers to psychotherapy among depressed and nondepressed primary care patients. *Annals of Behavioral Medicine, 32*(3), 254–258. https://doi.org/10.1207/s15324796abm3203_12

Morland, L. A., Poizner, J. M., Williams, K. E., Masino, T. T., & Thorp, S. R. (2015). Home-based clinical video teleconferencing care: Clinical considerations and future directions. *International Review of Psychiatry* 27(6), 504–512. https://doi.org/10.3109/09540261.2015.1082986

National Institute of Mental Health. (2023, July). *Technology and the future of mental health treatment.* U.S. Department of Health and Human Services, National Institutes of Health. https://www.nimh.nih.gov/health/topics/technology-and-the-future-of-mental-health-treatment

Nebeker, C. B., Bartlett Ellis, R. J., & Torus, J. (2020). Development of a decision-making checklist tool to support technology selection in digital health research. *Translational Behavioral Medicine, 10*(4), 1004–1015. https://doi.org/10.1093/tbm/ibz074

Olthuis, J. V., Watt, M. C., Bailey, K., Hayden, J. A., & Stewart, S. H. (2016). Therapist-supported Internet cognitive behavioural therapy for anxiety disorders in adults. *Cochrane Database of Systematic Reviews, 5*(3), CD011565. https://doi.org/10.1002/14651858.CD011565

Pote, H., Rees, A., Holloway-Biddle, C., & Griffith, E. (2021). Workforce challenges in digital health implementation: How are clinical psychology training programmes developing digital competences? *Digital Health, 7,* 1–11. https://doi.org/10.1177/2055207620985396

van der Vaart, R. W.-P., Witting, M., Riper, H., Kooistra, L., Bohlmeijer, E. T., & van Gemert-Pijnen, L. (2016). Blending online therapy into regular face-to-face therapy for depression: Content, ratio and preconditions according to patients and therapists using a Delphi study. *BMC Psychiatry, 14*(1), Article 355. https://doi.org/10.1186/s12888-014-0355-z

Weizenbaum, J. (1966). ELIZA—A computer program for the study of natural language communication between man and machine. *Communications of the ACM, 9*(1), 36–45. https://doi.org/10.1145/365153.365168

Wentzel, J., van der Vaart, R., Bohlmeijer, E. T., & van Gemert-Pijnen, J. (2016). Mixing online and face-to-face therapy: How to benefit from blended care in mental health care. *JMIR mental health. 3*(1), e9. https://doi.org/10.2196/mental.4534

CHAPTER 2

# STATUS OF TECHNOLOGIES

## Digital Tools

**Marco Baldetti**
***Sigmund Freud University, Milan***

Historically, there are numerous examples of how technology can offer new opportunities to psychotherapy and clinical psychology. For instance, as early as the 1940s, the possibility of using magnetic recorders was considered as a means of supporting analysis. If we take into consideration that this field of care is based mostly on communication between patient and clinician, this is exactly the type of field that is most suitable to benefit from new forms of communication that have gradually become available to people: from telephone, email, internet chat to videoconferencing systems (Goss & Anthony, 2003). New technologies have a novelty factor and some evident advantages for a common user, however, from a clinical point of view it is necessary to go beyond and evaluate every implication and potential drawback.

Recent data confirms that as the world's population and life expectancy increases, the number of mental health professionals remains scarce and below needs in both developing and high-income countries. The use of

*Digital Developments*, pages 17–35

technologies provides a potential means to maximize the delivery of care by making it more available and more efficient and scalable (World Health Organization, 2016).

To this end, numerous technologies have been used that allow for remote communication: the concept of Telehealth refers to "the use of telecommunications and information technologies to provide access to health information and services across a geographical distance" (Glueckauf et al., 2003, p. 160). The importance of these types of tools is also evident when we consider that, on the user side of health services, more than two-thirds of depressed patients report at least one practical barrier to regularly use psychotherapy, such as time constraints and transportation difficulties (Mohr et al., 2006).

An early form of distance therapy used the common telephone as a technological medium capable of providing synchronous verbal communication over distance. Despite the increasing diffusion of more advanced tools, the telephone has long been the only truly ubiquitous means of communication; for example, Brenes et al. (2011) report that until 2007, the telephone was present in 96% of American homes, compared to 62% of the Internet connection. From the report just mentioned, the diffusion of the Internet is still slow in most rural areas, moreover the use of the landline telephone does not require additional tools, specific skills, nor is subject to malfunctions or hiccups, which are typical of more modern and technologically based means of communication.

Despite some encouraging clinical research showing a good acceptability and effectiveness of telephone therapies, this medium still has limitations that pose some challenges. The most obvious is the clinician's lack of control over the environment and the mode of therapy. It is not possible, for example, to ensure that there are no intrusions or violations of the privacy of both the patient and the therapist. In addition to this, the impoverishment of communication caused by the total loss of visual data as well as the limited quality of sound, has cast doubt on the possibility of establishing a solid therapeutic alliance (e.g., Haas et al., 1996). Despite this, some empirical evidence over time has measured a satisfactory alliance quality and a bonding that is considered strong by patients in therapies conducted by telephone (e.g., Reese et al., 2002).

With the more recent spread of mobile phones, an additional means of communication has been observed in text messaging, including the pioneering short message service (SMS) form. This medium has become extremely popular and some of its clinical applications have been successfully tested, for example in increasing treatment adherence in schizophrenic patients (e.g., Montes et al., 2012). Recent research by Hull and Mahan (2017) investigated the usefulness of delivering treatment via asynchronous messaging, similar to SMS, although delivered via an app. In their research,

64% of the subjects (a group of 57 individuals between 18 and 60 years old, currently using the text therapy service) showed significant improvements in symptoms and reported a good therapeutic alliance with their remote therapist. These data may be surprising; however, it is known how some written exercises have been shown to be capable of stimulating psychological well-being (Baikie & Wilhelm, 2005). Moreover, the authors point out that treatment through messaging was beneficial to participants in several aspects: affordability, effectiveness, making progress, and receiving help when it is felt necessary and not according to a fixed appointment.

With the spread of the COVID-19 pandemic, remote mental health interventions via videoconferencing have become widespread very quickly even though these technologies have been available for many years. This type of service is described in the literature with various new terms such as telehealth, video to home (VTH) psychotherapy, video cognitive behavioral therapy (VCBT), or videoconferencing psychotherapy (VCP). From a strictly technological standpoint, the spread of broadband internet connections, computers, and smartphones with embedded cameras has facilitated the spread of video calling as a communication tool accessible to a growing population. The impact that this has on the provision of mental health services passes, for example, from the therapy setting: in some earlier implementations, in fact, a patient lacking appropriate tools or familiarity with technology meets the therapist on video, but going to their local health centre (primary care) and using a room set up for this purpose. More recently, the VTH form, in which the person does not have to move from home, has become more popular, thus overcoming other typical barriers to care, that include time and transportation difficulties or anonymity issues (Young, 2005).

The impact of video communication on the quality of psychotherapy has been much debated. Many authors have raised concerns related to the fact that neither the therapist nor the patient can access all the nonverbal information of the interlocutor such as posture, gestures, impoverishing or distorting the communication and consequently the alliance as well as therapeutic outcome. Nevertheless, any impoverishment of nonverbal communication does not appear to diminish the quality of the therapeutic alliance or of therapy outcomes as more and more research now confirms (Fletcher et al., 2018; Varker et al., 2019). In the context of psychiatric assessment, Zarate et al. (1997) found only a little difference in the quality of diagnostic assessment by comparing interviews conducted in person, on low-bandwidth video, and on high-bandwidth video. On the other hand, from the therapist's point of view, distrust and fears remain: Cataldo et al. (2021) suggest that this is due to the interferences that the computer produces during the encounter between therapist and patient. Indeed, according to these authors, it stands as an additional presence during the session, not only a means for communication. This presence materializes in the cognitive and emotional effort that the therapist must exert to prevent, control, or resolve all possible malfunctions that the computer can introduce into the communication and that would not occur if the encounters were face-to-face.

However, the distrust that clinicians continue to experience in using video conferencing technologies to deliver distance therapy seems to be a barrier that tends to thin out with experience and specific training. Clinicians with experience in VTH, for example, saw distance therapy as an opportunity to connect patients to care and reduce avoidant behaviors. Conversely, clinicians inexperienced in VTH see a potential risk in exacerbating these same avoidance conditions (Interian et al., 2018).

In addition to using technology to deliver therapy by making therapist–patient interaction easier and more accessible, clinicians have used it to try and reduce the time that they could spend on treatment so that they can provide their services to an increasing number of individuals.

This perspective is part of the "stepped care" view, where therapists propose, among the treatments deemed effective for the clinical problem presented, the treatment with the least impact in terms of resources needed (Bower & Gilbody, 2005). Among stepped care treatments for psychological disorders, some are self-help approaches, in which not only patients acquire information about their disorder as in simple education, but also about the principles of change, in order to stimulate clinical improvement on their own. With technological development, self-help interventions have been able to cross the boundaries of printed books and spread through different mediums: audiotapes, with detailed instructions for performing tasks such as relaxation; videotapes, in which problems and skills relevant to the patient are often illustrated in a documentary format; written materials in digital form such as downloadable pdfs and e-books (Williams, 2001). Finally, the spread of personal computers has made it possible to group all of these resources (text, images, audio, and video recordings) that were previously separated into different mediums and mix them inside interactive software. In the clinical setting, the computer has been used for numerous purposes, from automating assessment using structured questionnaires to monitor a patient's progress during a treatment or deliver the treatment itself even in the form of in vivo exposures, with the first practical experiments beginning in the late 1970s (Kaltenthaler et al., 2006). The computer could administer a self-help protocol in complete autonomy or be integrated with face-to-face therapy, in which the patient could use the computer before or after the session with the therapist by accessing a dedicated room in the same treatment facility.

The advent and the spread of the Internet have opened up new avenues for computer-based therapy, no longer tied to the use of a physical medium such as CD-ROMs. This has made it possible to experiment with new formats such as those of Internet-delivered cognitive behavioral therapy (iCBT), that is, "internet interventions" that are based on the consultation of dedicated web pages that convey content often similar to those already tested in computerized CBT software.

iCBTs via remotely accessible web pages began to develop around the mid-1990s (Ruwaard et al., 2011) and currently can be part of a therapy with different levels of intensity. Andersson et al. (2014) describes three of these levels: a basic level in which the system has only informational and educational purpose; a protocol-based level administered totally in self-help mode; and a "guided" mode level, in which a therapist supervises the work of the patient through brief email or telephone contacts. Automated alert and reminder systems are sometimes implemented in order to promote the patient's adherence, encouraging them to continue the program through messages of encouragement and support.

These iCBT interventions are based on online platforms accessible by both patients and clinicians. For example, one platform, developed at Linköping University in Sweden over nearly 2 decades, is called Iterapi and has been described in detail by Vlaescu et al. (2016), in order to allow other researchers and clinicians to implement similar services. The platform is designed to serve as a basic template and may be customized so that each treatment can have its own structure, its own webpage with specific URL to which participants can freely register, finding advertising in different media both electronic and traditional.

Clinicians, accessing the platform with their credentials, have the freedom to operate on multiple levels according to their role (e.g., the possibility or not to edit the pages of content and treatment programs). Therapists have access to an administrative section where they can see the list of their patients indexed by their summary information: for each patient, a user hub collects all the information grouping them into specific tabs based on their content (biographical information, completed questionnaires, therapy modules assigned, etc.). The activity of each patient is automatically summarized by the platform in user logs, which can be accompanied by text notes manually written by the therapist.

In order to participate in treatment, patients have to register to the platform through their personal email and fill in a form; after registration they can access the start page that contains a notification centre which guides the patient through the actions they can take, such as responding to messages from the therapist, filling in a questionnaire or carrying out a therapy form. The web pages of iCBT interventions such as Iterapi are often responsive, that is, capable of adapting to any web browser and thus being fully usable from desktops, tablets, and mobile phones. Treatment modules are often divided into chapters with textual content embedded in web pages or downloadable, accompanied by images or comics, video, and audio files.

Worksheets are used instead for the completion of homework, diaries, and quizzes. These can contain simple elements such as text boxes, where the patient can write their answers, or more interactive graphic elements such as sliders or radial buttons to show in an intuitive way, for example, the degree of intensity of an emotion or the degree of conviction of a thought.

A section for questionnaires is implemented allowing the distribution of automated assessment which are formatted to compute the scoring of the administration, its temporal trend also in the form of graphs and tables that are exportable.

The communication system within the system can provide both asynchronous written communications (similar to email and able to contain both text and elements attached) and synchronous (such as a chat in real time) that are thus maintained within the space of the platform without having to rely on external communications. More recent implementations have added synchronous audio–video communications systems so that both patient and therapist can use the same platform for each activity, eliminating the need for third-party applications and ensuring the standards of security and data protection necessary for clinical use.

The potential of responsive iCBT systems such as Iterapi, that are also adaptable for use on mobile device browsers, allows the implementation of ecological momentary assessment (EMA). In this case, a randomized or scheduled notification from the therapist is sent to the patient who will respond to short sets of questions measuring target variables such as mood or specific behaviors within daily life at different times of the day and thus increasing the understanding of various individual patient functioning, such as emotional, thoughts and behavior patterns (Heron & Smyth, 2010). This feature, made possible by the use of mobile web pages, shows how the latest electronic devices with mobile internet connectivity constitute a qualitative leap that has had a great impact in clinical applications.

A first example of experimentation with such devices emerged in the early 1990s with the use of palmtop computers. As summarized by Newman et al. (1997) these tools, forerunners of the more recent smartphones, made possible the recording of ecological information because patients could fill out questionnaires or clinical diaries in their environment and in different moments and conditions of their lives. This limit for the first time the bias of mnemonic recall and in the case of clinical diaries also reduced the possibility that data were modified to meet the expectations of the clinician, for example by pretending to have accurately completed a mood diary or a paper and pencil food diary (Stone et al., 2003).

With the introduction of smartphones and app stores the number of health-focused software has recently increased exponentially. To this date, there are an estimated 10,000 to 20,000 apps available on the topic of mental health (Clay, 2021) with a format that provides for both standalone and combined use with face-to-face treatments (Wilhelm et al., 2020). However, the popularity of these apps does not translate into equal clinical safety and efficacy; Lagan et al. (2021) recently showed that popularity in both user ratings and number of app downloads does not correlate with equal clinical relevance, nor with adequate levels of security and protection of user privacy. Kertz et al. (2017) showed, for example, that none of the 25 most popular iPhone apps for managing anxiety and brooding has referenced evidence-based treatments for these issues. It is precisely these critical issues that are part of the challenges that clinical psychology is currently facing in its relationship with technology and that need further development both technically and culturally, which we will continue to address in the next sections.

## HARDWARE

In a recent article by Zale et al. (2021), the authors analyzed the trends of technology applied to psychotherapy present in the last 40 years of the literature in the field. One of the contributions of the article is an interesting graph that shows the most recent technological milestones in this area: If we exclude virtual reality (VR) systems, that will be discussed elsewhere in this publication, smartphones are the most recent hardware to be part of this chronology, their debut in fact goes back to 2007 with the presentation of the first iPhone.

As we have previously mentioned, smartphones may constitute a means of fruition for iCBT interventions, but they have specific hardware features that have been exploited for clinical purposes over time, albeit in an alternating and often limited fashion. Miralles et al. (2020) conducted a review in which they point out that in most cases mental health apps still use traditional software whose features do not offer significant advancements over the past, such as education and learning interventions based on written text presentation, or prompting features based on SMS-like messages and reminders. However, the increased size and resolution of screens has allowed for the introduction of multimedia materials that were previously impossible to deliver on the move, or the introduction of more sophisticated notification and engagement systems. Most studies using apps, however, still do not fully exploit some hardware features now available such as GPS signal or Bluetooth or wi-fi proximity sensors for context awareness. Therefore, cases in which they are able to implement specific actions and stimuli based on the environment in which the patient is located are rare. This is the case of the ecological momentary intervention (EMI), which consists of momentary interventions provided via mobile technologies right when problems occur while people are engaged in their everyday life, as opposed to treatments provided only during appointments. Another recent hardware development, that has a potential impact on mental health applications, is that of wearable devices, such as fitness trackers or smartwatches, which are capable of connecting to smartphones and sharing with them and their applications the physiological parameters recordings. In 2022, 25% of Americans were already using a device of this type (Statistica, n.d.). Despite this, as Bauer et al. (2020) reported in a recent review, their accuracy is not high because they are not classified as medical devices and consequently are not bound to the highest quality standards. It can, therefore, be a problem to consider applying their use in mental health due to the quality of the sensors themselves, the applications that interpret the data and the suboptimal use by the users themselves. The gyroscopes and accelerometers of popular smartphones, for example, have biases that should be compensated by the applications through specific calibrations. In addition, sensors and components commonly used in industrial manufacturing, undergo numerous updates and revisions even within the same model, introducing potential new sources of inaccuracy in recorded data (Kos et al., 2016). The same problems are present in wearables sensors, for example, a review by Feehan et al. (2018) showed that the only truly reliable data among those measured was the number of steps. Similar results are reported by Bauer et al. (2020) regarding the accuracy of blood pressure, heart rate, sleep quality measurements: in many cases the comparison between the data reported by apps and the data measured by professional instruments indicated highly inaccurate measurements.

Smartphones and their set of sensors have also recently been used to perform a passive monitoring of some behaviors and parameters of the patient. The purpose of this type of passive monitoring is to perform a digital phenotyping that is able to recognize and assess the mental condition of patients without the need for their active involvement in providing responses or actions of any kind. The goal is to overcome the limitations of traditional assessments that cannot capture all the fluctuations that occur outside of clinical observation and that may be affected by self-monitoring and recalling bias on the part of the subject, even more so in those clinical conditions of high severity in which compliance and awareness of disease may be compromised. Precisely in the case of passive monitoring, sensor data available in smartphones and wearables are used to their full potential: Abdullah and Choudhury (2018) for example classify potentially usable signals into three categories. The first refers to behavioral signals such as location and mobility based on GPS, Bluetooth and wi-fi; speech patterns, based on listening to speech using microphones; technology use, directly measuring the duration and frequency with which the phone is used; and physical activity, using accelerometer and gyroscope sensors. A second category consists of physiological signals such as facial expressions, eye movements, and blinking, measured through the front camera of the phone; heart rate variability and electrodermal activity recorded through smartwatches. A final category of signals is social: social interactions, using Bluetooth and wi-fi sensors to assess proximity and location relative to other individuals; communication patterns (e.g., frequency and duration of phone calls and texts); and social media use.

These signals have shown potential in providing insights into the mental and clinical status of patients with severe psychological disorders, however, the authors themselves acknowledge that many of these measures were evaluated in a pilot research. Some recent reviews on the topic, for example, Seppälä et al. (2019), indicate similar conclusions to those already mentioned, that is, there are some potentially interesting findings but still premature and based on studies sometimes of limited numbers or with methodological difficulties that therefore require further research to demonstrate clinical utility.

In addition to the limitations of research in passive sensing, there are other issues that need to be addressed and that Abdullah and Choudhury (2018) summarize in their work. The researchers show how these types of recordings pose important issues related to privacy and confidentiality of the data collected because many data may incidentally concern other people besides the subject of the monitoring (e.g., in the case of social behavior or speech monitoring). Even user engagement is a relevant aspect to be considered, because even if the monitoring is passive, patients must still cooperate by making sure, for example, that the devices are always charged, properly worn, and kept with them in most situations, in order to achieve the desired clinical objectives.

## SOFTWARE

As we have seen above, one of the peculiar characteristics of the most recent phase of the technological development in the field of mental health is characterized by the presence of an exorbitant number of software in the form of apps for smartphones.

One of the recognized priorities, given the great variety of offerings, is to help clinicians and patients to consciously orient themselves in this mare magnum. For example, the need for guidelines has led to the development of assessment frameworks such as the Mobile App Rating Scale (Stoyanov et al., 2015) and mobile health index and navigation database (Lagan et al., 2021). However, as indicated by Roth et al. (2021), the appearance of various rating frameworks in the literature does not fully address the need for agile software selection tools. For this reason, easily understandable app rating and evaluation projects have been developed such as PsyberGuide: a nonprofit initiative that has been rating and reviewing mental health apps since 2013, also in collaboration with the University of California, Irvine, and Northwestern University.

To get an idea of what these apps are like, a recent review by Lagan et al. (2021) shows that the features most present in mental health apps are related to monitoring and education, such as mood tracking, jounraling, psychoeducation, symptoms tracking. Regarding the therapeutic principles, the one that appears most often is mindfulness (in about 130 apps among 278 surveyed), followed by deep breathing, with CBT appearing in just under 60 apps, while acceptance and commitment therapy and dialectical behavior therapy appear in less than 20 apps. Scholars also point out that in most cases these apps focus on one key feature, failing to provide more comprehensive tools to support the patient.

Studies related to apps tend to cover the most represented disorders in the population. The most common are apps for depression and anxiety, which are often referred to as emotional disorders, followed by apps for substance abuse and addiction disorders, disorders related to the psychosis spectrum, and apps for trauma and stress-related disorders; a similar proportion can be traced within iCBT software (Miralles et al., 2020).

As we have just seen, it seems that mental health researchers have become more and more interested in apps that deal with the clinical problems that afflict the majority of the population. However, the development and publication trends of these apps in app stores do not follow a similar logic. In Bauer et al. (2020), they examined reviews of apps related to various categories of mental health-related problems, and the most represented categories were found as followed: medication adherence (5,888 apps), anxiety (5,078 apps), prevent driving after drinking (2,907 apps), and sleep self-management (2,431 apps). On the other hand, the category related to depression was represented by "only" 310 apps (Huguet et al. 2016), on which Bauter and colleagues commented "despite the growing public demand, there is a concerning lack of appropriate CBT or BA apps, expecially from a clinical and legal point of view" (Bauter et al. 2020, p. 8). Bauer et al. (2020) concluded that, although many studies speak to the potential of mental health apps, the clinical evidence is small overall. Thus, the study calls for caution in the use of health apps, even more so if we consider that, despite attempts to index and evaluate apps through frameworks and expert reviews, personal research done directly on app stores remains a very common means for consumers to try and find their way around the field. In addition, there is a great risk for the consumers to run into content that is not sufficiently safe and sometimes they can be persuaded by claims of the app's scientificity that are not always entirely reliable (Larsen et al., 2019).

The initial enthusiasm, followed by caution in the adoption of mental health apps, also affected the English National Health Service (NHS).

They had launched a mental health app library in 2015 which was later removed due to concerns about the data security and clinical efficacy of the proposed solutions. The NHS replaced it with a new digital platform in 2017, but this app was also decommissioned in December 2021. Simmonds-Buckley et al. (2020) recently conducted a review to combine the clinical evidence regarding apps that the NHS had recommended for depression, anxiety, and stress in adults. Of the 48 apps listed, only seven had randomized controlled trials to evaluate their effectiveness; of these, only one was a smartphone app while the other six were web-based apps. Furthermore, only the latter had its technology development based on consultations by academic and clinical staff. The work of Simmonds-Buckley et al. (2020) gives an idea of how the galaxy of smartphone apps emerges from less clear and often commercial needs, while the development of web-based iCBT applications has been more academically centered, emerging from the scientific and clinical needs to disseminate evidence-based protocols often only partially automated (guided iCBT) and almost always under the supervision of a clinician.

Two contemporary examples of iCBT program implementation include MindSpot Clinic in Australia and the Internet psychiatry unit in Sweden, which have published numerous data regarding the success with which they are able to use iCBT programs in the routine clinic (Andersson et al., 2019). The implementation of iCBT interventions is often left to specialists in the field and centralized clinics interested in the topic. In some ways, this has on the one hand produced quality interventions but, on the other hand, limited their dissemination. This phenomenon is also often hindered by the well-documented fears of clinical stakeholders, especially in countries where these interventions are not yet widespread (Topooco et al., 2017). In the near future, overcoming such mistrust will be possible through direct practice and specific training.

Although many clinicians have not yet been trained in the use of digital interventions, such as iCBT or apps to support therapy, the years of the COVID-19 pandemic have forced most therapists to conduct at least some of their visits via videoconferencing platforms. This trend has brought into sharper focus the critical issues related to the security of the software that provides this service. Protecting patient data and anonymity is a key element of clinical practice and cannot be taken for granted. In the United States, the Health Insurance Portability and Accountability Act (HIPAA) regulates the protection of personal data and also regulates video conferencing programs that can be used in clinical settings. For this reason, only some softwares that provide video conferencing services are defined HIPAA-compliant because they must meet specific technical requirements that are not adopted by all providers. For this reason, the clinician should not use software just because it is very popular or easy to use but they should make sure that their software choice is legally compliant with the data protection laws in force in their country. A first requirement is the data encryption, the ability to make the transmission undecipherable except for those people who have the authorization, and who can authenticate themselves to the platform using specific personal credentials. Other technical requirements, which make data transmission secure and protect sensitive patient data, are peer to peer networking, a direct connection between users' terminals, without the use of intermediary servers that may not guarantee the same security. A further element of security required by the HIPAA data protection law concerns local file storage: the requirement that all data stored after its transmission can reside only in the clinician's terminals and not in storage media owned by the videoconferencing service provider. The local storage requirement makes it clear that, in addition to adopting software that meets legal requirements, clinicians must use good practices to avoid mistakes that could accidentally jeopardize the sensitive data they store and for which they are responsible. For this reason, in addition to the general guidelines that various professional associations may publish, it is important to provide clinicians with new trainings about the knowledge needed to be able to operate in a digital age.

## FUTURE DIRECTIONS/NEW SOLUTIONS

Despite the development and growth of increasingly refined technological solutions available to the clinic, one of the deepest and most important gaps to be filled remains that of the use of standardized measures in therapists' practice.

Currently, only 5% of clinicians uses measurement base care (MBC) practices in their most empirically accredited form (e.g., administering a measurement instrument at each session; Jensen-Doss et al., 2018). MBC is a practice that also introduces the ability to use reliable and valid measures of what is treated. We rely here not on instrumental or laboratory measures but on patient-reported outcomes, which often consist of the responses from self-administered scales used for measuring symptoms. The practice of MBC is capable of increasing the effectiveness of treatments, especially in patients deemed as nonresponders (Shimokawa et al., 2010). In fact, as Lewis et al. (2019) summarizes, MBC can foster greater patient involvement in treatment, greater understanding of their symptoms, and help clinicians to be more precise in their interventions.

Although the practice of MBC originated in a nonspecifically technological context, in which questionnaires were used in pen-and-paper mode, the use of softwares can now facilitate their effective use (Lyon et al., 2016). Measurement feedback systems are softwares that support the implementation of MBC, allowing for the automation of the administration of patient-reported outcomes, their scoring, and their organization into tables.

Today, many clinicians find themselves working in organizations where the use of electronic health records (EHRs) is necessary, and, as demonstrated by Steinfeld et al. (2016), simply having measurement feedback systems coexist with EHR systems can greatly increase the use of MBC practices, which is often hindered not by scepticism toward its usefulness, but by the work and organizational burden to which clinicians are subjected on a daily basis.

Even before using technology to modify and overcome the albeit significant scepticism toward iCBT protocols and telehealth practices, it could be an important goal to use technology to help psychologists deliver care in their traditional settings to the best of their ability, reducing the effectiveness problems sometimes attributable to therapist drift (Waller & Turner, 2016). On that note, some EHR software that implements MBC also introduces clinical decision support features that could be used in the future to support and increase the effectiveness of therapists' decision-making (Bauer et al., 2019).

The topic of measurement in mental health also has to do with the latest and most futuristic research directions, from which we can expect developments over the next few years. As somatic medicine has increasingly moved toward personalized care, this aspiration within mental health needs to move beyond the traditional boundaries of a statistical approach that investigates disorders according to homogeneous groupings, such as diagnoses and homogeneous groups of patients. Even if this approach has contributed to the advancement of the discipline for decades, it still continues to view individual variation more as a source of statistical noise than a useful resource for clinical characterization (Verhagen et al., 2022).

EMA, also called experience sampling method, emerged in the 1980s with the use of paper diaries. Nowadays, they consist in the use of mobile technology to collect information at the moment in which target events occur in order to increase the reliability and ecological validity of the measurements. EMA has the potential to facilitate personalized care pathways based on data collected through such structured diaries aimed at reliably and ecologically recording a whole range of aspects related to the patient's mental state. Smartphone-based applications of this kind are already available for research and clinical use, and help develop an understanding of micro correlations between different symptoms and between contexts and symptoms (van Os et al., 2017). Such developments require not only structured and reliable data collection but also an equally powerful statistical analysis of data (Borsboom & Cramer, 2013), capable of extracting patterns that are also useful for predicting future events such as symptomatic lapse and relapse.

A further advancement that we can expect in the future is related to the maturation of previously mentioned EMI or its newer subclass called just-in-time adaptive interventions (JITAI). These are interventions not only tailored to the individual patient, but also delivered at specific times by adapting to an individual's changing internal and contextual state (Nahum-Shani et al., 2018). For example, since smokers who have recently quit smoking can relapse in stressful situations, a JITAI intervention consists in monitoring their level of stress with an electronic wristband that activates an app that prompts the user with a stress reduction exercise as soon as a high-stress level is detected (Nahum-Shaniet al., 2021). The distinguishing feature of JITAI, compared to EMI, is the use of statistical methods to improve and tailor the interventions for a given individual over time. The field of JITAI is still in its preliminary evolution, if we take into consideration that the majority of studies are focused only on anxiety and substance abuse disorders, with other major topics still poorly explored. Moreover, it is also necessary to further explore what technical solutions and components of interventions work best (Balaskas et al., 2021).

Whatever the technological evolutions of the future will be, they will probably be as surprising and disruptive as those in the recent past have been. However, the integration of these tools in mental health will most likely require a whole new series of innovations that professionals in our field will have to be ready to learn and make their own. An example is the development of new experimental models such as micro-randomized trials (Klasnja et al., 2015). In micro-randomized trials, differently to randomized controlled trials, individuals are randomized hundreds of times over the course of a single study to address research questions about the effects of JITAI options, and whether their effects vary according to different conditions. New technological evolutions and implementations in our field will also require the deployment of many multidisciplinary efforts involving not only clinicians and behavioral scientists, but also engineers, statisticians, computer scientists, and human–computer interaction specialists (Nahum-Shani et al., 2018).

## REFERENCES

Abdullah, S., & Choudhury, T. (2018). Sensing technologies for monitoring serious mental illnesses. *IEEE MultiMedia, 25*(1), 61–75. https://pac.cs.cornell.edu/pubs/SensingTechnologiesForSeriousMentalIllnesses.pdf

Andersson, G., Cuijpers, P., Carlbring, P., Riper, H., & Hedman, E. (2014). Guided Internet-based vs. face-to-face cognitive behavior therapy for psychiatric and somatic disorders: A systematic review and meta-analysis. *World Psychiatry 13*(3), 288–295. https://doi.org/10.1002/wps.20151

Andersson, G., Titov, N., Dear, B. F., Rozental, A., & Carlbring, P. (2019). Internet-delivered psychological treatments: From innovation to implementation. *World psychiatry: Official Journal of the World Psychiatric Association (WPA), 18*(1), 20–28. https://doi.org/10.1002/wps.20610

Baikie, K. A., & Wilhelm, K. (2005). Emotional and physical health benefits of expressive writing. *Advances Psychiatric Treatment, 11*, 338–346. https://doi.org/10.1192/apt.11.5.338

Balaskas, A., Schueller, S. M., Cox, A. L., & Doherty, G. (2021). Ecological momentary interventions for mental health: A scoping review. *PloS one, 16*(3), e0248152. https://doi.org/10.1371/journal.pone.0248152

Bauer, M., Glenn, T., Geddes, J., Gitlin, M., Grof, P., Kessing, L. V., Monteith, S., Faurholt-Jepsen, M., Severus, E., & Whybrow, P. C. (2020). Smartphones in mental health: A critical review of background issues, current status and future concerns. *International Journal Bipolar Disorders, 8*(2). https://doi.org/10.1186/s40345-019-0164-x

Bauer, M., Monteith, S., Geddes, J., Gitlin, M. J., Grof, P., Whybrow, P. C., Glenn, T. (2019). Automation to optimise physician treatment of individual patients: Examples in psychiatry. *Lancet Psychiatry, 6*(4), 338–349. https://doi.org/10.1016/S2215-0366(19)30041-0

Borsboom, D., & Cramer, A. O. J. (2013). Network analysis: An integrative approach to the structure of psychopathology. *Annual Review of Clinical Psychology, 9*, 91–121. https://doi.org/10.1146/annurev-clinpsy-050212-185608

Bower, P., & Gilbody, S. (2005). Stepped care in psychological therapies: Access, effectiveness, and efficiency: Narrative literature review. *The British Journal of Psychiatry: The Journal of Mental Science, 186*, 11–17. https://doi.org/10.1192/bjp.186.1.11

Brenes, G. A., Ingram, C. W., & Danhauer, S. C. (2011). Benefits and challenges of conducting psychotherapy by telephone. *Professional Psychology: Research and Practice, 42*(6), 543–549. https://doi.org/10.1037/a0026135

Cataldo, F., Chang, S., Mendoza, A., & Buchanan, G. (2021). A perspective on client-psychologist relationships in videoconferencing psychotherapy: Literature review. *JMIR Mental Health, 8*(2), e19004. https://doi.org/10.2196/19004

Clay, R. A. (2021). Mental health apps are gaining traction: Self-help apps are leading more people to therapy rather than replacing it, psychologists say. *Monitor on Psychology, 52*(1). www.apa.org/monitor/2021/01/trends-mental-health-apps

Feehan, L. M., Geldman, J., Sayre, E. C., Park, C., Ezzat, A. M., Yoo, J. Y., Hamilton, C. B., & Li, L. C. (2018). Accuracy of Fitbit devices: Systematic review and narrative syntheses of quantitative data. *JMIR Mhealth Uhealth, 6*(8), e10527. https://doi.org/10.2196/10527

Fletcher, T. L., Hogan, J. B., Keegan, F., Davis, M. L., Wassef, M., Day, S., & Lindsay, J. A. (2018). Recent advances in delivering mental health treatment via video to home. *Current Psychiatry Reports, 20*(8), 56. https://doi.org/10.1007/s11920-018-0922-y

Glueckauf, R. L., Pickett, T. C., Ketterson, T. U., Loomis, J. S., & Rozensky, R. H. (2003). Preparation for the delivery of telehealth services: A self-study framework for expansion of practice. *Professional Psychology: Research and Practice, 34*(2), 159–163. https://doi.org/10.1037/0735-7028.34.2.159

Goss, S. P., & Anthony, K. (Eds.). (2003). *Technology in counselling and psychotherapy: A practitioner's guide*. Palgrave.

Haas, L. J., Benedict, J. G., & Kobos, J. C. (1996). Psychotherapy by telephone: Risks and benefits for psychologists and consumers. *Professional Psychology: Research and Practice, 27*, 154–160. https:doi.org/10.1037/0735-7028.27.2.154

Heron, K. E., & Smyth, J. M. (2010). Ecological momentary interventions: Incorporating mobile technology into psychosocial and health behaviour treatments. *British Journal of Health Psychology, 15*(Pt 1), 1–39. https://doi.org/10.1348/135910709X466063

Huguet, A., Rao, S., McGrath, P. J., Wozney, L., Wheaton, M., Conrod, J., Rozario, S. (2016). A systematic review of cognitive behavioral therapy and behavioral activation apps for depression. *PLoS ONE, 11*(5), e0154248. https://doi.org/10.1371/journal.pone.0154248

Hull, T. D., & Mahan, K. (2017). A study of asynchronous mobile-enabled SMS text psychotherapy. *Telemedicine and e-Health, 23*(3), 240–247. https://doi.org/10.1089/tmj.2016.0114

Interian, A., King, A. R., St Hill, L. M., Robinson, C. H., & Damschroder, L. J. (2018). Evaluating the implementation of home-based videoconferencing for providing mental health services. *Psychiatric Services, 69*(1), 69–75. https://doi.org/10.1176/appi.ps.201700004

Jensen-Doss, A., Haimes, E., Smith, A. M., Lyon, A. R., Lewis, C. C., Stanick, C. F., & Hawley, K. M. (2018). Monitoring treatment progress and providing feedback is viewed favorably but rarely used in practice. *Administration and Policy in Mental Health, 45*(1), 48–61. https://doi.org/10.1007/s10488-016-0763-0

Kaltenthaler, E., Brazier, J., De Nigris, E., Tumur, I., Ferriter, M., Beverley, C., Parry, G., Rooney, G., & Sutcliffe, P. (2006). Computerised cognitive behaviour therapy for depression and anxiety update: a systematic review and economic evaluation. *Health technology assessment (Winchester, England), 10*(33), 1–168. https://doi.org/10.3310/hta10330

Kertz, S. J., Kelly, J. M., Stevens, K. T., Schrock, M., Danitz, S. B. (2017). A review of free iPhone applications designed to target anxiety and worry. *Journal of Technology in Behavioral Science, 2*(2), 61. https://doi.org/10.1007/s41347-016-0006-y

Klasnja, P., Hekler, E. B., Shiffman, S., Boruvka, A., Almirall, D., Tewari, A., & Murphy, S. A. (2015). Microrandomized trials: An experimental design for developing just-in-time adaptive interventions. *Health Psychology: Official Journal of the Division of Health Psychology, 34S*(0), 1220–1228. https://doi.org/10.1037/hea0000305

Kos, A., Tomažič, S., Umek, A. (2016). Evaluation of smartphone inertial sensor performance for cross-platform mobile applications. *Sensors (Basel), 16*(4), 477. https://doi.org/10.3390/s16040477

Lagan, S., D'Mello, R., Vaidyam, A., Bilden, R., & Torous, J. (2021). Assessing mental health apps marketplaces with objective metrics from 29,190 data points from 278 apps. *Acta Psychiatrica Scandinavica, 144*(1), 201–210. https://doi.org/10.1111/acps.13306

Larsen, M. E., Huckvale, K., Nicholas, J., Torus, J., Birrell, L., Li, E., & Reda, B. (2019). Using science to sell apps: Evaluation of mental health app store quality claims. *NPJ Digital Medicine*, 2, Article 18. https://doi.org/10.1038/s41746-019-0093-1

Lewis, C. C., Boyd, M., Puspitasari, A., Navarro, E., Howard, J., Kassab, H., Hoffman, M., Scott, K., Lyon, A., Douglas, S., Simon, G., & Kroenke, K. (2019). Implementing measurement-based care in behavioral health: A review. *JAMA Psychiatry, 76*(3), 324–335. https://doi.org/10.1001/jamapsychiatry.2018.3329

Lyon, A. R., Wasse, J. K., Ludwig, K., Zachry, M. Bruns, E. J., Unützer, J., & McCauley, E. (2016). The contextualized technology adaptation process (CTAP): Optimizing health information technology to improve mental health systems. *Administration and Policy in Mental Health, 43*(3), 394–409. https://doi.org/10.1007/s10488-015-0637-x

Miralles, I., Granell, C., Díaz-Sanahuja, L., Van Woensel, W., Bretón-López, J., Mira, A., Castilla, D., & Casteleyn, S. (2020). Smartphone apps for the treatment of mental disorders: Systematic review. *JMIR mHealth and uHealth, 8*(4), e14897. https://doi.org/10.2196/14897

Mohr, D. C, Hart, S. L., Howard, I., Julin, L., Vella, L., Catledge, C, & Feldman, M. D. (2006). Barders to psychotherapy among depressed and nondepressed primary care patients. *Annals of Behavioral Medicine, 32*(3), 254–258. https://doi.org/10.1207/s15324796abm3203_12

Montes, J. M, Medina, E., Gomez-Beneyto, M., & Maurino, J. A (2012). A short message service (SMS)-based strategy for enhancing adherence to antipsychotic medication in schizophrenia. *Psychiatry Research, 200*(2–3), 89–95. https://doi.org/10.1016/j.psychres.2012.07.034

Nahum-Shani, I., Potter, L. N., Lam, C. Y., Yap, J., Moreno, A., Stoffel, R., Wu, Z., Wan, N., Dempsey, W., Kumar, S., Ertin, E., Murphy, S. A., Rehg, J. M., & Wetter, D. W. (2021). The mobile assistance for regulating smoking (MARS) micro-randomized trial design protocol. *Contemporary Clinical Trials, 110*, 106513. https://doi.org/10.1016/j.cct.2021.106513

Nahum-Shani, I., Smith, S. N., Spring, B. J., Collins, L. M., Witkiewitz, K., Tewari, A., Murphy, S. A. (2018). Just-in-time adaptive interventions (JITAIs) in mobile health: Key components and design principles for ongoing health behavior support. *Annals of Behavioral Medicine, 52*(6), 446–462. https://doi.org/10.1007/s12160-016-9830-8

Newman, M. G., Consoli, A., & Taylor, C. B. (1997). Computers in assessment and cognitive behavioral treatment of clinical disorders: Anxiety as a case in point. *Behavior Therapy, 28*(2), 211–235. https://doi.org/10.1016/S0005-7894(97)80044-5

Reese, R. J., Conoley, C. W., & Brossart, D. F. (2002). Effectiveness of telephone counseling: A field-based investigation. *Journal of Counseling Psychology, 49*, 233–242. https://doi.org/10.1037/0022-0167.49.2.233

Roth, C. B., Papassotiropoulos, A., Brühl, A. B., Lang, U. E., & Huber, C. G. (2021). Psychiatry in the digital age: A blessing or a curse? *International Journal of Environmental Research and Public Health, 18*(16), 8302. https://doi.org/10.3390/ijerph18168302

Ruwaard, J., Lange, A., Schrieken, B., & Emmelkamp, P. (2011). Efficacy and effectiveness of online cognitive behavioral treatment: A decade of interapy research. *Studies in Health Technology and Informatics, 167*(1), 9–14. https://doi.org/10.3233/978-1-60750-766-6-9

Seppälä, J., De Vita, I., Jämsä, T., Miettunen, J., Isohanni, M., Rubinstein, K., Feldman, Y., Grasa, E., Corripio, I., Berdun, J., D'Amico, E., M-RESIST Group, & Bulgheroni, M. (2019). Mobile phone and wearable sensor-based mhealth approaches for psychiatric disorders and symptoms: Systematic review. *JMIR Mental Health, 6*(2), e9819. https://doi.org/10.2196/mental.9819

Shimokawa, K., Lambert, M. J., Smart, D. W. (2010). Enhancing treatment outcome of patients at risk of treatment failure: meta-analytic and mega-analytic review of a psychotherapy quality assurance system. *Journal of Consulting and Clinical Psychology, 78*(3), 298–311. https://doi.org/10.1037/a0019247

Simmonds-Buckley, M., Bennion, M. R., Kellett, S., Millings, A., Hardy, G. E., & Moore, R. K. (2020). Acceptability and effectiveness of NHS-recommended e-therapies for depression, anxiety, and stress: Meta-analysis. *Journal of Medical Internet Research, 22*(10), e17049. https://doi.org/10.2196/17049

Statistica. (n.d.). *Adult wearable users penetration rate in the United States from 2016 to 2022.* https://www.statista.com/statistics/793800/us-adult-wearable-penetration/

Steinfeld, B., Franklin, A., Mercer, B., Fraynt, R., Simon, G. (2016). Progress monitoring in an integrated health care system: Tracking behavioral health vital signs. *Administration and Policy in Mental Health, 43*(3), 369–378. https://doi.org/10.1007/s10488-015-0648-7

Stone, A. A., Shiffman, S., Schwartz, J. E., Broderick, J. E., & Hufford, M. R. (2003). Patient compliance with paper and electronic diaries. *Controlled Clinical Trials, 24*(2), 182–199. https://doi.org/10.1016/s0197-2456(02)00320-3

Stoyanov, S. R., Hides, L., Kavanagh, D. J., Zelenko, O., Tjondronegoro, D., & Mani, M. (2015). Mobile app rating scale: A new tool for assessing the quality of health mobile apps. *JMIR mHealth uHealth, 3*(1), e27. https://doi.org/10.2196/mhealth.3422

Topooco, N., Riper, H., Araya, R. Berking, M. Brunn, M., Chevreul, K., Cieslak, R., Ebert, D. D., Etchmendy, E., Herrero, R., Kleiboer, A., Krieger, T., García-Palacios, A., Cerga-Pashoja, A., Smoktunowicz, E., Urech, A., Vis, C., & Andersson, G. (2017). Attitudes towards digital treatment for depression: A European stakeholder survey. *Internet Interventions, 8,* 1–9. https://doi.org/10.1016/j.invent.2017.01.001

van Os, J., Verhagen, S., Marsman, A., Peeters, F., Bak, M., Marcelis, M., Drukker, M., Reininghaus, U., Jacobs, N., Lataster, T., Simons, C., ESM-MERGE Investigators PhD, Lousberg, R., Gülöksüz, S., Leue, C., Groot, P. C., Viechtbauer, W., & Delespaul, P. (2017). The experience sampling method as an mHealth tool to support self-monitoring, self-insight, and personalized health care in clinical practice. *Depression and Anxiety, 34*(6), 481–493. https://doi.org/10.1002/da.22647

Varker, T., Brand, R. M., Ward, J., Terhaag, S., & Phelps, A. (2019). Efficacy of synchronous telepsychology interventions for people with anxiety, depression, posttraumatic stress disorder, and adjustment disorder: A rapid evidence assessment. *Psychological Services, 16*(4), 621–635. https://doi.org/10.1037/ser0000239

Verhagen, S., van Os, J., & Delespaul, P. (2022). Ecological momentary assessment and other digital technologies for capturing daily life in mental health. In D. J. Stein, N. A. Fineberg, & S. R. Chamberlain (Eds.), *Mental health in a digital world* (pp. 81–108). Elsevier.

Vlaescu, G., Alasjö, A., Miloff, A., Carlbring, P., & Andersson, G. (2016). Features and functionality of the Iterapi platform for internet-based psychological treatment. *Internet Interventions, 6,* 107–114. https://doi.org/10.1016/j.invent.2016.09.006

Waller, G., & Turner, H. (2016). Therapist drift redux: Why well-meaning clinicians fail to deliver evidence-based therapy, and how to get back on track. *Behaviour Research and Therapy, 77,* 129–137. https://doi.org/10.1016/j.brat.2015.12.005

Wilhelm, S., Weingarden, H., Ladis, I., Braddick, V., Shin, J., & Jacobson, N.C. (2020). Cognitive-behavioral therapy in the digital age: Presidential address. *Behavioral Therapy, 51*(1), 1–14. https://doi.org/10.1016/j.beth.2019.08.001

Williams, C. (2001). Use of written cognitive–behavioural therapy self-help materials to treat depression. *Advances in Psychiatric Treatment, 7*(3), 233–240. https://doi.org/10.1192/apt.7.3.233

World Health Organization. (2016). *Global diffusion of eHealth: Making universal health coverage achievable: Report of the third global survey on eHealth.* World Health Organization. https://www.who.int/publications/i/item/9789241511780

Young, K. S. (2005). An empirical examination of client attitudes towards online counseling. *Cyberpsychology & Behavior, 8*(2), 172–177. https://doi.org/10.1089/cpb.2005.8.172

Zale, A., Lasecke, M., Baeza-Hernandez, K., Testerman, A., Aghakhani, S., Muñoz, R. F., & Bunge, E. L. (2021). Technology and psychotherapeutic interventions: Bibliometric analysis of the past four decades. *Internet Interventions, 25,* 100425. https://doi.org/10.1016/j.invent.2021.100425

Zarate, C. A, Weinstock, L., Cukor, P., Morabito, C., Leahy, L., Burns, C., & Baer, L. (1997). Applicability of telemedicine for assessing patients with schizophrenia: Reliability and acceptance. *Journal of Clinical Psychiatry, 58*(1), 22–25. https://doi.org/10.4088/jcp.v58n0104

# SECTION II

VIDEO GAMES

CHAPTER 3

# DIGITAL GAME PSYCHOLOGY

## Roots, Dynamics, and Beyond

**Armin Klaps**
***Sigmund Freud University***

**Birgit Ursula Stetina**
***Sigmund Freud University***

### UNCOVERING THE PSYCHOLOGICAL DYNAMICS OF GAMING POPULARITY

*There is no path. Beyond the scope of light, beyond the reach of Dark . . . what could possibly await us? And yet, we seek it, insatiably . . . Such is our fate.*

—Wyche & Bosso, 2022

Unexplored endless worlds with fascinating landscapes and wildest varieties of creatures, inviting social structures and endless possibilities to be and become who one always wanted to be, completely independent from the boundaries of the real world.

Sounds unrealistic?

Well, it is not, not for gamers.

*Digital Developments,* pages 39–52

Sounds dangerous?

Well, it depends on how the multifaceted possibilities are used.

The introduction of the Internet gaming disorder (IGD) diagnosis in DSM-5 (research diagnosis) and ICD-11 (diagnosis) marks the first time that the mass phenomenon of gaming has been clinically addressed. Classification manuals differ in regards to the new construct IGD. Escapism and avoidance are constructs measured by standardized tests that play a central role in the diagnosis of IGD. Of course, these two important terms are not only found in the new diagnosis of IGD but also, for example, in the complete spectrum of anxiety disorders (Melodia et al., 2020). Regarding mental health, professional gaming is not considered a "positive" activity by the general public and in the worst case it is used to explain extreme psychopathological behaviors of violent offenders in mass shootings. No school shooting goes without press coverage of the killer's preferred ego-shooter, leaving out any (and in those cases crucial) explanations on causal relations. The topic of gaming leads to a broad spectrum of very emotional responses and it is still uncommon to openly discuss preferred games in the same way as preferred sports or books (Andrade & Ho, 2009).

Scientifically, the theory of game psychology accepts the fascination and tries to explain the enjoyment of games. A certain behavior lies beneath all that, and it needs to be explained and understood as well. One of behaviorism's godfathers proposed valuable theories that can still be applied and show an astonishing fit regarding gaming. Thorndike (1905) placed a cat in a puzzle box and encouraged it to escape and reach the food that was placed outside. After the cat was placed in the box, the time it took the cat to escape from the box was measured. The cats experimented with different ways to escape from the puzzle box to reach the food. After several attempts, they touched the lever that opened the cage. When the cat escaped, it was put back into the box and the time was measured again. In the following trials, the cats learned that touching the lever created a favorable starting position, so they adopted this behavior and touched the lever faster and faster. Edward Thorndike established his famous "law of effect" which states that any behavior that produces pleasant consequences is likely to be repeated, and any behavior that produces unpleasant consequences is likely to be discontinued. As this is not new to any psychologist, the application to gaming is easy and fascinating at the same time. Applied to gaming, we propose Thorndike's law means that once players have figured out a part of a game's mechanics, they will use that behavior again and again. Programmers can take advantage of this property and change game mechanics to dynamically adjust the level of difficulty in games. This can be motivating but also frustrating. Games like World of Warcraft are good examples of how bosses (as final challenges of a level in the game) have their own game mechanics and can change them over the course of a fight.

This means that players can only adapt to a certain behavior to a limited extent, and the same behavior does not always lead to the desired result. Players today need to be cognitively able to envision and execute multiple solutions, and this makes many games attractive by being challenging. This argumentation is the consequent continuation of the intellectual nature of the idea of Thorndike's law.

Since the rise of online games, several ideas with regards to the underlying dynamics have been published. Most seem to be based on motivational theories such as the one of Nick Yee (2007), who proposed three motivational components of online gaming, that have been used widely in the scientific community since then. His motivational framework includes the three major components, that are: achievement, social, and immersion, with 10 underlying aspects, all of them applicable to a large variety of games' genres. The well-known study of Boyle and colleagues (2011) uses the construct of the self-determination theory, with the factor's competence, autonomy, and relatedness, that seem to be the prerequisite to enjoy activities, including gaming, of course (Boyle et al., 2011).

These are the underlying theories and approaches the following text is subsequently trying to use to shed light on unexplored dynamics. After a first insight into gaming dynamics, a new video trend is introduced (Let's Play Videos) to lead the reader into a historical overview of the start and evolution of video games. Returning to the present, the dynamics of microtransactions and in-game purchases are discussed including the highly problematic aspects related to the trends that are found all over a variety of gaming genres.

The fascination of digital games is based on several factors such as the gaming experience itself and the existing gaming culture, in which social networks and streaming platforms also play a role (Gros et al., 2017). Yee's (2021) current model shows how motivation in gaming can be classified on a continuum and how many constructs contribute to motivation. These are not always equally present and vary between games. A whole subfield of gaming research focuses on the study of gaming motivation alone. A recent study by the well-known gaming researcher Yee shows the possibilities of games and which constructs can be combined respectively which are perceived by players (see Table 3.1). The most common combinations and a possible explanation of the motivation behind them were described (Yee, 2021).

**TABLE 3.1 Game Motivation Model**

| Action | Social | Mastery | Achievement | Immersion | Creativity |
|---|---|---|---|---|---|
| Destruction | Competition | Challenge | Completion | Fantasy | Design |
| Excitement | Community | Strategy | Power | Story | Discovery |

*Source:* Yee, 2021

The action–social combination concerns players who are interested in immediacy and the rush of adrenaline. Players in this cluster look for excitement through high scores in the game itself or in interaction with other players. Players who prefer the mastery–achievement combination are looking to play long term and with calculation. Game mechanics should be cumulative so that, for example, cities grow and become more complex over time. Immersion creativity is a play style that seeks expansive and expressive worlds. One is curious and tests the limits of the game. Classic for this are open-world scenarios.

## ONLINE GAMES AS SOCIAL NETWORKS

Online games have now developed into virtual places of social interaction, where people chat or communicate via headsets. They arrange to meet friends in online games, with the game world receding into the background. Mannerisms from digital games are also being transferred to real life. A prominent example are dances from Fortnite (Fortnite is a survival game where 100 players fight against each other in player versus player combat to be the last one standing. It is a fast-paced, action-packed game, where strategic thinking is a must in order to survive) which are now even performed by professional soccer players as a form of goal celebration.

Despite, or perhaps because of, their popularity, many online games include challenges similar to those faced by classic social networks. Phenomena such as cyberbullying, fake news, and hate speech can also be found in online games. There is also a phenomenon called griefing. When players in multiplayer games deliberately act against the server rules or community guidelines and in this way rob other players of the game fun and prevent the game progress. Above all, the anonymity of users by using avatars and nicknames creates a breeding ground for such phenomena. Avatars and nicknames give players the chance to disappear into anonymity to do things that would be harder to do in real life. Directly insulting someone is easier with filters interposed (Ichino et al., 2022).

## VIDEO GAMES SINCE THE BEGINNING

To get an idea of video games, their potential, meaning the power that lies within, it is crucial to understand their historical development. The first appearance of video games was in the 1950s. The first video game was a computer simulation of tic-tac-toe which was developed for the Electronic Delay Storage Automatic Calculator (EDSAC). The next big step was Pong, an electronic table-tennis simulation game. Pong was the first video game for a generation in the 1970s and is nowadays a symbol of early video games (Egenfeldt-Nielsen, 2008). Pong is a very interesting topic because it created an interface to use complex machines with motor skills in a time before personal computers were available for the public. The evolution of video games until now roots in simple tools, which became complex big online worlds that can communicate cultural values, knowledge, human relationships, and soft skills.

The second relevant historical step was arcade games, which appeared in the early 1970s. Arcade games were coin-operated, and the first model was Space Wars. For the general public the game was too difficult to control and another problem was the steep learning curve. As a reaction Atari created a much more usable arcade game with Pong and started the success story of their well-known brand. The next step was that Atari placed Pong in bars beside pinball machines and some other games. At the end of 1970s more arcade games were created and their popularity was rising (Forster, 2015; Kent, 1997).

In 1972, Ralph Baer licensed the first video game console Magnavox for televisions. The Magnavox Odyssey was programmable but without cartridges. Every game needed a change of the wiring in the Odyssey. Naturally the next big step was the development of game cartridges, which eliminated the need for rewiring the console. The cartridges stored the games. After this revolution many groups released their version of cartridge consoles, but only Atari's 2600 console was able to reach the public. One reason was that many people who bought the Atari 2600 knew the brand as the arcade machines in the 1970s. Games like Pac-Man and Space Invaders made Atari successful (Forster, 2015).

The first computer for consumers' homes was built in 1975. The concept was to sell a complete set for the public which included monitor, central unit, disc-drive, and software. The selling started years after home consoles and addressed home users and not professional users. In 1977, two very important brands entered the market of home computers. The Commodore PET and Apple II (Forster, 2015). Home computers allowed the development of more complex games. The processors were more powerful and so the games could have extended plots and storylines. The users were involved in a narrative for the first time. Solving problems and moving through landscapes assisted the early appearance of immersion and narrative. The players were able to develop a new form of interaction in relation to the complex stories in the games, which was the start of a new era. To understand current developments, one must always look at the history of their origins. This is characterized by successes and also failures. In the end, gaming has become a cultural phenomenon. The term Esport as the latest development in the field of gaming (also spelled E-Sport, eSports or e-Sport) refers to professional competition in computer and video games. As with classic sports, esports are also about competing or measuring oneself against others in a discipline. Many highly interesting psychological questions can be derived from this history (Loftus & Loftus, 1983). Loftus and Lotus (1983) already wrote about mental health in relation to gaming and defined three questions for this purpose:

- Is the behavior good for the person?
- Is the person in touch with reality?
- Is the person's behavior markedly different from the norm?

These questions are precise and you can see from this that you have dealt with the phenomenon early on. The third question is a very relevant one because it takes up the concept of norm in the field of clinical psychology, which is often about norms. At what point do we speak of abnormal behavior? That's why the diagnostic and statistical manual (DSM) and international classifications of diseases (ICD) are important indicators so that we can communicate internationally. But these norms are subject to permanent change. As an example, it should be mentioned again that ICD-11 and DSM-5 each include the IGD, but the concurrent classification differs.

## THE RAPID EVOLUTION OF VIDEO GAMES

In the 1980s and 1990s the hardware of consoles and home computers was getting better and better. More new brands entered the market (see Table 3.2) and video games entered millions of living rooms and households. At this time point the games and their dynamics started to influence

**TABLE 3.2 Sales Figures for the World's Best-Selling Game Consoles by the End of October 2022**

| Device (rollout Europe) | Million per Piece |
|---|---|
| Playstation 2 (2000) | 157.68 |
| Nintendo DS (2005) | 154.90 |
| Game Boy (1990) | 118.69 |
| Playstation 4 (2013) | 116.82 |
| Nintendo Switch (2017) | 102.76 |
| Xbox 360 (2005) | 85.50 |
| Nintendo Entertainment System (NES) (1986) | 61.91 |
| Sega Genesis (1990) | 29.54 |
| Atari 2600 (1982) | 27.64 |

*Source:* Statista, 2022b

culture, perception, and social dynamics. A look at the social side of video games naturally leads to seeing games as examples of what social scientists call collective behavior. We usually speak of collective behavior when many people have a common goal with common direction. Participants in such behaviors do not necessarily have to be together, for example, as in a soccer stadium. Similar to the analogy of watching a football game on television. A common focus or direction may be based on a desire to effect lasting social change, as in the nuclear phase-out movement. Or it could be pure entertainment, as in a rock concert (Loftus & Loftus, 1983).

Today online games have continued to develop and are therefore attracting a huge number of players every day. In 2010, the massively multiplayer online role-playing game (MMORPG) World of Warcraft had 12 million active players on their servers (Statista, 2022a). But it is neither the only popular game, nor is there only one console. Gamers today have many options. The gaming industry has developed into a huge market. There are several gaming consoles available, video games for home computers, virtual reality headsets (for home computers and consoles), augmented reality headsets and cloud gaming are also possible. From a clinical psychologist perspective, there is one special device in the focus. VR-headsets and AR-headsets may have a great impact for treatment because of a new level of immersion. Interaction in AR and VR will be able to embody a new structure of using technologies in the virtual environment (Cipresso et al., 2018).

## TRENDS AND RISKS

Current trends in games show risks as well as opportunities that are worth exploring from a psychological point of view and can be categorized into aspects of education, microtransactions, downloadable contents (DLCs), in-game currencies, virtual items, loot boxes, and dealing with in-game purchases in general.

### Education

Even though digital games are an integral part of the everyday lives of many children and young people, they still play a subordinate role in the educational context. Yet digital games have great potential for teaching and learning scenarios. Complex content can be visualized in a realistic way via digital games. In addition, game scenarios can have a motivating effect and get students excited about rather difficult or non-attractive learning material. Gamification is a motivational learning tool that, when properly designed and used, can enhance the learning process. It has the potential to increase motivation, engagement, and participation, improve cognitive performance, support personalized learning, reduce student absenteeism, and develop a range of skills (Acosta-Medina et al., 2020). In addition, schools must also have the technical prerequisites to use digital games. Depending on the game, this can be done with smartphones, tablets, laptops, or desktop PCs, for example. But it is not just the games themselves that need to be the focus of the lessons. In this way, media literacy can also be promoted with a view to other forms of media work. In addition, teachers can use this to facilitate interdisciplinary learning.

Examples of digital games that can bring new ideas into the classroom are manifold and range exemplarily from Assassins Creed to Minecraft.

- Assassin's Creed Origins: The game has an education mode that allows players to freely explore the world of the ancient Egyptians. The game provides historical information about important buildings and cultural customs. For this purpose, the game offers themed tours without any time pressure or combat.
- Valiant Hearts: Valiant Hearts is set in the First World War in terms of content and offers a mixture of puzzle game and adventure game. The game is based on real letters and historical materials from the war period. It tells the story of four characters who experience wartime in their own way. The game was awarded by a French historical commission for its historical accuracy.
- Minecraft: Minecraft is a kind of construction kit game with the goal of forming various shapes from blocks. Among other things, buildings, tools, but also animals and plants can be created from the blocks. The building block system makes it possible to transfer topics from the subject lessons to the virtual world. For example, students can recreate certain buildings or illustrate complex facts such as the structure of a molecule with the help of the blocks.
- Scratch: Scratch is not a game in the classic sense, but a programming environment that allows students to create animations and digital applications. For example, students can program their own computer game or use Scratch to define command sequences for robots. The programming interface is clearly and simply designed, so that even beginners can quickly find their way around and gain a first insight into the world of programming.

The listed games offer the possibility to use them in the sense of gamification especially when focusing on the context. Possibilities of use in the educational sector have already been briefly explained. Psychological questions can also be derived from thinking about the possibilities consistently. In the field of educational and developmental psychology. Quasi-experimental settings for research in the education sector might include children taught using traditional materials and others taught by means of gamification. Future research questions seem without limit.

However, depending on which game is chosen, there are also pitfalls that have been built in by the game companies. The keyword here is microtransactions. This type of monetization is intended to get players to pay small amounts of money for additional game content. This is a fact that is well known and has led to the fact that even countries have begun to ban this type of payment.

## Microtransactions/In-Game Purchase

A box full of "smurf berries," an additional level, or a new costume for the hero: Virtually purchasable goods in computer games can be found in a wide variety of manifestations and the range is constantly increasing. Whether on the computer, on the game console, or on the mobile device: So-called in-game purchases have become an indispensable part of many computer games today. The main reason is that they have become a profitable source of income for the gaming industry. The actual main game can be free of charge (so-called free-to-play games) or subject to a charge. Free-to-play games are most common in the form of browser games and apps. In-game purchases within apps are also known as in-app purchases. The term in-game purchase basically refers to the acquisition of virtual services or goods within computer games. In-game purchases were established as a common business model for PC and console games. Unlike apps and browser games, however, the main game usually must be purchased. Generally, there are different types of in-game purchases, which are briefly presented below.

1. Downloadable Contents (DLCs): The abbreviation DLC stands for downloadable content and refers to downloadable add-on content for games. These expansion packs usually include additional game missions, levels, or characters for a particular computer game. A download is possible, for example, via the distribution platforms of the game consoles, but also via common sales portals such as eBay or Amazon. Most DLCs are priced between 10 and 20 EUR. The appeal of such additional content lies primarily in extending or expanding the gameplay experience of the main game.
2. In-Game Currencies: The use of game currencies is particularly widespread in apps and browser games, affecting games for all age groups. Although the download and the first use of many apps and browser games are free of charge, the game mechanisms are often designed in such a way that the use of digital currencies gives users

advantages: This can manifest itself, for example, in shortening waiting times in the game or making it easier to solve particularly difficult levels. Some games might even be difficult to play without additional purchases. The purchase process takes place within the in-game store (a store that can be accessed via the game menu), where the currency can be purchased for real money. In their presentation, the digital goods are often deliberately abstracted so that the players have no direct reference to the expenditures made. Typical game currencies are in addition to in-game money or gold, food or raw materials. Examples of apps that use virtual currencies are "Clash of Clans" (jewels), "The Simpsons Springfield" (donuts), "Smurf Village" (smurf berries), or "Candy Crush Saga" (gold). An example of a browser game is "Farmerama" (tulip guilders).

3. Virtual Items: Virtual items often appear in games with role-playing elements. In this type of game, players take on the role of a virtual character, an avatar, which they accompany in its development and advance its abilities. Objects that can be acquired in the game are, for example, weapons or pieces of equipment. One role-playing game that relies on such a sales system is "Diablo 3." The game has already made headlines due to the use of an auction house for buying and selling virtual items, as particularly rare pieces of equipment were purchased by buyers here, sometimes for several thousand euros. This circumstance led to criticism of the system used—but the appealing feeling of being able to call an item as rare as possible one's own still motivates many players to buy it.
4. Loot boxes: Loot boxes are virtual boxes in computer games that contain a randomly determined selection of items. These include, for example, game weapons or rare items of equipment for the game character. Loot boxes are often used in so-called free-to-play games. The use of free-to-play games is free of charge, but the purchase of loot boxes is often a prerequisite for progress in the game. In addition to mobile games, cross-platform game titles such as FIFA and Overwatch now also rely on this source of revenue. So-called loot boxes were also used in a certain mode in the game Fortnite. However, these were removed again at the beginning of 2019.

The broad variety of in-game purchases show that certain strategies are needed for gamers to be able to navigate the jungle of endless possibilities to spend a fortune in tiny increments. For children and adolescents, as one of the main target groups, dealing with virtual goods represents a major challenge. They are often unable to properly assess the amount of expenditure made digitally. An important point here is the fact that many online stores, or sales platforms of game consoles, rely on payment by credit card. After entering the card data once, all payment processes are child's play. The findings support that the use of loot boxes may be associated with problem gambling due to increased participation in video games. Certain subtypes of adolescent gamblers may develop symptoms of gambling disorder due to the use of loot boxes and intensive use of video games. The practical implications of prevention and treatment are discussed (Primi et al., 2022). From a clinical psychology perspective, it is important to consider these mechanisms in both research and treatment.

## GAMING AND GENRES

For clinical psychology it is important that the DSM-5 (American Psychiatric Association, 2013) describes gambling disorder and IGD. These classifications play a role when discussing online gaming. Many games are played with other gamers online in immersive big virtual worlds and these games can also have gambling characteristics (loot-boxes). Research today is focusing on the gaming genres. Stetina et al. (2016) grouped the recent trends into the seven most played genres: (a) MMORPG, (b) shooter (including MMO & tactical), (c) casual (handy games), (d) action RPGs (incl. horror/survival), (e) multi play online battle arenas (MOBA), (f) simulation, and (g) real-timeime strategy (RTS/S).

All those genres differ with regards to Yee's motivational framework and clinical aspects with the most relevant clinical predictor for problematic gaming behavior being the subscale escapism. Most studies show a low percentage of participants suffering from clinical problems. But in all gamers (dependent and recreational) significant differences between males and females are reported with female gamers showing significantly fewer problematic behaviors but in some studies more loneliness. The relevant differences in gameplay motivation might be a key construct for further understanding of problematic gaming behavior in the future. Most online gaming genres also offer numerous possibilities for intervention in the sense of the first and second wave of cognitive behavior therapy. Each genre of games offers a different possibility or already does so in the form of learning the necessary skills to succeed in the games.

## A CLINICIAN'S VIEW AND OUTLOOK

A variety of genres offer possibilities in terms of cognitive behavioral therapy because of the game mechanics on which these games are based. Cognitive skills are trained in the areas of perception, thinking, memory, problem solving, imagination, and creativity. The social and emotional competences are promoted solely by the fact that certain online games do not offer the gaming experience if one does not play in a group. This makes it necessary to join groups and to submit to social conventions. Along with this, players need emotional competences to be able to deal with the demands of the group. This concerns above all the understanding of emotions, emotion regulation, and the ability to empathize. These skills can be promoted through online gaming. It is not possible to generalize, but it is possible to identify genres that have more potential to promote skills. Online gaming, like other games, is based on the principle of many factors (Yee, 2021). However, the ratio varies greatly between the many different games. A professional who uses gaming as a therapeutic tool needs the concurrent knowledge to be able to navigate the gaming jungle.

This ratio might become a trap when it comes to microtransactions. With those microtransactions and certain types of them one enters the realm of gambling. Engagement in gambling is related to increased psychological stress (Li et al., 2019). It becomes gambling as soon as customers no longer know what they can get for their money.

Games can offer progress and success: visible progress and success and the rules for success and rewards are very clear. One needs to add that in real life that is often quite complicated and not so clear at all. Yet, through these games it is amongst other positive effects possible to build resilience to pursue and ultimately achieve a certain goal. If a professional works with techniques that focus on change and goal orientation this is just one example of how, within the therapeutic setting, these experiences of people can be used and applied to therapeutic goals. In terms of cognitive behavioral therapy in general, this means that professionals who are willing to use games in their treatments have to explore whether online gaming is or was an issue and to what intensity. This is important because there is an IGD in the ICD-11 and at the same time it can be an indication that people from this area are cognitively accessible and have already consciously experienced the principle of reinforcement and conditioning to a certain extent. Self-efficacy can also be retrieved through successes in the various games. Technology evolves and so do people. Gaming as a trend with all its facets should be researched and the diagnosis of IGD should also be considered. However, it should not be forgotten that humans are adaptive beings and can adopt technology without harm. Gaming can be an opportunity for development and coping.

## REFERENCES

Acosta-Medina, J. K., Torres-Barreto, M. L., & Alvarez-Melgarejo, M. (2020). Literature mapping about gamification in the teaching and learning processes. *Espacios,*

*41*(11), 26. https://www.researchgate.net/publication/340789969_Literature_mapping_about_gamification_in_the_teaching_and_learning_processes

American Psychiatric Association. (2013). *Diagnostic and statistical manual of mental disorders* (5th ed.). https://doi.org/10.1176/appi.books.9780890425596

Andrade, E. B., & Ho, T. H. (2009). Gaming emotions in social interactions. *Journal of Consumer Research, 36*(4), 539–552. https://doi.org/10.1086/599221

Boyle, E., Connolly, T. M., & Hainey, T. (2011). The role of psychology in understanding the impact of computer games. *Entertainment Computing, 2*(2), 69–74. https://doi.org/10.1016/j.entcom.2010.12.002

Cipresso, P., Giglioli, I., Raya, M. A., & Riva, G. (2018). The past, present, and future of virtual and augmented reality research: A network and cluster analysis of the literature. *Frontiers in Psychology, 9*, 2086. https://doi.org/10.3389/fpsyg.2018.02086

Egenfeldt-Nielsen, S., Heide Smith, J., & Pajares Tosca, S. (2008). *Understanding video games: The essential introduction* (3rd ed.). Taylor & Francis.

Forster, W. (2015). *Spielekonsolen und Heimcomputer: 1972–2015* (5th ed.) [Games consoles and home computers: 1972–2015]. Gameplan.

Gros, D., Wanner, B., Hackenholt, A., Zawadzki, P., & Knautz, K. (2017). World of streaming: Motivation and gratification on Twitch. In G. Meiselwitz (Ed.), *Social computing and social media: Human behavior* (pp. 44–57). Springer.

Ichino, J., Ide, M., Yokoyama, H., Asano, H., Miyachi, H., & Okabe, D. (2022). "I've talked without intending to": Self-disclosure and reciprocity via embodied avatar. Proceedings of the *ACM on Human-Computer Interaction, 6*(CSCW2), Article 482. https://doi.org/10.1145/3555583

Kent, S. (1997, September 1997). *Super Mario nation.* American Heritage. https://www.americanheritage.com/super-mario-nation

Li, W., Mills, D., & Nower, L. (2019). The relationship of loot box purchases to problem video gaming and problem gambling. Addictive Behaviors, *97*, 27–34. https://doi.org/10.1016/j.addbeh.2019.05.016

Loftus, G. R., & Loftus, E. F. (1983). *Mind at play: The psychology of video games.* Basic Books.

Melodia, F., Canale, N., & Griffiths, M. D. (2020). The role of avoidance coping and escape motives in problematic online gaming: A systematic literature review. *International Journal of Mental Health and Addiction, 20,* 996–1022. https://doi.org/10.1007/s11469-020-00422-w

Primi, C., Sanson, F., Vecchiato, M., Serra, E., & Donati, M. A. (2022). Loot boxes use, video gaming, and gambling in adolescents: Results from a path analysis before and during COVID-19-pandemic-related lockdown in Italy. *Frontiers in Psychology, 13,* 5909. https://doi.org/10.3389/fpsyg.2022.1009129

Statista. (2022a, July 27). *Anzahl der Abonnenten von World of Warcraft weltweit vom 1. Quartal 2005* [Number of World of Warcraft subscribers worldwide as of Q1 2005]. Statista. https://de.statista.com/statistik/daten/studie/208146/umfrage/anzahl-der-abonnenten-von-world-of-warcraft/

Statista. (2022b, December 11). *Verkaufszahlen der weltweit meistverkauften Spielekonsolen bis Ende Oktober 2022* [Sales figures for the world's best-selling game consoles until the end of October 2022]. https://de.statista.com/

statistik/daten/studie/160549/umfrage/anzahl-der-weltweit-verkauften-spielkonsolen-nach-konsolentypen/

Stetina, B. U., Klaps, A., Kovacovsky, Z., Aden, J., Bendas, C., Daude, A., Kluss, K., & Lehenbauer-Baum, M. (2016, March 2–4). *Gaming-genres and motivation: Why do we play what we play?* [Oral presentation]. 18th General Online Research Conference, Dresden, Germany. https://www.researchgate.net/publication/296696459_GAMING-GENRES_AND_MOTIVATION_WHY_DO_WE_PLAY_WHAT_WE_PLAY

Thorndike, E. L. (1905). *The elements of psychology.* A. G. Seiler.

Wyche, J., & Bosso, A. N. (2022, April 1). *Dark souls: 16 moments unforgettable quotes from the series. thegamer.com.* https://www.thegamer.com/dark-souls-games-memorable-quotes/

Yee, N. (2007). Motivations for play in online games. *Cyberpsychology & Behavior, 9*(6), 772–775. https://doi.org/10.1089/cpb.2006.9.772

Yee, N. (2021, December 12). *A closer look into the 12 gamer motivations–ironSource LevelUp.* Medium. https://medium.com/ironsource-levelup/a-closer-look-into-the-12-gamer-motivations-8d156ff0151a

CHAPTER 4

# VIDEO GAMING FOR YOUR WELL-BEING

## What We Know From 20 Years of Research

**Claudia Carissoli**
***Universitá Cattolica del Sacro Cuore***

**Daniela Villani**
***Universitá Cattolica del Sacro Cuore***

Video games (VGs) represent a very widespread activity among people. According to the Statista report 2021,[1] there are 3.24 billion gamers across the globe. Most of them are adolescents and children: In Europe 76% of children aged 6–14 and 90% of teens aged 13–17[2] in the United States play VGs.

Despite the risks associated with their use (see Chapter 2, this volume), the enjoyment and intrinsic motivation make VGs a valuable and attractive medium able to promote well-being and even offer psychological support to people (Pallavicini et al., 2018). During the lockdown period due to the COVID-19 virus pandemic, the number of gamers and the time spent

*Digital Developments*, pages 53–70

in playing has dramatically increased (Johannes et al., 2021; Wiederhold, 2021). In fact, VGs represented a fun way to spend time and to stay connected with other people, overcoming the sense of isolation. Moreover, for good or ill, they have offered a unique mood-boosting and stress-reducing solution to deal with anxiety and uncertainty (Johannes et al., 2021; Wiederhold, 2021), loneliness (Kaye et al., 2017), and the negative emotional effects experienced due to pandemic issues (Barr & Copeland-Stewart, 2021; Viana & Barbosa de Lira, 2020).

VGs are artefacts developed through a digital visual medium, with the aim to provide entertainment through rules and objective gameplay and/or interactive narrative (Tavinor, 2009). Their components, such as setting, story, and objects interact according to a specific set of rules, which will eventually lead to the final outcome (Salen & Zimmerman, 2005). Moreover, technological evolution transformed VGs from simple interactive activities into real multisensory experiences (visual, auditory, proprioceptive), which even allow the manipulation of affective states through the experience of intense and realistic emotions. During the game, gamers feel fully immersed in the virtual world of the game, in which they can move and with which they can interact freely through their avatars, the gamer's alter-ego (Gaggioli et al., 2014; Triberti et al., 2017; Triberti & Argenton, 2013; Wiederhold & Wiederhold, 2005), through sensations, emotions, and behaviors typical of everyday reality, experiencing a sense of immersion, transparency of the medium, presence and interactivity (Di Letizia, 2014; Villani, Grassi, Cognetta, et al., 2011). The avatar turns into "a vicarious identity," embodied, to the point of being endowed with a brain, with its own emotional life. The player is responsible for what happens in the game, for the actions and even their consequences in the virtual world. The game world becomes, thus, a space for experimentation, in which the player engages and evolves (Janssen & Tortolano, 2010).

Thanks to their features, VGs may offer many opportunities to promote individuals' positive functioning and to develop new life skills. Starting from these premises, the purpose of this chapter, without claiming to be exhaustive, is to analyze VGs as positive technologies, offering suggestions for their use and future research.

## VIDEO GAMES, POSITIVE TECHNOLOGIES

According to Riva et al. (Botella et al., 2012; Riva et al., 2012; Villani, Grassi, & Riva, 2011) it is possible to combine the goals of positive psychology with technology in a new paradigm: positive technology. Positive technology aims to use technology "to modify the characteristics of our personal experience—structuring, augmenting, or replacing it with synthetic environments—in order to improve the quality of our personal experience, and increase well-being in individuals, organizations, and societies" (Riva et al., 2012, p. 69). According to this paradigm, three different types of technologies can be used to reach this goal:

- hedonic well-being, technologies used to induce positive and pleasant experiences, such as casual VGs that are able to alter gamers' mood inducing positive and pleasant emotions (Russoniello et al., 2009);
- eudaimonic well-being, technologies used to support people in achieving engaging and self-realizing experiences, such as VR protocol developed to help people to cope with the negative psychological effects of COVID-19 (anxiety, depression and reduced social connectedness; Riva, Bernardelli et al., 2020); and
- social/interpersonal well-being, technologies used to support and improve social integration and/or connectedness between individuals, groups, and organizations, such as "My Country Talks"[3] that is an international social sharing platform where people can discuss one-on-one with similar or different viewpoints, eliciting a sense of connectedness (Riva, Mantovani et al., 2020).

VGs are able to generate meaningful experiences for individuals of a hedonic, eudaimonic, and interpersonal nature (Ferguson & Olson, 2012; Granic et al., 2014), as illustrated in the next paragraphs, and that is why they can be included among positive technologies (Triberti & Argenton, 2013).

## HEDONIC VIDEO GAMES EXPERIENCE

According to the hedonic perspective, subjective well-being is represented by the presence of positive emotional states and the absence of negative ones. VGs can promote positive emotional states (Anolli et al., 2010; Argenton et al., 2014) and emotions: enjoyment and fun are often the main reasons to play (Chou & Tsai, 2007; Connolly et al., 2012; Yee, 2006). Numerous studies found a causal relationship between playing one's favorite VGs and improvements in mood and positive emotions (Russoniello et al., 2009; Ryan et al., 2006), relief from stress and boredom while creating a feeling of relaxation (Pine et al., 2020). A recent study based on the broaden-and-build theory, found that playing the mobile game *Pokémon Go* induced positive affect such as nostalgic feelings, and friendship initiation and intensification (Bonus et al., 2017). According to the broaden-and-build theory, adolescents' game experiences can broaden their mental states and enhance resources such as knowledge, self-insight, or social connections that fulfil their specific needs, benefiting their healthy development process (Fredrickson, 2004).

However, VGs can also induce negative emotions, elicited by the structure or narrative content of VGs, typically sadness, anxiety, and fear. In this case, pleasure and positive emotions can derive from the mere enjoyment of the artifact, related not to the terrifying or tragic object, but to the narrative structure and style that characterize the game's structure. On the other hand, based on the classical theory of catharsis, enjoying tragic plays might allow one to purge oneself of negative emotions such as pity or fear and this is undeniably a desirable and absolutely rational purpose (Barbero, 2008). Furthermore, aggressive playing can be a way to vent and get rid of negative emotions such as anger, guilt, or frustration in a "safe" way, avoiding aggressive real-life behavior (Colwell, 2007; Ferguson & Rueda, 2010). Also failure, often experienced in VGs and associated with frustration and anger can turn into positive emotions because VGs allow the gamer to overcome the sense of inadequacy that they themselves have generated (Juul, 2013; Triberti, 2016).

## EUDAIMONIC VIDEO GAMES EXPERIENCE

VGs possess high quality, emotionally complex, and involving *narratives* that can promote eudaimonic game experiences (Kümpel & Unkel, 2017; Oliver et al., 2016; Rogers et al., 2017). Recent studies, based on Self Determination Theory, reported that video gaming allowed gamers to satisfy their universal psychological needs (autonomy, a sense of competence, and relatedness), that are essential to psychological growth, integrity, and well-being (Przybylski et al., 2009, Przybylski et al., 2014; Ryan & Deci, 2000).

As any player knows, gaming often elicits negative emotions, mainly due to the frequent failures they generate. Experiencing negative emotions may play a positive role in expanding emotional regulation skills (Granic et al., 2014; Villani et al., 2018). In fact, through frequent failures, players train themselves to cope with and modulate negative emotions in order to continue the game and achieve the desired outcome (Granic et al., 2014; Ventura et al., 2013). Specifically, the logic of play may promote adaptive emotion regulation strategies such as cognitive revaluation. This feature represents a crucial dimension that allows use of VGs as tools to enhance emotional intelligence by helping adolescents to evaluate, express, and to manage their own emotions (Carissoli & Villani, 2019).

Furthermore, in the game, individuals can express aspects of themselves that do not find expression in everyday life (Przybylski et al., 2012), and discover more about themselves, simply by observing their own reactions (Daneels et al., 2020). It is known that discrepancies between the real self (the representation of the characteristics one believes themselves to actually possess) and the ideal self (the representation of the characteristics one would ideally like to have) are associated with feelings of depression and disappointment (Higgins, 1989). Embodying one's ideals through an avatar may lead to increased self-esteem and a higher sense of attainability of the ideal self by reducing the self-discrepancy (Fong, 2017; Klimmt et al., 2009; Ryan & Deci, 2000; Triberti, 2016). Moreover, through the avatar features, gamers can express different aspects of their personality (Leroux, 2019) and bring about changes in the real self (Shupeng et al., 2020). Indeed, the actions performed (agency), and the type of avatar impersonated can affect the gamers' real-life behavior: this is called the Proteus effect, named by Yee and Bailenson in honor of the Greek god who could change his physical form at will (Yee & Bailenson, 2007). In a VR environment, such as VGs, people modify their behavior based on how they think others expect them to behave; people are influenced by their digital representation and, typically, their behavior changes depending on the appearance of the representation (Yee & Bailenson, 2007). The Proteus effect extends to real life as well: subjects, who in the online virtual environment had been assigned an avatar resembling a superhero, were more likely to help others in the real world (Yee et al., 2009).

Moreover, VGs allows gamers to experience flow, a state characterized by intense absorption in one's activities, a feeling of fulfilment and a purely intrinsic motivation for the activity. The flow state experienced during VGs can generate positive emotions (Bassi & Fave, 2004; Granic et al., 2014) and psychological well-being (Bassi et al., 2013), thus helping individuals cope better with stressful situations, (even the feeling of isolation during the quarantine due to COVID-19 pandemic; Sweeny et al., 2020).

## INTERPERSONAL VIDEO GAMES EXPERIENCE

One of the main reason to play is to socialize (Kim & Kim, 2020): playing with others, chatting about strategies (Liang et al., 2014), and meeting new people and making friends through games (Cole & Griffiths, 2007; Granic et al., 2014; Hussain & Griffiths, 2009; Utz et al., 2012) allow gamers to meet the psychological need of relations (Elson et al., 2014; Rogers et al., 2017).

Playing can help individuals in overcoming social difficulties, such as shyness or loneliness (Colwell & Kato, 2003; Domahidi et al., 2018; Roy & Ferguson, 2016; Shang & Zhuang, 2008). For example, multiplayer role-playing games, such as "World of Warcraft,"[4] can train gamers in social skills and encourage prosocial behaviors. Furthermore, VGs can trigger empathy (Granic et al., 2014): playing prosocial VGs may enhance interpersonal empathy, increase cooperation as well as prosocial behavior in children and adolescents

(Harrington & O'Connell, 2016; Saleem et al., 2012). Habitual experiences of prosocial play, in which prosocial behavior is experienced and rewarded by game logic, may impact players' cognitive, affective, and behavioral processes (Greitemeyer, 2022; Shoshani et al., 2022). Indeed, several studies have shown an effect on reducing the social accessibility of aggressive cognitions, and antisocial affect (Wulansari et al., 2020) and on promoting prosocial thoughts, positive attitudes and stereotypes, and affective traits such as kindness or empathy (Gentile et al., 2009; Shoshani et al., 2022).

A new emerging aspect in VGs research is moral positioning. Moral choices and dilemmas are increasingly present in VGs and represent a real element of game play, determining effects on players (Triberti et al., 2015). During the game, gamers can actively make moral choices that impact on the progress of the game. Thus, this can lead them to reflect on themselves while taking others' perspectives and reflecting on societal issues. In particular, multiplayer role-playing games can expose players to ethics in a controlled environment, and thanks to the sense of agency experienced in the game, gamers can be guided to think about real-life experiences and to learn about human nature (Nordlinger, 2010).

VGs can also encourage cooperation, mutual aid, and commitment to social causes which lays the foundation for developing these behaviors in the real world as well (Granic et al., 2014). Adolescents who have experiences with participatory and social multiplayer games reported much higher levels of civic and political engagement than adolescents who did not play (Lenhart et al., 2008). For example, the serious game "It's a Deal" can enhance students' intercultural communication competence, thanks to its educational content and clear pedagogical goals (Guillén-Nieto & Aleson-Carbonell, 2012).

## HOW TO USE VIDEO GAMES IN PSYCHOTHERAPY

Young people are fascinated with VGs, and no child psychotherapist can ignore this. The use of play in therapy is not new. Games have been used for a long time, since the work of both Anna Freud (1928) and Melanie Klein (1932) and commercial VGs have been used since the early 1980s to treat different mental health problems. However, the use of these tools is still considered innovative, as many therapists have not enough knowledge about the world of VGs nor how to use them in practice (Ceranoglu, 2010; Leroux, 2019; Virole, 2021). The VG is not a cure in itself, but the guidance of the therapist allows the VG to condense dreams, fantasies, impulses, and actions, that can be thus actualized in a possible fiction, an "as if" shared in the session (Haza, 2019, p. 343).

First of all, VGs and serious games can be excellent tools for *motivating and engaging children* and adolescents during psychotherapy sessions, because they are fun and enjoyable (Barnes & Prescott, 2018). For example, *"gNats Island"*[5] is a gamified cognitive behavioral therapy intervention for adolescents used to deal with anxiety disorder (O'Reilly et al., 2016). Adolescents that played the game with the therapist judged the game more fun and engaging than "just talking" (Coyle et al., 2011; Van Der Meulen et al., 2019). Playing VGs is an excellent opportunity for gathering clinical material to be analyzed and discussed during the psychotherapy (Haza, 2020), regardless of therapeutic orientations. Even commercial VGs can be used to increase engagement, promote problem solving skills and insight of adolescent patients (Gardner, 1991); playing VGs can lead patients to reflect on themselves and find a way to manage their emotional, social, and cognitive problems (Virole, 2021). Moreover, the interaction about the games provides a common ground—the virtual world of the VG—between the therapist and the patients. The game can also provide a structure to the therapeutic session itself (Aharoni et al., 2008; Coyle et al., 2011).

It is known that the ability to alter physical and physiological parameters can decrease ADHD, depressive, and anxiety symptoms (Knox et al., 2011). VGs can be used *to train the ability to regulate physiological activation levels, inducing a state of relaxation.* Numerous serious games[6] based on biofeedback technology were developed, and tested for teaching this skill; for example, "Relax to Win" is a serious competitive game developed to teach the regulation of physiological activation in children and adolescents to manage anxiety (Sharry et al., 2003); "RAGE-Control" (regulate and gain emotional control) game, based on the arcade Space Invaders game (a classic arcade game in which you need to shoot down all the aliens), teaches adolescents how to manage physiological activation due to anger. If physiological activation rises above a certain threshold, the spaceship fires blanks and starts to move uncontrollably; when the player regains emotional control (heart rate) the ship returns to firing under their control (Kahn et al., 2013).

The world of the VG can be used as *a space for the projection, symbolization and possible realization of desires of the patient* (Jung & Gillet, 2021). The experiential dimension of the game may facilitate individuals' emotional expression and elaboration and identification of conflicts (Virole, 2021). Especially in adolescence, VGs can represent a transitional space (Tisseron, 2009a), a safe place in which the interchange of thinking processes between the therapist and the patient can be promoted (Hojman, 2020). Furthermore, the avatar, specifically, can represent in turn an interface of communication with oneself or with others, the incarnation of the ideal or real self, a real person, or even a vector of symbolization (Tisseron, 2009b). The space of the game can represent a sort of "identity laboratory," in which gamers can explore different identities, playing different roles and new identities, projecting the self or aspects of the self onto their avatar.

VGs can be a useful strategy *to promote relationship closeness* (Pecchioni & Osmanovic, 2018): playing a prosocial VG together can promote parents' participation in a child-directed activity (McNeil & Hembree-Kigin, 2010) and facilitate positive intergenerational connections (Jordan, 2014; Pecchioni & Osmanovic, 2018; Zhang & Kaufman, 2016).

VGs can also be used to convey mental health basic concepts such as the distinction between thoughts, feelings, and behavior, the impact of thoughts on our feelings or the concept of useful and useless thoughts, such as in "Treasure Hunt," "Ricky" and "The Spider," or "gNnats' Island," based on cognitive-behavioral treatment (Brezinka, 2014).

Furthermore, VGs can offer the opportunity to expose patients to difficult psychological contexts or situations, such as racism, immigration, grief ("Grif"),[7] or depression ("Depression Quest")[8] in a safe context, providing the therapist with behavioral rehearsal and feedback to shape behavior in the functional direction (Bowman & Lieberoth, 2018).

More role-playing can be facilitated by VGs. Patients in VGs may practice social identities and roles, experiencing the emotions of different characters. This increases their ability to reappraise emotional experiences, in turn helping them to deal with negative emotion in an adaptive way, to develop new social skills, and to increase empathy for others (Bowman & Lieberoth, 2018; Granic et al., 2014).

The roles played, the game mechanics, the emotions and feelings experienced, and behaviors can be the object of discussion with the patient, allowing the therapist to draw parallels to how these roles can be related to the patient's personality and psychological struggles (Bean, 2020).

Recently, young people's mental health is becoming a top priority due to COVID-19 negative effects. According to UNICEF, "Children and young people could feel the impact of COVID-19 on their mental health and well-being for many years to come."[9] To deal with the emergency, serious games can represent a promising solution to promote mental health in the young (David et al., 2021; Van Der Meulen et al., 2019). For example "REThink"[10] (David et al., 2021) is a therapeutic VG developed to be used as a stand-alone application aimed to promote emotional resilience in children and adolescents. It is based on rational emotive behavior therapy, a short-term form of psychotherapy (Ellis, 2002), focused on self-defeating thoughts and feelings, challenging and replacing them with more functional beliefs. This game was demonstrated to be effective in reducing emotional problems, irrational beliefs, and negative automatic thoughts with young people aged from 10 to 16 years (David et al., 2010).

## CONCLUSIONS

VGs, as positive technologies, can support the pursuit of eudaimonic well-being as well, as they are able to generate engaging and self-fulfilling experiences (Villani, Grassi, Cognetta, et al., 2011).

VGs, both commercial and serious, allow for enhanced mood and positive experiences, but also allow for meaningful experiences that can satisfy the basic psychological needs (autonomy, competence, and connectedness) that underlie individuals' well-being (Ryan & Deci, 2000; Tamborini et al., 2010; Triberti & Argenton, 2013). The experience of VGs allows players to see themselves faced with complex, sometimes morally difficult choices and to evaluate the effects of their choices in a virtual environment. This can become a safe, structured, and controlled base from which to start to explore, feel, imagine, relive sensations and thoughts (present or past), and thus activate a learning process of skills and competences, exportable beyond the game. Players can experience in a "practica" way the idea they have of themself and of the world and question their beliefs, a necessary condition for change (Riva et al., 2016).

Despite VGs having entered fully into the therapeutic setting for years, more research is needed to investigate their effects on clinical outcome. In fact, it is essential to start to consider VGs not as simple entertainment products, but also as a sort of technology-enabled tool to support therapeutic interventions that can be adapted according to the orientation of the clinician. They can be a useful option among many from which therapists will choose (Van Der Meulen et al., 2019).

## NOTES

1. https://www.statista.com/topics/868/video-games/#dossierKeyfigures
2. https://www.pewresearch.org/internet/2018/05/31/teens-social-media-technology-2018/
3. https://www.mycountrytalks.org/
4. https://worldofwarcraft.com
5. In gNats Island, players visit a tropical island and meet a team of wildlife explorers who explain some mental health concepts through spoken conversations, embedded animations, videos, and questions regarding the player's own situation. Automatic negative thoughts are presented as small creatures called gNats that can sting people, causing negative thoughts. There are nine types of gNats. For example, the sting of a black-and-white gNat can cause people to think in extremes. Conversations with game characters allow players to think about possible strategies to identify and defuse negative thoughts. To this end, strategies are illustrated through concrete metaphors

such as catching, trapping, and driving away gNats. For more information, visit http://www.davidcoyle.org/gnats-island/.

6. VGs developed for a primary purpose other than pure entertainment
7. https://store.steampowered.com/app/683320/GRIS
8. http://www.depressionquest.com/
9. https://www.unicef.org/press-releases/impact-covid-19-poor-mental-health-children-and-young-people-tip-iceberg
10. https://rethinkplatform.ro/the-rethink-game/

## REFERENCES


Aharoni, E., Beall, A., Denni, M., Dollman, A., German, T., Hoyt, C., Loomis, J., Swinth, K., Weisbuch, M., & Bailenson, J. N. (2008). Self-representations in immersive virtual environments. *Journal of Applied Social Psychology, 38*(11), 2673–2690. https://doi.org/10.1111/j.1559-1816.2008.00409.x

Anolli, L., Mantovani, F., Confalonieri, L., Ascolese, A., & Peveri, L. (2010). Emotions in serious games: From experience to assessment. *International Journal of Emerging Technologies in Learning, 5*(SI3), 7. https://doi.org/10.3991/ijet.v5s3.1496

Argenton, L., Triberti, S., Serino, S., Muzio, M., & Riva, G. (2014). Serious games as positive technologies for individual and group flourishing. In A. L. Brooks, S. Brahnam, & L. C. Jain (Eds.), *Technologies of inclusive well-being: Serious games, alternative realities, and play therapy* (pp. 221–244). Springer. https://doi.org/10.1007/978-3-642-45432-5_11

Barbero, C., & Carola. (2008). Il paradosso del terrore. *Rivista di estetica, 39*, 43–55. https://doi.org/10.4000/estetica.2023

Barnes, S., & Prescott, J. (2018). Empirical evidence for the outcomes of therapeutic video games for adolescents with anxiety disorders: Systematic review. *JMIR Serious Games, 6*(1), e3. https://doi.org/10.2196/GAMES.9530

Barr, M., & Copeland-Stewart, A. (2021). Playing video games during the COVID-19 pandemic and effects on players' well-being. *Games & Culture, 17*(1), 122–139. https://doi.org/10.1177/15554120211017036

Bassi, M., & Fave, A. D. (2004). Adolescence and the changing context of optimal experience in time: Italy 1986–2000. *Journal of Happiness Studies, 5*(2), 155–179. https://doi.org/10.1023/B:JOHS.0000035914.66037.b5

Bassi, M., Steca, P., Monzani, D., Greco, A., & Delle Fave, A. (2013). Personality and optimal experience in adolescence: Implications for well-being and development. *Journal of Happiness Studies, 15*(4), 829–843. https://doi.org/10.1007/S10902-013-9451-X

Bean, A. (2020). Therapeutic use of video games. *The Video Game Debate 2*, 81–94. https://doi.org/10.4324/9780429351815-7

Bonus, J. A., Peebles, A., Mares, M. L., & Sarmiento, I. G. (2017). Look on the bright side (of Media Effects): Pokémon go as a catalyst for positive life experiences. *Media Psychology, 21*(2), 263–287. https://doi.org/10.1080/15213269.2017.1305280

Botella, C., Riva, G., Gaggioli, A., Wiederhold, B. K., Alcaniz, M., & Baños, R. M. (2012). The present and future of positive technologies. *Cyberpsychology, Behavior, and Social Networking, 15*(2), 78–84. https://doi.org/10.1089/cyber.2011.0140

Bowman, S. L., & Lieberoth, A. (2018). Psychology and role-playing games. In S. Deterding & J. Zagal (Eds.), *Role-playing game studies* (pp. 245–264). Routledge. https://doi.org/10.4324/9781315637532-13

Brezinka, V. (2014). Computer games supporting cognitive behaviour therapy in children. *Clinical Child Psychology and Psychiatry, 19*(1), 100–110. https://doi.org/10.1177/1359104512468288

Carissoli, C., & Villani, D. (2019). Can videogames be used to promote emotional intelligence in teenagers? Results from EmotivaMente, a School Program. *Games for Health Journal, 8*(6). https://doi.org/10.1089/G4H.2018.0148

Ceranoglu, T. A. (2010). Video games in psychotherapy. *Review of General Psychology, 14*(2), 141–146. https://doi.org/10.1037/a0019439

Chou, C., & Tsai, M.-J. (2007). Gender differences in Taiwan high school students' computer game playing. *Computers in Human Behavior, 23*(1), 812–824. https://doi.org/10.1016/J.CHB.2004.11.011

Cole, H., & Griffiths, M. D. (2007). Social interactions in massively multiplayer online role-playing gamers. *CyberPsychology & Behavior, 10*(4), 575–583. https://doi.org/10.1089/cpb.2007.9988

Colwell, J. (2007). Needs met through computer game play among adolescents. *Personality and Individual Differences, 43*(8), 2072–2082. https://doi.org/10.1016/j.paid.2007.06.021

Colwell, J., & Kato, M. (2003). Investigation of the relationship between social isolation, self-esteem, aggression and computer game play in Japanese adolescents. *Asian Journal of Social Psychology, 6*(2), 149–158. https://doi.org/10.1111/1467-839X.t01-1-00017

Connolly, T. M., Boyle, E. A., MacArthur, E., Hainey, T., & Boyle, J. M. (2012). A systematic literature review of empirical evidence on computer games and serious games. *Computers & Education, 59*(2), 661–686. https://doi.org/10.1016/J.COMPEDU.2012.03.004

Coyle, D., McGlade, N., Doherty, G., & O'Reilly, G. (2011). Exploratory evaluations of a computer game supporting cognitive behavioural therapy for adolescents. In *Proceedings of the SIGCHI Conference on Human Factors in Computing Systems* (pp. 2937–2946). https://doi.org/10.1145/1978942.1979378

Daneels, R., Vandebosch, H., & Walrave, M. (2020). "Just for fun?": An exploration of digital games' potential for eudaimonic media experiences among Flemish adolescents. *Journal of Children and Media, 14*(3), 285–301. https://doi.org/10.1080/17482798.2020.1727934

David, D., Lynn, S., & Ellis, A. (Eds.). (2010). *Rational and irrational beliefs: Research, theory, and clinical practice.* Oxford.

David, O. A., Predatu, R., & Cardoș, R. A. I. (2021). Effectiveness of the REThink therapeutic online video game in promoting mental health in children and adolescents. *Internet Interventions, 25*, 100391. https://doi.org/10.1016/J.INVENT.2021.100391

Di Letizia, R. (2014). *Ludosofia. Cosa la filosofia ha da dirci sui videogiochi* [Ludosophy. What philosophy has to tell us about video games]. Universitalia. https://www.libreriauniversitaria.it/ludosofia-cosa-filosofia-ha-dirci/libro/9788865077009

Domahidi, E., Breuer, J., Kowert, R., Festl, R., & Quandt, T. (2018). A longitudinal analysis of gaming- and non-gaming-related friendships and social support among social online game players. *Media Psychology, 21*(2), 288–307. https://doi.org/10.1080/15213269.2016.1257393

Ellis, A. (2002). Rational emotive behavior therapy. *Encyclopedia of Psychotherapy*, 483–487. https://doi.org/10.1016/B0-12-343010-0/00177-X

Elson, M., Breuer, J., Ivory, J. D., & Quandt, T. (2014). More than stories with buttons: Narrative, mechanics, and context as determinants of player experience in digital games. *Journal of Communication, 64*(3), 521–542. https://doi.org/10.1111/jcom.12096

Ferguson, C. J., & Olson, C. K. (2012). Friends, fun, frustration and fantasy: Child motivations for video game play. *Motivation and Emotion, 37*(1), 154–164. https://doi.org/10.1007/S11031-012-9284-7

Ferguson, C. J., & Rueda, S. M. (2010). The hitman study: Violent video game exposure effects on aggressive behavior, hostile feelings, and depression. *European Psychologist, 15*(2), 99–108. https://doi.org/10.1027/1016-9040/a000010

Fong, K. A. (2017). *Reflecting and shaping the self through avatars: The relationship between avatars, identity, and personal needs.* https://yorkspace.library.yorku.ca/xmlui/handle/10315/34329

Fredrickson, B. L. (2004). The broaden-and-build theory of positive emotions. *Philosophical Transactions of the Royal Society of London: Biological Sciences, 359*(1449), 1367–1378. https://doi.org/10.1098/rstb.2004.1512

Freud, A. (1928). On the theory of child analysis. *The Psychoanalytic Review, 15*(85). https://www.proquest.com/openview/6fe50800ffe89ef88f3e9a74732a33c7/1?pq-origsite=gscholar&cbl=1820903

Gaggioli, A., Pallavicini, F., Morganti, L., Serino, S., Scaratti, C., Briguglio, M., Crifaci, G., Vetrano, N., Giulintano, A., Bernava, G., Tartarisco, G., Pioggia, G., Raspelli, S., Cipresso, P., Vigna, C., Grassi, A., Baruffi, M., Wiederhold, B., & Riva, G. (2014). Experiential virtual scenarios with real-time monitoring (interreality) for the management of psychological stress: A block randomized controlled trial. *Journal of Medical Internet Research, 16*(7), e167. https://doi.org/10.2196/jmir.3235

Gardner, J. E. (1991). Can the Mario Bros. help? Nintendo games as an adjunct in psychotherapy with children. *Psychotherapy, 28*(4), 667–670. https://doi.org/10.1037/0033-3204.28.4.667

Gentile, D. A., Anderson, C. A., Yukawa, S., Ihori, N., Saleem, M., Lim Kam Ming, Shibuya, A., Liau, A. K., Khoo, A., Bushman, B. J., Rowell Huesmann, L., & Sakamoto, A. (2009). The effects of prosocial video games on prosocial behaviors: International evidence from correlational, longitudinal, and experimental studies. *Personality and Social Psychology Bulletin, 35*(6), 752–763. https://doi.org/10.1177/0146167209333045

Granic, I., Lobel, A., E, C. M., & Engels, R. C. M. E. (2014). The benefits of playing video games. *American Psychologist, 69*(1), 66–78. https://doi.org/10.1037/a0034857

Greitemeyer, T. (2022). The dark and bright side of video game consumption: Effects of violent and prosocial video games. *Current Opinion in Psychology, 46,* 101326. https://doi.org/10.1016/j.copsyc.2022.101326

Guillén-Nieto, V., & Aleson-Carbonell, M. (2012). Serious games and learning effectiveness: The case of It's a Deal! *Computers & Education, 58*(1), 435–448. https://doi.org/10.1016/J.COMPEDU.2011.07.015

Harrington, B., & O'Connell, M. (2016). Video games as virtual teachers: Prosocial video game use by children and adolescents from different socioeconomic groups is associated with increased empathy and prosocial behaviour. *Computers in Human Behavior, 63,* 650–658. https://doi.org/10.1016/J.CHB.2016.05.062

Haza, M. (2019). Médiations numériques: Jeux vidéo et jeux de transfert [Digital mediations: Video games and transfer games]. ERES. https://doi.org/10.3917/ERES.HAZA.2019.01

Haza, M. (2020). Du jeu vidéo en psychothérapie? Un habile mélange de récits et de sensorialités [Video games in psychotherapy? A clever mix of stories and sensorialities]. *Enfances & Psy,* (N°85), 119. https://doi.org/10.3917/ep.085.0119

Higgins, E. T. (1989). Self-discrepancy theory: What patterns of self-beliefs cause people to suffer? *Advances in Experimental Social Psychology, 22,* 93–136. https://doi.org/10.1016/S0065-2601(08)60306-8

Hojman, H. (2020). The positive use of video games and media in psychodynamic psychotherapy. *The Brown University Child and Adolescent Behavior Letter, 36*(7), 1–6. https://doi.org/10.1002/CBL.30474

Hussain, Z., & Griffiths, M. D. (2009). The attitudes, feelings, and experiences of online games: A qualitative analysis. *CyberPsychology & Behavior, 12*(6), 747–753. https://doi.org/10.1089/cpb.2009.0059

Janssen, C., & Tortolano, S. (2010). Mondes virtuels et capacité d'illusion: Les avatars du lien [Virtual worlds and the capacity for illusion: The avatars of the link]. *Cahiers de psychologie clinique, 35*(2), 57. https://doi.org/10.3917/cpc.035.0057

Johannes, N., Vuorre, M., & Przybylski, A. K. (2021). Video game play is positively correlated with well-being. *Royal Society Open Science, 8*(2). https://doi.org/10.1098/rsos.202049

Jordan, N. A. (2014). Video games: Support for the evolving family therapist. *Journal of Family Therapy, 36*(4), 359–370. https://doi.org/10.1111/j.1467-6427.2012.00593.x

Jung, J., & Gillet, G. (2021). Psychotherapy mediated by videogames. *International Journal of Psychoanalysis, 102*(2), 281–296. https://doi.org/10.1080/00207578.2020.1847601

Juul, J. (2013). *The art of failure: An essay on the pain of playing video games.* MIT Press.

Kahn, J., Ducharme, P., Rotenberg, A., & Gonzalez-Heydrich, J. (2013). "RAGE-control": A game to build emotional strength. *Games for Health Journal, 2*(1), 53–57. https://doi.org/10.1089/g4h.2013.0007

Kaye, L. K., Kowert, R., & Quinn, S. (2017). The role of social identity and online social capital on psychosocial outcomes in MMO players. *Computers in Human Behavior, 74,* 215–223. https://doi.org/10.1016/j.chb.2017.04.030

Kim, J., & Kim, M. (2020). Spectator e-sport and well-being through live streaming services. *Technology in Society, 63.* https://doi.org/10.1016/j.techsoc.2020.101401

Klein, M. (1932). *The psychoanalysis of children: The international psycho-analytical library No. 22).* Hogarth.

Klimmt, C., Blake, C., Hefner, D., Vorderer, P., & Roth, C. (2009). *Player performance, satisfaction, and video game enjoyment* [Conference paper]. In S. Natkin & J. Dupire (Eds.), *Entertainment computing–ICEC 2009. Lecture notes in computer science, vol. 5709.* Springer. https://doi.org/10.1007/978-3-642-04052-8_1

Knox, M., Lentini, J., Cummings, T. S., McGrady, A., Whearty, K., & Sancrant, L. (2011). Game-based biofeedback for paediatric anxiety and depression. *Mental Health in Family Medicine, 8*(3), 195–203. https://www.ncbi.nlm.nih.gov/pmc/articles/PMC3314276/

Kümpel, A. S., & Unkel, J. (2017). The effects of digital games on hedonic, eudaimonic and telic entertainment experiences. *Journal of Gaming and Virtual Worlds, 9*(1), 21–37. https://doi.org/10.1386/JGVW.9.1.21_1

Lenhart, A., Kahne, J., Middaugh, E., Rankin Macgill, A., Evans, C., & Vitak, J. (2008). *Teens, video games, and civics: Teens' gaming experiences are diverse and include significant social interaction and civic engagement.* Pew Internet & American Life Project. https://files.eric.ed.gov/fulltext/ED525058.pdf

Leroux, Y. (2019). Le jeu vidéo comme miroir dans la relation thérapeutique [The video with a view of the therapeutic relationship]. In *Médiations numériques: Jeux vidéo et jeux de transfert* (pp. 137–159). Érès. https://doi.org/10.3917/ERES.HAZA.2019.01.0137

Liang, S., Li, H., & Yang, X. (2014). The video game from the perspective of positive psychology. *Open Journal of Social Sciences, 2,* 57–60. https://doi.org/10.4236/jss.2014.28009

McNeil, C. B., & Hembree-Kigin, T. L. (2010). *Parent–child interaction therapy.* Springer. https://doi.org/10.1007/978-0-387-88639-8

Nordlinger, J. (2010). Virtual ethics: Ethics and massively multiplayer online games. In *Ethics and game design: Teaching values through play* (pp. 102–108). IGI Global. https://www.igi-global.com/chapter/ethics-game-design/41314

O'Reilly, G., Coyle, D., & Tunney, C. (2016). Even Buddhist monks use a gong: A mindfulness skills programme for young people delivered through the "Mindful Gnats" computer Game and app. *International Journal of Game-Based Learning, 6*(4), 39–51.

Oliver, M. B., Bowman, N. D., Woolley, J. K., Rogers, R., Sherrick, B. I., & Chung, M.-Y. (2016). Video games as meaningful entertainment experiences. *Psychology of Popular Media Culture, 5*(4), 390–405. https://doi.org/10.1037/ppm0000066

Pallavicini, F., Ferrari, A., & Mantovani, F. (2018). Video games for well-being: A systematic review on the application of computer games for cognitive and emotional training in the adult population. *Frontiers in Psychology, 9,* 2127. https://doi.org/10.3389/fpsyg.2018.02127

Pecchioni, L. L., & Osmanovic, S. (2018). Play it again, grandma: Effect of intergenerational video gaming on family closeness. In *Human aspects of IT for the aged population: Acceptance, communication, and participation* (pp. 518–531). Springer Link. https://doi.org/10.1007/978-3-319-92034-4_39

Pine, R., Sutcliffe, K., McCallum, S., & Fleming, T. (2020). Young adolescents' interest in a mental health casual video game. *Digital Health, 6.* https://doi.org/10.1177/2055207620949391

Przybylski, A. K., Rigby, C. S., Deci, E. L., & Ryan, R. M. (2014). Competence-impeding electronic games and players' aggressive feelings, thoughts, and behaviors. *Journal of Personality and Social Psychology, 106*(3), 441–457. https://doi.org/10.1037/a0034820

Przybylski, A. K., Ryan, R. M., & Rigby, C. S. (2009). The motivating role of violence in video games. *Personality and Social Psychology Bulletin, 35*(2), 243–259. https://doi.org/10.1177/0146167208327216

Przybylski, A. K., Weinstein, N., Murayama, K., Lynch, M. F., & Ryan, R. M. (2012). The ideal self at play: The appeal of video games that let you be all you can be. *Psychological Science, 23*(1), 69–76. https://doi.org/10.1177/0956797611418676

Riva, G., Baños, R. M., Botella, C., Mantovani, F., & Gaggioli, A. (2016). Transforming Experience: The potential of augmented reality and virtual reality for enhancing personal and clinical change. *Frontiers in Psychiatry, 7,* 164. https://doi.org/10.3389/fpsyt.2016.00164

Riva, G., Baños, R. M., Botella, C., Wiederhold, B. K., Gaggioli, A., Baños, R. M., Botella, C., Wiederhold, B. K., & Gaggioli, A. (2012). Positive technology: Using interactive technologies to promote positive functioning. *Cyberpsychology, Behavior, and Social Networking, 15*(2), 69–77. https://doi.org/10.1089/cyber.2011.0139

Riva, G., Bernardelli, L., Browning, M. H. E. M., Castelnuovo, G., Cavedoni, S., Chirico, A., Cipresso, P., de Paula, D. M. B., Di Lernia, D., Fernández-Álvarez, J., Figueras-Puigderrajols, N., Fuji, K., Gaggioli, A., Gutiérrez-Maldonado, J., Hong, U., Mancuso, V., Mazzeo, M., Molinari, E., Moretti, L. F., . . . Wiederhold, B. K. (2020). COVID feel good—An easy self-help virtual reality protocol to overcome the psychological burden of coronavirus. *Frontiers in Psychiatry, 11.* https://www.frontiersin.org/articles/10.3389/fpsyt.2020.563319

Riva, G., Mantovani, F., & Wiederhold, B. K. (2020). Positive technology and COVID-19. *Cyberpsychology, Behavior, and Social Networking, 23*(9), 581–587. https://doi.org/10.1089/cyber.2020.29194.gri

Rogers, R., Woolley, J., Sherrick, B., Bowman, N. D., & Oliver, M. B. (2017). Fun versus meaningful video game experiences: A qualitative analysis of user responses. *The Computer Games Journal, 6*(1–2), 63–79. https://doi.org/10.1007/s40869-016-0029-9

Roy, A., & Ferguson, C. J. (2016). Competitively versus cooperatively? An analysis of the effect of game play on levels of stress. *Computers in Human Behavior, 56,* 14–20. https://doi.org/10.1016/J.CHB.2015.11.020

Russoniello, C. V., O'Brien, K., & Parks, J. M. (2009). EEG, HRV, and psychological correlates while playing Bejeweled II: A randomized controlled study. *Studies in Health Technology and Informatics, 144*(1), 189–192. https://pubmed.ncbi.nlm.nih.gov/19592761/

Ryan, R. M., & Deci, E. L. (2000). Self-determination theory and the facilitation of intrinsic motivation, social development, and well-being. *The American Psychologist, 55*(1), 68–78. https://doi.org/10.1037/0003-066X.55.1.68

Ryan, R. M., Rigby, C. S., & Przybylski, A. K. (2006). The Motivational pull of video games: A self-determination theory approach. *Motivation and Emotion, 30*(4), 344–360. https://doi.org/10.1007/s11031-006-9051-8

Saleem, M., Anderson, C. A., & Gentile, D. A. (2012). Effects of prosocial, neutral, and violent video games on children's helpful and hurtful behaviors. *Aggressive Behavior, 38*(4), 281–287. https://doi.org/10.1002/ab.21428

Salen, K., & Zimmerman, E. (2005). Game design and meaningful play. In J. Raessens & J. Goldstein (Eds.), *Handbook of computer game studies* (pp. 59–79). MIT Press.

Shang, J. J., & Zhuang, S. Y. (2008). Value research of the game's applications in education. *Distance Education Journal, 6,* 63–68. https://www.scirp.org/reference/referencespapers?referenceid=1267743

Sharry, J., Mcdermott, M., & Condron, J. (2003). 'Relax to win'—Treating children with anxiety problems with a biofeedback video game. *Eisteach,* 2(2), 22–26. https://citeseerx.ist.psu.edu/document?repid=rep1&type=pdf&doi=72494de08fffc0ffd0b257244dd3b85965a6e62a

Shoshani, A., Nelke, S., & Girtler, I. (2022). Tablet applications as socializing platforms: The effects of prosocial touch screen applications on young children's prosocial behavior. *Computers in Human Behavior, 127,* 107077. https://doi.org/10.1016/j.chb.2021.107077

Shupeng, H., Huanfang, Z., Cuiying, F., & Zongkui, Z. (2020). The impacts of virtual avatar in video game on users' self-concept. *Advances in Psychological Science, 28*(5), 810–823. https://doi.org/10.3724/SP.J.1042.2020.00810

Sweeny, K., Rankin, K., Cheng, X., Hou, L., Long, F., Meng, Y., Azer, L., Zhou, R., & Zhang, W. (2020). Flow in the time of COVID-19: Findings from China. *PLOS ONE, 15*(11), e0242043. https://doi.org/10.1371/JOURNAL.PONE.0242043

Tamborini, R., Bowman, N. D., Eden, A., Grizzard, M., & Organ, A. (2010). Defining media enjoyment as the satisfaction of intrinsic needs. *Journal of Communication, 60*(4), 758–777. https://doi.org/10.1111/j.1460-2466.2010.01513.x

Tavinor, G. (2009). *The art of videogames.* Wiley-Blackwell.

Tisseron, S. (2009a). L'ado et ses avatars. *Adolescence, 69*(3), 591. https://doi.org/10.3917/ado.069.0591

Tisseron, S. (2009b). L'avatar, voie royale de la thérapie, entre espace potentiel et déni [The avatar, the royal road of therapy, between potential space and denial]. *Adolescence, T. 27 n°3*(3), 721–731. https://doi.org/10.3917/ado.069.0721

Triberti, S. (2016). This drives me nuts! In D. Villani, P. Cipresso, A. Gaggioli, & G. Riva (A c. Di), *Integrating technology in positive psychology practice* (pp. 266–289). IGI Global. https://doi.org/10.4018/978-1-4666-9986-1.ch012

Triberti, S., & Argenton, L. (2013). *Psicologia dei videogiochi: Come i mondi virtuali influenzano mente e comportamento* [Video game psychology: How virtual worlds influence mind and behavior]. https://www.ibs.it/psicologia-dei-videogiochi-come-mondi-libro-stefano-triberti-luca-argenton/e/9788838787034

Triberti, S., Durosini, I., Aschieri, F., Villani, D., & Riva, G. (2017). Changing avatars, changing selves? The influence of social and contextual expectations on digital rendition of identity. *Cyberpsychology, Behavior, and Social Networking, 20*(8), 501–507. https://doi.org/10.1089/cyber.2016.0424

Triberti, S., Villani, D., & Riva, G. (2015). Moral positioning in video games and its relation with dispositional traits: The emergence of a social dimension. *Computers in Human Behavior, 50*, 1–8. https://doi.org/10.1016/j.chb.2015.03.069

Utz, S., Jonas, K. J., & Tonkens, E. (2012). Effects of passion for massively multiplayer online role-playing games on interpersonal relationships. *Journal of Media Psychology, 24*(2), 77–86. https://doi.org/10.1027/1864-1105/a000066

Van Der Meulen, H., McCashin, D., O'Reilly, G., & Coyle, D. (2019). Using computer games to support mental health interventions: Naturalistic deployment study. *JMIR Mental Health, 6*(5), e12430. https://doi.org/10.2196/12430

Ventura, M., Shute, V., & Zhao, W. (2013). The relationship between video game use and a performance-based measure of persistence. *Computers and Education, 60*(1), 52–58. https://doi.org/10.1016/j.compedu.2012.07.003

Viana, R., & Barbosa de Lira, C. A. (2020). Exergames as coping strategies for anxiety disorders during the COVID-19 quarantine period. *Games for Health Journal, 9*(3), 147–149. https://doi.org/10.1089/g4h.2020.0060

Villani, D., Carissoli, C., Triberti, S., Marchetti, A., Gilli, G., & Riva, G. (2018). Videogames for emotion regulation: A systematic review. *Games for Health Journal, 7*(2), 85–99. https://doi.org/10.1089/g4h.2017.0108

Villani, D., Grassi, A., Cognetta, C., Toniolo, D., Cipresso, P., & Riva, G. (2011). Self-help stress management training through mobile phones: An experience with oncology nurses. *Psychological Services, 10*(3), 315–322. https://doi.org/10.1037/a0026459

Villani, D., Grassi, A., & Riva, G. (2011). *Tecnologie emotive: Nuovi Media per migliorare la qualità della vita e ridurre lo stress* [Emotive technology: New media to improve the quality of life and relieve stress]. https://www.cattolicanews.it/Qualita-della-vita-riduzione-dello-stress-473.pdf

Virole, B. (2021). Jeux vidéo en psychothérapie: Une métapsychologie du virtuel [Video games in psychotherapy: A metapsychology of the virtual]. *Nouvelle Revue de l'Enfance et de l'Adolescence, N° 5*(2), 53–57. https://doi.org/10.3917/nrea.005.0053

Wiederhold, B. K. (2021). Kids will find a way: The benefits of social video games. *Cyberpsychology, Behavior, and Social Networking, 24*(4), 213–214. https://doi.org/10.1089/CYBER.2021.29211.EDITORIAL

Wiederhold, B. K., & Wiederhold, M. D. (2005). *Virtual reality therapy for anxiety disorders: Advances in evaluation and treatment.* American Psychological Association. https://doi.org/10.1037/10858-000

Wulansari, O. D. E., Pirker, J., Kopf, J., & Guetl, C. (2020). Video games and their correlation to empathy: How to teach and experience empathic emotion. In *The impact of the 4th industrial revolution on engineering education* (pp. 151–163). Spring Link. https://doi.org/10.1007/978-3-030-40274-7_16

Yee, N. (2006). Motivations for play in online games. *CyberPsychology & Behavior, 9*(6), 772–775. https://doi.org/10.1089/cpb.2006.9.772

Yee, N., & Bailenson, J. (2007). The proteus effect: The effect of transformed self-representation on behavior. *Human Communication Research, 33*(3), 271–290. https://doi.org/10.1111/j.1468-2958.2007.00299.x

Yee, N., Bailenson, J. N., & Ducheneaut, N. (2009). The proteus effect: Implications of transformed digital self-representation on online and offline behavior.

*Communication Research, 36*(2), 285–312. https://doi.org/10.1177/0093650208330254

Zhang, F., & Kaufman, D. (2016). A review of intergenerational play for facilitating interactions and learning. *Gerontechnology, 14*(3), 127–138. https://doi.org/10.4017/gt.2016.14.3.002.00

CHAPTER 5

# THE ROLE OF VIDEO GAMES IN CLINICAL PSYCHOLOGY

## Benefits, Risks, and Future Directions

**Christiane Eichenberg**
***Sigmund Freud Private University, Vienna***

**Jessica Huss**
***Asklepios Hospital Teupitz, Germany***

Clinical psychology addresses video games from different perspectives. For a long time, the focus was primarily on negative aspects, such as etiopathogenesis and treatment of addictive use. Research interest has only recently shifted to positive effects, such as motor (e.g., hand–eye coordination), cognitive (e.g., promotion of problem-solving skills), and social (e.g., networking in multiplayer games) aspects as well as therapeutic usage options. Those interactive computer or video games used for preventing and treating mental health disorders are called serious games. The current available (digital) serious games are extremely profiting from the enormous success of digital or video games for leisure purposes. For instance, the

*Digital Developments*, pages 71–84

Entertainment Software Association (2019) stated—based on their annual survey—that 75% of U.S. Americans ($N = 4{,}000$) had at least one active gamer within their household or family. Moreover, 164 million U.S. American adults regularly play commercial video games. The same applies to Germany: About 34.5 million Germans played games (on smartphones) in 2018 (The German Games Association, 2019). However, the largest gaming market is currently claimed by China (see importance of e-sports, video game tournaments; Ma et al., 2020).

Despite the high appreciation for the digital gaming medium and the therapeutic opportunities that serious games offer (see Chapter 2), clinical psychology as a field of research and practice also covers the risks for mental health resulting from video games (see Chapter 3). Hence, the opportunities of video games for clinical-psychological and psychotherapeutic treatment will be elaborated by showing how computer games are used within the therapy setting, especially in child and adolescent psychotherapeutic practice. Chapter 3 is also dedicated to the clinically relevant risks of video games and focuses on problematic modes of use in which addictive gaming dominates. Computer game addiction, which also includes addicted video game playing, has been intensively researched over the past 20 years. As a result, knowledge is now available on epidemiology (e.g., prevalence), etiopathogenesis (e.g., risk factors, models explaining the development of computer game addiction), and evidence-based treatment approaches.

Finally, Chapter 4 provides an outlook for new research directions, such as the analysis of the representation of mental health disorders in video games.

## POTENTIAL BENEFITS

Video games offer a number of options for clinical psychology and psychotherapy. On the one hand, they can serve as common medium in child and adolescent psychotherapy, on the other hand, there are serious games that are particularly suitable for the target group of children and adolescents.

### Computer Games in Child and Adolescent Psychotherapy

The COVID-19 pandemic is an accelerator of digitization in psychotherapy (Eichenberg, 2021). The majority of psychotherapists switched to the video setting due to the pandemic (for Germany see e.g., Rabe-Menssen et al., 2020) which has been resulting in positive experiences (e.g., Beck-Hiestermann et al., 2021). However, it turned out that this does not apply to the treatment of children and adolescents, since a survey among psychotherapists (Rabe-Menssen et al., 2020) showed that this age group had the greatest concerns about psychotherapy in the video setting. However, Sindelar (2020) suggests playing computer games (together), embedded in a video conference, since the selection of the game character, playing together or against each other also, and so on, offer the psychotherapist intervention opportunities (e.g., therapeutic techniques of mirroring, verbalizing, marking feelings, etc.). The prerequisite for this is, of course, that the therapists are aware of the opportunities offered by computer games (Eichenberg et al., 2016).

## Serious Games

Abt (1970) was among the first to use the term serious games within his work for the military context:

> Games may be played seriously or casually. We are concerned with serious games in the sense that these games have an explicit and carefully thought-out educational purpose and are not intended to be played primarily for amusement. This does not mean that serious games are not, or should not be, entertaining. (p. 9)

In accordance with Abt (1970), various definitions resulted from the original coining of serious games, also largely depending on different stakeholders in research, game design and development, and economics. Despite all the differing approaches, serious games usually combine three aspects: technology, entertainment, and education (Laamarti et al., 2014).

Serious games as novel E-mental health technology applications can be used for the prevention, treatment, and rehabilitation of mental health disorders. They can be either standalone or self-management tools or combined with traditional therapy (Eichenberg et al., 2017). Serious games train, build, and improve cognitive-(behavioral), social, and emotional skills (Eichenberg et al., 2016). The application scope of serious games includes various age groups ranging from children to older adults in different treatment phases (Fleming et al., 2016).

A prominent serious game developed for mental health concerns addressing adolescents (between 12 and 19 years) with depression is called SPARX. Due to its success and positive (treatment) results, revised versions of SPARX were developed addressing general mental health without clinically relevant depression or sexual minority youth struggling with depression. Merry et al. (2012) and her New Zealand research team created SPARX, a cognitive behavioral therapy (CBT) self-help program with video game-specific characteristics, even though it is mainly utilized via computers. SPARX includes seven modules with different tasks to solve by including psychoeducation, information for relapse prevention, relaxation exercises, or social competence training. SPARX is not only extremely popular, especially in English-speaking countries, but also well evaluated with a significant body of evidence. A randomized-controlled study involving 187 young persons with depression demonstrated that SPARX is as effective as traditional face-to-face therapy. Of those, 94 were allocated to the SPARX-intervention and 93 to the control group (treatment as usual). In the SPARX intervention conditions, circa 44% ($N = 31$) of the young study participants recovered from their depressive symptoms in contrast to only 26% ($N = 19$) in the treatment-as-usual group (difference 17.3%, 95% confidence interval 1.6% to 31.8%; $p = 0.030$).

In contrast to other serious games, users can create an avatar according to their preferred and individual wishes who accompanies users throughout the game. In accordance with Blinka (2008), transmissive attachment processes and projective dynamics can be enabled by users and their relationship with their customized avatar. Hence, SPARX even offers the flexibility of various treatment approaches, applications, and scopes.

Besides SPARX several serious games have been developed in the past years (see systematic overviews by Eichenberg et al., 2017 and Halldorsson et al., 2021), but only few contain rigorous study designs. Despite the promising and well-proven treatment effects as well as chances serious games offer for the psychotherapy setting, serious games are still not frequently used until this day. This is mainly due to the lacking knowledge of serious games among mental health professionals and patients despite their promising and well-proven treatment effects. Therefore, still little awareness by especially mental health clinicians, important gatekeepers for patients' therapy motivation and openness to new treatment methods hinder the successful integration of serious games into clinical and routine practice (Halldorsson et al., 2021).

Fleming et al. (2016) mention three main chances of video games for the psychotherapeutic context. Firstly, video games can reach those who are reluctant to seek professional mental health support in the traditional setting. This automatically helps to reduce the current treatment gap: In accordance with Andrade et al. (2014), who stated that many people suffering from psychological problems and mental health concerns are not receiving psychological assistance, caused by cost factors, shortage of mental health professionals, or attitudinal barriers. Moreover, serious (video) games offer a low-threshold and anonymous support bypassing obstacles occurring in the face-to-face setting. Secondly, serious games contain intrinsically motivating and engaging potential, especially in contrast with Internet-based interventions which are commonly accompanied by high attrition rates (Fleming et al., 2016). In this regard, serious games have the chance to strengthen adherence due to curiosity-increasing (e.g., story narrative, avatar, etc.) and gaming-specific competitive behaviors (e.g., goals, rules, feedback, etc.). Thirdly and finally, video games are considered as effective for any behavior or learning change by including adaptive gameplay (that is, task difficulty is matched to user's personal skills) in order to avoid frustrating experiences resulting from the game play (Fleming et al., 2016). Adaptive game play also enables video games to be individualized with customized objectives which further increases motivation, compliance, and completion of the respective psychological online (video) programs (Fleming et al., 2016).

## POTENTIAL RISK

One of the main risks of video games is their excessive use.

### Diagnostic Criteria

Computer game addiction is conceptualized as a substance-free addictive disorder, that is, a behavioral addiction. It has only recently been incorporated into mainstream diagnostic classification systems. As a new research diagnosis, Internet gaming disorder (IGD), which refers to problematic use of computer games (both online and offline), has been included in Section III of the current version of the Diagnostic and Statistical Manual of Mental Disorders (DSM-5-TR; American Psychiatric Association, 2022). The diagnosis is based on nine criteria (see Table 5.1), derived from the criteria used to diagnose pathological gambling and substance addictions (Petry et al., 2015), since studies have demonstrated the neurobiological similarities

**TABLE 5.1 Diagnostic Criteria for Internet Gaming Disorder According to DSM-5-TR**

| Diagnostic Criteria of Internet Gaming Disorder According to DSM-5 |
|---|
| Preoccupation with gaming |
| Withdrawal symptoms when gaming is taken away or not possible (sadness, anxiety, irritability) |
| Tolerance, the need to spend more time gaming to satisfy the urge |
| Inability to reduce playing, unsuccessful attempts to quit gaming |
| Giving up other activities, loss of interest in previously enjoyed activities due to gaming |
| Continuing to game despite problems |
| Deceiving family members or others about the amount of time spent on gaming |
| The use of gaming to relieve negative moods, such as guilt or hopelessness |
| Risk, having jeopardized or lost a job or relationship due to gaming |

*Source:* American Psychiatric Association, 2022

between substance and behavioral addictions (Wölfling et al., 2011). To be diagnosed with IGD according to DSM-5 standards, at least five of nine criteria must have been met in the past 12 months (American Psychiatric Association, 2022). Both clinical interviews and screening instruments help to assess IGD according to the DSM-5.

In the ICD-11 (International Classification of Diseases—11th revision), behavioral addictions (disorders due to addictive behaviors) are subdivided into the categories "gambling disorder" (6C50) and "gaming disorder" (6C51) and are generally subordinated to "disorders due to substance use or addictive behaviors." For other behavioral addictions, there are additional coding options in "other specified disorders due to addictive behaviours (6C5Y)" and "disorders due to addictive behaviors, unspecified (6C5Z)" (Rumpf & Mann, 2018).

## Prevalence and Risk Factors

Epidemiological studies determine the prevalence rates of mental disorders; for computer game addiction, these figures vary greatly among countries, but also largely depending on the test instruments used and thus underlying diagnostic criteria. Meta-analyses attempt to summarize the available studies. For example, Paulus et al. (2018) concluded that an average of 2% of children and adults are addicted to computer games or the Internet. Asian countries have the most severely gaming addicted individuals. Lowest numbers were reported in Norway (0.6%). Sugaya et al. (2019) analyzed prevalence studies of computer game addiction and came up with a global prevalence of IGD of 1.2–5.9%. Among them, male gender (Wartberg et al., 2017), young age, lower school education (Wartberg et al., 2020), and users of so-called massively multiplayer online role-playing games (Eichenbaum et al., 2015) are particularly considered to be at risk. Accordingly, computer game addiction is a widespread and serious problem. With the average prevalence rates found, computer game addiction is one of the most highly prevalent mental disorders, especially in adolescence.

Clinical findings show that many of those affected by addiction suffer a high degree of distress. For example, a sample of Asian adolescents addicted to computer games and the Internet showed that they were significantly more psychopathologically burdened compared to unaffected adolescents (significantly increased symptom burden on the scales somatization, obsessiveness, insecurity in social contact, depressiveness and anxiety, aggressiveness, phobic anxiety, and psychoticism according to SCL-90; Franke, 2000). Common comorbidities of computer game addiction have been found to be anxiety disorders, hyperactivity/impulsivity, and suicidality in children (Ünsel Bolat et al., 2021) and depression in adolescents (Wartberg et al.,

2020) and adults (Wang et al., 2018) and higher illicit drug use compared to non-addicted gamers. A recent review (Bussone et al., 2020) highlights the moderating role of early childhood relationship factors (e.g., parent–child relationship, childhood maltreatment, experiencing (cyber)bullying) in the development of IGD. Payam and Mirzaeidoostan (2019) also showed that parenting style as well as narcissistic personality traits and cognitive dysfunction significantly predicted students' addiction to online games. Another review (Chia & Zhang, 2020) proves that sufferers of IGD show certain cognitive distortions and furthermore tend to use dysfunctional coping strategies, such as distraction and avoidance, so that video games seem to be a means of coping with problems and difficulties (Milani et al., 2018; see also case study Box 5.1, which illustrates the typical symptoms of IGD).

The mother of F (14) desperately seeks help and reports that she no longer knows how to deal with her son. He has only one interest or purpose in life: playing computer games. Various attempts to regulate his gaming behavior have failed. He does not adhere to agreements to limit play time to 1 hour per day. Even when the family was eating dinner, he would not interrupt the game and reacted aggressively when asked if he did not want to eat. At school, he could hardly keep up, the teachers had already asked for a talk, because F would only spend the school day overtired. The mother reported that she had even switched off the electricity at night so that F would not play, but then he would run out of the house to friends. She herself could not even read in the evening when she turned off the electricity. The whole family suffers from F's gaming addiction, there are only arguments. He would no longer go to his soccer training. Pocket money reduction as a punitive measure was of no use. Offers to spend a nice vacation if he gave up gaming also did not work. Basically, everything was getting worse and F's behavior was becoming more and more excessive. The mother reported that F himself stated that the computer game helped him to distract himself from his worries, as he did not feel integrated in his class and therefore often felt depressed.

These findings—summarized in etiopathogenetic models—offer starting points for psychotherapeutic treatment.

Following integrative explanatory approaches for addiction to psychotropic substances, complex etiopathogenetic models are also suggested for computer game addiction (for an overview of integrative models with a focus on learning theory and neurobiological mechanisms, taking personality traits into account, see Wölfling et al., 2011; for psychodynamic considerations, see Stavrou, 2018). In addition, the neurobiological basis of IGD is currently under intense scrutiny (see review by Petry et al., 2015).

The extreme prevalence rates in the Asian region resulted in the founding of specialized departments, much earlier than in Europe. But also in German-speaking countries, corresponding specialized clinics (e.g., Psychosomatische Klinik Kloster Dießen in Germany, www.psychosomatik-diessen.de/internet-und-computerspielsucht; Anton Proksch Institute in Vienna, Austria, https://www.api.or.at/sucht-abhaengigkeit/internet-und-gaming sucht/) and outpatient clinics (see, e.g., the outpatient clinics for gambling addiction at the University Hospital Mainz, Germany, https://www.unimedizin-mainz.de/psychosomatik/patienten/poliklinik-und-hochschulambulanzen/ambulanz-fuer-spielsucht.html) have been founded. Moreover, manuals for disorder-specific treatments have been published, for example, by Wölfling et al. (2013). This cognitive-behavioral treatment program includes 15 group and eight individual therapy sessions. The individual therapy sessions are designed to reinforce the group sessions, but are basically open-ended. The behaviorally oriented therapy components of the group program include motivation building, psychoeducation, development of a functional conditioning model, strategies for dealing with craving, development of alternative activities, improvement of self-esteem and social competence, reference to biographical background, problem-solving strategies, exposure exercises, and relapse prevention.

In Asia, so-called treatment camps dominate. Rumpf et al. (2015) describe the most well-known camps in China: The camp is designed to treat Internet addiction more broadly, but the vast majority of patients report gaming as their primary problem. This camp applies group, individual, and family therapy to increase motivation to change and improve social and cognitive-behavioral control over gaming. Therapists actively promote and encourage alternative activities, including participation in work and physical fitness programs. In addition, adjunctive pharmacotherapies are used primarily to treat comorbid mental illness.

The treatment approaches referenced as examples have in common that they either push for passive total technology abstinence (Cash et al., 2012) or push for such abstinence as it relates to addiction-related play (Wölfling et al., 2011).

Overall, the evidence base for treatment approaches to IGD is rather weak. Only a few randomized-controlled evaluation studies exist, which are mainly cognitive-behavioral oriented or refer to medication-based treatment (Zajac et al., 2020), but are also of limited value due to low methodological standards (Rehbein et al., 2015).

Given the high prevalence of IGD, it is not surprising that various programs have been developed for reasons of prevention. These are mostly targeted at students (King et al., 2018), using gamification approaches (Chau et al., 2019). But they should also target parents, as studies have demonstrated the influence of family factors in the development of IGD

(Schneider et al., 2017). Overall, evaluation studies suggest that these programs are effective, but there is a lack of a stringent strategy in collaboration among health policy and care stakeholders to implement them broadly and sustainably (King et al., 2018).

## FUTURE DIRECTIONS

IGD has been included in DSM-5 in Section III. This means that more clinical research is needed before it can be included as a formal disorder in the main body. Most importantly, more high-quality randomized-controlled trials are required, which more favourably include treatment approaches other than CBT. Thus, although psychodynamically oriented studies exist on the aetiology of Internet addiction which particularly examine attachment theory relationships (e.g., Eichenberg et al., 2017), these findings have not yet been reflected in treatment manuals yet.

Especially the case for serious games, longitudinal study designs are vital for an effective and long-term success of serious games in the psychotherapeutic setting. Hennemann et al. (2016) pointed out that those longitudinal studies are further necessary to detect barriers and drivers regarding serious games usage. Acceptance research demands more studies and scales measuring favorable and sceptical views on serious games use by also including cross-cultural or gender-specific characteristics (Clough et al., 2019). Female gaming is explored to a much lesser extent in comparison to male gaming characteristics (Lopez-Fernandez et al., 2019). The few existing studies demonstrated that female players prefer light and funny games with the opportunity to interact and connect with others (Eichenberg et al., 2016). Hence, further research must explore if cross-cultural and gender-specific user characteristics also apply to serious games usage within the psychotherapeutic context. Adverse effects—such as gaming addiction, feeling of isolation, and so on—meet evolving needs of larger assessment. Mostly positive views on serious games have been investigated by research so far by leaving out negatively shaped perspectives or the risk of addictive behavior (Clough et al., 2019).

Another intersection of clinical psychology and computer games is the study of stigma. This includes the portrayal of mental health disorders in video games. A study by Ferrari et al. (2019) aimed to investigate the impact of commercial video games on the transmission and shaping of knowledge about mental illness. Hence, the authors analyzed nearly 800 video games from a gaming platform, of which 100 games addressed mental illness. They concluded that 97 of them portrayed the illnesses in a completely negative and incurable way. This shows that an important area of research and practice is to involve clinical psychologists and psychotherapists in game development so that mental illnesses are portrayed realistically in video games, thus helping to destigmatize those affected. Second, the issue of stigmatization concerns sufferers of IGD themselves. Peter et al. (2019) found that this is highly prevalent in public perception and strategies need to be developed and tested with the wider population. At the same time, approaches now exist to design video games that explicitly aim to reduce the stigma of mental illness (for a positively evaluated use in school-based contexts, see Cangas et al., 2017).

Apart from the requiring need for more thorough study designs, video and serious games usage within psychotherapy are still rarely taught among practitioners. Standardized education and knowledge about novel (psychotherapeutic) tools, such as video and serious games, should be integrated into psychotherapy training curricula or ethical guidelines (Titov et al., 2018). Then, mental health professionals will be able to properly support patients with the selection, guidance, and handling of video games for psychological purposes.

To conclude: Because of the interfaces between video games and clinical psychology and psychotherapy, it seems crucial that practitioners are informed about the opportunities but also the risks. In addition, the significance of video games in all their constructive but also destructive facets should also be addressed in training of mental health professionals.

## REFERENCES

Abt, C. C. (1970). *Serious games.* The Viking Press.

American Psychiatric Association. (2022). *Diagnostic and Statistical Manual of Mental Disorders: DSM-5-TR.* (5th ed.).

Andrade, L. H., Alonso, J., Mneimneh, Z., Wells, J. E., Al-Hamzawi, A., Borges, G., Bromet, E., Bruffaerts, R., de Girolamo, G., de Graaf, R., Florescu, S., Gureje, O., Hinkov, H. R., Hu, C., Huang, Y., Hwang, I., Jin, R., Karam, E. G., Kovess-Masfety, V., Levinson, D., . . . Kessler, R. C. (2014). Barriers to mental health treatment: Results from the WHO World Mental Health surveys. *Psychological Medicine, 44*(6), 1303–1317. https://doi.org/10.1017/S0033291713001943

Beck-Hiestermann, F., Kästner, D., & Gumz, A. (2021). Onlinepsychotherapie in Zeiten der Corona-Pandemie: Querschnittsbefragung deutscher Psychotherapeuten [Online psychotherapy in times of coronavirus pandemic: Cross-sectional survey of German psychotherapists]. *Psychotherapeut, 66,* 372–381. Advance online publication. https://doi.org/10.1007/s00278-021-00519-0

Blinka, L. (2008). The relationship of players to their avatars in MMORPGs: Differences between adolescents, emerging adults and adults. *Cyberpsychology: Journal of Psychosocial Research on Cyberspace, 2*(1), 1–9. https://cyberpsychology.eu/article/view/4211/3252

Bussone, S., Trentini, C., Tambelli, R., & Carola, V. (2020). Early-life interpersonal and affective risk factors for pathological gaming. *Frontiers in Psychiatry, 11,* 423. https://doi.org/10.3389/fpsyt.2020.00423

Cangas, A. J., Navarro, N., Parra, J., Ojeda, J. J., Cangas, D., Piedra, J. A., & Gallego, J. (2017). Stigma-stop: A serious game against the stigma toward mental health in educational settings. *Frontiers in Psychology, 8,* 1385. https://doi.org/10.3389/fpsyg.2017.01385

Cash, H., Rae, C. D., Steel, A. H., & Winkler, A. (2012). Internet addiction: A brief summary of research and practice. *Current Psychiatry Reviews, 8*(4), 292–298. https://doi.org/10.2174/157340012803520513

Chau, C. L., Tsui, Y. Y., & Cheng, C. (2019). Gamification for Internet gaming disorder prevention: Evaluation of a wise IT-use (WIT) program for Hong Kong primary students. *Frontiers Psychology, 10,* 2468. https://doi.org/10.3389/fpsyg.2019.02468

Chia, D., & Zhang, M. (2020). A scoping review of cognitive bias in Internet addiction and internet gaming disorders. *International Journal of Environmental Research and Public Health, 17*(1), 373. https://doi.org/10.3390/ijerph17010373

Clough, B. A., Zarean, M., Ruane, I., Mateo, N. J., Aliyeva, T. A., & Casey, L. M. (2019). Going global: Do consumer preferences, attitudes, and barriers to using e-mental health services differ across countries? *Journal of Mental Health, 28*(1), 17–25. https://doi.org/10.1080/09638237.2017.1370639

Eichenbaum, A., Kattner, F., Bradford, D., Gentile, D. A., & Green, C. S. (2015). Role-playing and real-time strategy games associated with greater probability of Internet gaming disorder. *Cyberpsychology, Behavior and Social Networking, 18*(8), 480–485. https://doi.org/10.1089/cyber.2015.0092

Eichenberg, C. (2021). Onlinepsychotherapie in Zeiten der Coronapandemie [Online psychotherapy in times of the Corona pandemic]. *Psychotherapeut, 66*(3), 195–202. https://doi.org/10.1007/s00278-020–00484-0

Eichenberg, C., Küsel, C., & Sindelar, B. (2016). Computerspiele im Kindes- und Jugendalter: Geschlechtsspezifische Unterschiede in der Präferenz von Spielgenres, Spielanforderungen und Spielfiguren und ihre Bedeutung für die Konzeption von Serious Games [Computer games in children and adolescents: Gender-specific differences in the preference of game genres, game requirements and game characters and their significance for the conception of serious games]. *Merz. Zeitschrift für Medienpädagogik, 60*(6), 97–109. https://www.merz-zeitschrift.de/alle-ausgaben/pdf/christiane-eichenberg-cornelia-kuesel-und-brigitte-sindelar-computerspiele-im-kindes-und-jugendalter/?preview=1%27%5B0%5D&hc=0&cHash=0d9b2023c9dbf3a5b2295121ef20aca2

Eichenberg, C., Schott, M., Decker, O., & Sindelar, B. (2017). Attachment style and Internet addiction: An online survey. *Journal of Medical Internet Research, 19*(5), e170. https://doi.org/10.2196/jmir.6694

Entertainment Software Association. (2019). *Essential fact about the computer and video game industry.* https://www.theesa.com/wp-content/uploads/2019/05/2019-Essential-Facts-About-the-Computer-and-Video-Game-Industry.pdf

Ferrari, M., McIlwaine, S., Jordan, G., Shah, J., Lal, S., & Iyer, S. (2019). Gaming with stigma: Analysis of messages about mental illnesses in video games. *JMIR Mental Health, 6*(5), e12418. https://doi.org/10.2196/12418

Fleming, T. M., de Beurs, D., Khazaal, Y., Gaggioli, A., Riva, G., Botella, C., Baños, R. M., Aschieri, F., Bavin, L. M., Kleiboer, A., Merry, S., Lau, H. M., & Riper, H. (2016). Maximizing the impact of e-therapy and serious gaming: Time for a paradigm shift. *Frontiers in Psychiatry, 7*(65). https://doi.org/10.3389/fpsyt.2016.00065

Franke, G. H. (2000). *BSI: Brief symptom inventory* [Deutsche version, manual]. Beltz. https://www.researchgate.net/publication/260614093_Franke_GH_2000_BSI_Brief_Symptom_Inventory_-_Deutsche_Version_Manual_Gottingen_Beltz

Halldorsson, B., Hill, C., Waite, P., Partridge, K., Freeman, D., & Creswell, C. (2021). Annual research review: Immersive virtual reality and digital applied gaming interventions for the treatment of mental health problems in children and young people: The need for rigorous treatment development and clinical evaluation. *Journal of Child Psychology and Psychiatry, and Allied Disciplines, 62*(5), 584–605. https://doi.org/10.1111/jcpp.13400

Hennemann, S., Beutel, M. E., & Zwerenz, R. (2016). Drivers and barriers to acceptance of web-based aftercare of patients in inpatient routine care: A cross-sectional survey. *Journal of Medical Internet Research, 18*(12), e337. https://doi.org/10.2196/jmir.6003

King, D. L., Delfabbro, P. H., Doh, Y. Y., Wu, A., Kuss, D. J., Pallesen, S., Mentzoni, R., Carragher, N., & Sakuma, H. (2018). Policy and prevention approaches for disordered and hazardous gaming and Internet use: An international perspective. *Prevention Science: The Official Journal of the Society for Prevention Research, 19*(2), 233–249. https://doi.org/10.1007/s11121-017-0813-1

Laamarti, F., Eid, M., & El Saddik, A. (2014). An overview of serious games. *International Journal Computer Games Technology, 2014,* 1–15. https://doi.org/10.1155/2014/358152

Lopez-Fernandez, O., Williams, A. J., & Kuss, D. J. (2019). Measuring female gaming: Gamer profile, predictors, prevalence, and characteristics from psychological and gender perspectives. *Frontier Psychology, 10,* 898. https://doi.org/10.3389/fpsyg.2019.00898

Ma, W., Peng, N., Zhang, P., & Renwick, A. (2020). Impact of Internet use on economic well-being of rural households: Evidence from China. *Review of Development Economics, 2,* 503–523. https://doi.org/10.1111/rode.12645

Merry, S. N., Stasiak, K., Shepherd, M., Frampton, C., Fleming, T., & Lucassen, M. F. G. (2012). The effectiveness of SPARX. A computerised self help intervention for adolescents seeking help for depression: Randomised controlled non-inferiority trial. *British Medical Journal, 344,* e2598. https://doi.org/10.1136/bmj.e2598

Milani, L., Torre, G. L., Fiore, M., Grumi, S., Gentile, D., Ferrante, M., Miccoli, S., & Blasio, P. D. (2017). Internet gaming addiction in adolescence: Risk factors and maladjustment correlates. *International Journal of Mental Health and Addiction, 16,* 888–904. https://doi.org/10.1007/s11469-017-9750-2

Paulus, F. W., Ohmann, S., von Gontard, A., & Popow, C. (2018). Internet gaming disorder in children and adolescents: A systematic review. *Developmental Medicine and Child Neurology, 60*(7), 645–659. https://doi.org/10.1111/dmcn.13754

Payam, A. Z., & Mirzaeidoostan, Z. (2019). Online game addiction relationship with cognitive distortion, parenting style, and narcissistic personality traits in students. *Iranian Journal of Psychiatry and Clinical Psychology, 25*(1), 72–83. https://doi.org/10.32598/ijpcp.25.1.72

Peter, S. C., Li, Q., Pfund, R. A., Whelan, J. P., & Meyers, A. W. (2019). Public stigma across addictive behaviors: Casino gambling, eSports gambling, and Internet gaming. *Journal of Gambling Studies, 35*(1), 247–259. https://doi.org/10.1007/s10899-018-9775-x

Petry, N. M., Rehbein, F., Ko, C. H., & O'Brien, C. P. (2015). Internet gaming disorder in the DSM-5. *Current Psychiatry Reports, 17*(9), 72. https://doi.org/10.1007/s11920-015-0610-0

Rabe-Menssen, C., Ruh, M., & Dazer, A. (2020). *Psychotherapeutische Videobehandlungen.* Wissenschaft und Forschung. https://www.dptv.de/fileadmin/Redaktion/Bilder_und_Dokumente/Wissensdatenbank_oeffentlich/Umfragen/DPtV_Umfrage_Videobehandlung_Mai_2020.pdf

Rehbein, F., Kliem, S., Baier, D., Mößle, T., & Petry, N. M. (2015). Prevalence of Internet gaming disorder in German adolescents: Diagnostic contribution of the nine DSM-5 criteria in a state-wide representative sample. *Addiction, 110*(5), 842–851. https://doi.org/10.1111/add.12849

Rumpf, H. J., & Mann, K. (2018). Gaming disorder in ICD-11: Pathologisation or clinical need? *Sucht-Zeitschrift Fur Wissenschaft Und Praxis, 64*(4), 181–183. https://doi.org/10.1024/0939-5911/a000548

Rumpf, H. J., Tao, R., Rehbein, F., & Petry, N. M. (2015). Internet addiction: A future addictive disorder? In N. M. Petry (Ed.), *Behavioral addictions: DSM-5 and beyond* (Chapter 4). Oxford University Press.

Schneider, L. A., King, D. L., & Delfabbro, P. H. (2017). Family factors in adolescent problematic Internet gaming: A systematic review. *Journal of behavioral addictions, 6*(3), 321–333. https://doi.org/10.1556/2006.6.2017.035

Sindelar, B. (2020). Kinder- und Jugendlichenpsychotherapie: Online in Zeiten der Corona-Krise [Child and adolescent psychotherapy: Online in times of the Corona crisis]. In C. Eichenberg & R. Bering (Hrsg.), *Die Psyche in Zeiten der Corona-Krise: Herausforderungen und Lösungsansätze für Psychotherapeuten und soziale Helfer* [The psyche in times of the Corona crisis: Challenges and solutions for psychotherapists and social helpers] (pp. 83–97). Klett-Cotta.

Stavrou, P.-D. (2018). Addiction to video games: A case study on the effectiveness of psychodynamic psychotherapy on a teenage addict struggling with low self-esteem and aggression issues. *Psychology, 9*(10), 2436–2456. https://doi.org/10.4236/psych.2018.910140

Sugaya, N., Shirasaka, T., Takahashi, K., & Kanda, H. (2019). Bio-psychosocial factors of children and adolescents with Internet gaming disorder: A systematic review. *BioPsychoSocial Medicine, 13,* Article 3. https://doi.org/10.1186/s13030-019-0144-5

The German Games Industry Association. (2019). *The German games industry 2019. Insights, facts and reports.* https://www.game.de/wp-content/uploads/2017/02/2019-10-31-Guide-to-the-German-Games-Industry_NEU.pdf

Titov, N., Dear, B., Nielssen, O., Staples, L., Hadjistavropoulos, H., Nugent, M., Adlam, K., Nordgreen, T., Bruvik, K. H., Hovland, A., Repål, A., Mathiasen, K., Kraepelien, M., Blom, K., Svanborg, C., Lindefors, N., & Kaldo, V. (2018). ICBT in routine care: A descriptive analysis of successful clinics in five countries. *Internet Interventions, 13,* 108–115. https://doi.org/10.1016/j.invent.2018.07.006

Ünsel Bolat, G., Çelik, D., Özgül, S., & Ercan, E., S. (2021). Psychiatric correlates of Internet gaming disorder in children. *The Turkish Journal on Addictions, 8*(1), 45–50. https://www.addicta.com.tr/Content/files/sayilar/29/45-50(1).pdf

Wang, H. R., Cho, H., & Kim, D. J. (2018). Prevalence and correlates of comorbid depression in a nonclinical online sample with DSM-5 Internet gaming disorder. *Journal of Affective Disorders, 226,* 1–5. https://doi.org/10.1016/j.jad.2017.08.005

Wartberg, L., Kriston, L., & Kammerl, R. (2017). Associations of social support, friends only known through the Internet, and health-related quality of life with Internet gaming disorder in adolescence. *Cyberpsychology, Behavior and Social Networking, 20*(7), 436–441. https://doi.org/10.1089/cyber.2016.0535

Wartberg, L., Kriston, L., & Thomasius, R. (2020). Internet gaming disorder and problematic social media use in a representative sample of German adolescents: Prevalence estimates, comorbid depressive symptoms and related psychosocial aspects. *Computers in Human Behavior,* 103, 31–36. https://doi.org/10.1016/j.chb.2019.09.014

Wölfling, K., Mörsen, C. P., Duven, E., Albrecht, U., Grüsser, S. M., & Flor, H. (2011). To gamble or not to gamble: At risk for craving and relapse—Learned motivated attention in pathological gambling. *Biological psychology, 87*(2), 275–281. https://doi.org/10.1016/j.biopsycho.2011.03.010

Zajac, K., Ginley, M. K., & Chang, R. (2020). Treatments of Internet gaming disorder: A systematic review of the evidence. *Expert review of neurotherapeutics, 20*(1), 85–93. https://doi.org/10.1080/14737175.2020.1671824

# SECTION III

## VIRTUAL REALITY

CHAPTER 6

# VIRTUAL REALITY AND ITS APPLICATIONS IN CLINICAL SETTINGS, BETWEEN RISKS AND BENEFITS

**Tommaso Ciulli**
***Idego Digital Psychology***

## WHAT IS VIRTUAL REALITY?

Today, we could define virtual reality (VR) as that technology that allows human beings to be projected within an artificial and fictitious environment but perceived by our brain as strongly real. The expression VR was coined by Lanier in 1989.1 Composed of a set of electronic devices that allow a new kind of human–computer interaction (Steuer, 1992), VR is defined as a realistic simulation of a verisimilar place that the user experiences and perceives in the same way as in the real world. Conceptualized as a revolutionary device, VR was initially a research prerogative. Currently, the use of this technology has extended to other fields: recreational, medical,

*Digital Developments*, pages 87–100

educational, sports (Lazzeri & Porzia, 2021), or for the development and use of functional programs in psychology.

Understanding VR can be quite difficult. Very often, terms such as "augmented reality" (AR) or "mixed reality" (MR) are superimposed, assuming that they mean the same thing. However, these three expressions have particular differences between them. In particular:

> *Virtual reality (VR)* is a digital environment processed by computers in which people can interact in an alternative reality to the real one that can be manipulated in the same way as otherwise used in the real world. The experience of the subject involved radical changes: from a simple observer of an action, they become an active protagonist (Lazzeri, 2011). Visual and auditory stimuli are perceived through the use of visors or head mounted displays. According to the output tools used, it is possible to distinguish between three types of VR: immersive, non-immersive and semi-immersive. In immersive VR, the subject is sensory immersed in the computer-generated three-dimensional environment. Immersion is made possible through visors and position sensors (trackers). Non-immersive VR consists of three-dimensional environments generated by the computer, but shown on a 2D screen that is perceived by the user as a kind of window. To limit this effect, special glasses are used to enable stereoscopic viewing. Finally, semi-immersive VR is a small room in which the walls, ceiling, and floor are replaced by rear-projected screens. In the room, the user's movements are detected by special sensors allowing them to update the three-dimensional environment displayed on the walls. CAVEs or automatic virtual environments belong to this category (Cruz-Neira et al., 1992).
>
> *Augmented reality (AR)*, is a visual and interactive method of presenting relevant digital information (video, computer graphics, audio) in the real world (Azuma, 1997). In contrast to VR, the virtual objects present are not manipulable by the person. However, the user has the ability to observe and hear sounds produced by the surrounding environment. To take advantage of AR content, the tools available are tablets, smartphones, or visors with lenses similar to those of glasses that allow you to see the surrounding reality. AR has only become dominant since 2016 thanks to the popularity of the mobile game Pokémon Go (Lazzeri, 2017a). AR finds its use in areas that are not only playful, though: this technology is used in medicine, education, military, and many other areas (Schmalstieg & Hollerer, 2016).
>
> *Mixed Reality (MR)* consists of the integration of the real world and virtual objects. Digital objects are in this case manipulated by the user. The visors that support mixed reality are not many, the most known is Microsoft Hololens, now (i.e., 2022) in its second version.[2]

Regardless of the VR technology used, the clinical potential of VR is supported by clinical outcomes. Its use in clinical psychology has been shown to be effective in the treatment of social anxiety, eating disorders, pain management, addiction treatment, as well as with autism (Riva, 2020).

Like any new technology, VR is not exempt from limitations and disadvantages. Despite the recent accessibility of visors at low cost such as Meta Quest 2 or Pico 4, the price of the first headsets was initially very high. Originally available only for research, Google has played a very important role in VR with its Google Cardboard, even if it wasn't exactly a viewer like those we know today. However, the problem of cost will still remain one of the limitations of visors; the presence on the market of performing VR devices, like the Quest Pro, will be for the benefit and consumption for a niche consumer market. Today a further limitation of headsets is their weight. All VR devices are heavy and prolonged use can generate headaches and neck pains. This is the reason behind consumers' tendency towards AR. Finally, another limitation to pay attention to concerns the graphical limitations inherent in VR (Girdhar, 2022). Many applications, for instance, have severe rendering problems and this causes a reduction to the sense of presence characteristic of VR.

Despite its various limitations, a great deal of research has been conducted using VR for the treatment of various disorders as discussed in the next section.

## STATE OF THE ART

Before exploring the state of the art of VR, it is necessary to understand how one of the most effective therapies in the treatment of phobias, anxiety disorders, or obsessive-compulsive disorder works, namely exposure therapy (ET; Choy et al., 2007; Ougrin, 2011; Law & Boisseau, 2019); a psychological therapy where VR has been used the most. In ET the patient is exposed in a controlled way to situations that generate emotions of anxiety or fear until these emotions are reduced. The first step is to select a series of stimuli (e.g., situations, objects, or animals) that are potentially anxiogenic and then put them in order according to their level of activation (subjective unit of discomfort) from lowest to highest on a scale from 0 to 100.

Once the exposure hierarchy has been constructed, the therapist helps the subject to expose (in imagination and then in vivo) gradually to the selected stimuli, starting with the lowest step until anxiety is reduced and then moving on to the next one.

One of the main limitations of ET is that it cannot always identify appropriate stimuli. For example, for the fear of flying one of the steps could be to enter the cabin of an airplane without it taking off, in the real world this might be impossible or difficult. In this case, the use of a virtual scenario could be very useful to use instead of a real one or as an intermediate step before an in vivo exposure. When computer-generated virtual scenarios are used in ET, it is called virtual reality exposure therapy (VRET).

The efficacy of VR treatment was first documented more than 20 years ago, when Barbara Rothbaum and her collaborators demonstrated that VRET had been effective in the treatment of acrophobia (Rothbaum et al., 1995). In their study, 20 academic students with acrophobia, subdivided into 12 males and 8 females, were randomly assigned to a VRET treatment (12) and a wait-listed comparison group (8). Seventeen students completed the study. Each individual VR exposure session was conducted for 8 weeks, with a time duration between 35–45 minutes. The students spent as much time as necessary in each situation to decrease anxiety; everyone progressed at their personal rhythm. The virtual environments were: (a) three walkways that were located 7, 50, and 80 meters above the water; (b) four outside balconies that were located on the ground, second, 10th and 20th floors; and (c) a glass lift that simulated the Atlanta Marriott Marquis hotel which could rise 49 floors to 147 meters. The researchers' conclusions showed that the group subjected to the VRET improved significantly after 8 weeks, while the comparison group remained unchanged. Following the research conducted by Rothbaum and her colleagues, there were many studies and applications, carefully documented in the literature, that used VRET in the treatment of phobias, but not limited to (Maples-Keller et al., 2017). From the beginning and over time VR has proven to be a tool with considerable capacity in the treatment of a person's psychological well-being (Rothbaum et al., 1995).

Many studies have shown how VR, when used in combination with cognitive behavioral therapy (CBT) can be an excellent tool to help people cope with certain phobias (Maples-Keller et al., 2017). For example, acrophobia (fear of heights), amaxophobia (fear of driving), or agoraphobia are just a few of the many phobias that can be treated these days through VRET.

To date, the effectiveness of VRET has proven useful in the treatment of other specific phobias, as in the case of selachophobia. Those suffering from this phobia have serious difficulties in swimming in the open sea, to practice water sports even in places where certainly there are no sharks (e.g., lakes), to make a boat trip or visit aquariums or zoos. In very severe cases the fear extends even to swimming in a pool or to photos or films depicting sharks. In the study of Malbos and colleagues (Malbos et al., 2020), the use of VRET not only led to a reduction in the symptoms of the patient affected by this phobia, but also showed a benefit that was maintained over time even after a follow up at a distance of 12 months.

Many studies on the use of VR in clinical psychology have focused on anxiety disorders. Few studies have investigated the use of VR in the treatment of, for example, schizophrenia. The goal of these studies was to test the effectiveness of using VR to facilitate subjects in managing persecution deliriums and social anxiety during interactions with others. Thus, employing VR as a tool to increase learning of social skills in conjunction with standard methodologies. Although few in number, these studies appear to be very promising (Maples-Keller et al., 2017).

VR has also proven to be a pioneering solution in eating disorders. Through the practice of frame shifting (Akhtar et al., 2017; Riva et al., 2011), it was noted that it was possible to modify the individual's body self-awareness as well as reorganize their body-related memories (Osimo et al., 2015; Riva et al., 2011). To accomplish this, the subject relives a negative body-related situation in VR in both first and third person.

This approach has been successfully used in several randomized trials with obese patients (Cesa et al., 2013; Manzoni et al., 2016), allowing them to both update body memory content and improve clinical outcomes compared to traditional CBT.

VR (Strickland et al., 1996) has also been used to improve social skills, nonverbal communication, and emotional skills in children with autism (Lorenzo et al., 2019). Simulated real-life scenarios, such as taking the bus or crossing a street intersection, are used to train youth with autism thereby improving their social interaction skills (Moon & Ke, 2019). During the VR experience, they must initiate interactions and talk with simulated actors in order to achieve training goals while building their personal and social identity. Another use of VR is based on improving the emotional skills of the children themselves. Through social stories developed in VR (Ghanouni et al., 2019), young people with autism can get in touch with their emotions in a gradual way.

VR has also proved effective for those problems not directly related to merely psychological aspects.

For example, for pain management, VR interventions have been used synergistically with healthcare interventions and pharmacological approaches (Chan et al., 2018). The most common approach used through VR is distraction. The computer-generated virtual world redirects the patient's attention away from incoming pain signals (Ahmadpour et al., 2019; Hoffman et al., 2006) and appears to change the way the brain processes incoming signals from pain receptors (Lazzeri & Porzia, 2021).

Another area is the use of VR in pain treatment of people affected by the phantom limb syndrome. A study was conducted in Sweden on the effectiveness of VR therapy in the treatment of pain due to phantom limb syndrome (Catalan et al., 2016). Specifically, muscle signals from the amputated limb were used to control augmented and virtual environments. Electrical signals in the muscles are detected by electrodes on the skin. Artificial intelligence algorithms translate the signals into movements of a virtual arm in real time. Patients see themselves on a screen with the virtual arm in place of their missing arm, and can control it as they would control their biological arm. The results of the study indicated a significant decrease in pain, stable over time, in a large number of study participants. The use of VR induced the amputee's brain to think that it was still in control of the missing limb, thus reducing their suffering.

In an article recently written by psychologists Lazzeri and Porzia (2021), it is explained how VR is now also used in fields other than clinical psychology, such as sport (Torkington et al., 2001) or hospital therapy. As regards the latter, the case of SnowWorld should be mentioned. SnowWorld, developed at the University of Washington in collaboration with the Harborview Burn Center, was the first immersive VR software designed specifically for pain reduction. It moves the patient's focus away from pain into an ice-cold virtual environment, where their only task is to throw snowballs at an endlessly advancing group of penguins and puppets (Lazzeri & Porzia, 2021). It might sound silly, but the results speak for themselves: burn patients experienced 35 to 50% less pain when immersed in VR (Hoffman et al., 2011), about the same reduction as a moderate dose of painkillers.

Last but not least is the possibility of using VR in addiction treatment as well. By inducing in a safe, monitorable, and controlled environment the effect of craving in people addicted to alcohol, drugs, nicotine, or gambling (Segawa et al., 2019), VR would increase the patient's insight and ability to make alternative choices with full awareness in the real world.

## POTENTIAL RISK

VR is becoming more and more mainstream. However, despite its countless uses, there are some risks involved in using a VR viewer that are worth knowing about. The first issue to be aware of is cybersickness (McCauley & Sharkey, 1992), a feeling of loss of orientation, dizziness, nausea, and headaches. Seeing oneself, for example, inside a virtual cockpit without our nervous system feeling the real sensations of movement leads to a perceptual imbalance and a consequent state of discomfort. Although the body remains stationary, the sensation of moving in space is all too realistic, since the reference points are no longer on a two-dimensional screen but run alongside and in three dimensions.

Although modern VR devices have attempted to address this problem by opting to upgrade processing, head tracking, and graphics (Rheingold, 1991), unfortunately this problem still remains (Stanney et al., 2020a, 2020b).

A recent Oregon State University study (Penumudi et al., 2020) evaluated how some common VR movements contribute to muscle strain and discomfort. Long, prolonged interaction with environments, games, or applications that involve extending the arm outward causes the user to experience shoulder discomfort. This can lead to serious health problems such as the "gorilla arm"[3] and rotator cuff injuries. In addition, the weight exerted by the visor can place a load on the cervical spine, risking increased neck fatigue (Penumudi et al., 2020).

Current warnings in the use of VR usually refer to physical and sensory ailments, such as cybersickness (Lazzeri, 2017b). However, what unknown risks, outside the clinical context, could this tool entail? A consistent topic of discussion is the intrinsic capacity of VR to induce dissociative states (Van Heugten-van der Kloet et al., 2018). However, this possibility has been frugally explored by the scientific literature, as opposed to its therapeutic benefits.

Furthermore, recent studies have shown how children are more vulnerable when they come to VR technologies, as they may be unable to distinguish between the real world and the virtual world. For example, in a 2009 study by Segovia and Bailenson, some elementary school children watched their virtual doppelgangers swim with killer whales. When these children were questioned a week later, they said they believed their virtual experience was real. The sense of immersion offered by this technology, can also lead a child to develop a false memory (Segovia & Bailenson, 2009). In this research, on 55 preschool and elementary children, it was noted that those immersed in virtual environments increased the production of false memories compared to the group placed in a condition of inactivity. A final risk to be aware of is an increased sense of dissociation and a reduced sense of presence of objective reality (Aardema et al., 2010). Indeed, in a study conducted by Ardeema and colleagues, a sample of 30 people were administered a test to assess their level of dissociation, sense of presence, and immersion before and after an exposure in a virtual environment. Results indicated an increase in dissociative experience (depersonalization and derealization), including a decreased sense of presence in objective reality as a result of exposure to VR. Higher preexisting levels of dissociation and a tendency to become more immersed and absorbed in a virtual environment were associated with greater increases in dissociative symptoms resulting from VR immersion. Recent studies have shown how some VR settings can elicit or intensify negative emotions in users' experiences (Lavoie et al., 2021). In the research conducted by Lavoie and staff, an interactive scenery was designed to elicit low to moderate amounts of negative emotions. Participants in the experiment had interacted with the scenery or in VR, using an HTC Vive, or with a laptop. The participants who had been exposed to the scene with VR reported higher levels of absorption, which increased the intensity of their negative emotions. A questionnaire given many hours later showed that the intensified negative emotions had a significant correlation with negative rumination as a result of VR.

Because VR is now also used by children and teenagers in video games, Kaimara and colleagues (2022) conducted a review to discuss ethical issues and concerns. They analyzed three domains: physical, cognitive, and psychosocial. The review revealed contradictory results especially for the psychosocial domain, but in general, the recommendations and research on children's well-being are reassuring if health, safety, and time constraints are adhered to.

## POTENTIAL BENEFITS

However, VR is a highly flexible tool that allows you to program an enormous variety of ways to treat psychological distress. The possibility of structuring a large number of controlled stimuli and at the same time to be able to monitor the possible physiological responses induced in the subject exposed to VR, offers a great increase in the possibility of therapeutic efficacy, compared to traditional procedures.

In general, the possibility of allowing patients to experience potentially infinite scenarios an infinite number of times allows for a significant reduction in costs. For example, people can try out various scenarios for their fear of flying without the excessive costs of in vivo exposure. In a study conducted on the fear of flying using the computer-assisted exposure approach (Breton-Lopez et al., 2015), the researchers verified that VR with a viewer garnered a higher preference than VR on a PC monitor. The researchers divided the subjects into three groups. One group used exposure with a VR viewer (VRET), one group exposure on a PC monitor with a therapist, and one group with autonomous monitor exposure without a therapist. The participants in the VR group interacted within a virtual world on certain scenarios (airport, aircraft takeoff and landing). The other two groups viewed real static images associated with the typical sounds of that image.

At the end of the expositional exercises, the participants were given a demonstration of the alternatives. They then had to indicate their level of perceived efficacy, whether or not they suggested this tool and their perceived sense of adversity. In general, although VRET was perceived as more aversive, it was the condition perceived as most effective, recommended, and preferred.

Another important factor to consider is the dropout rate of ETs. In a study (Garcia-Palacios et al., 2007), the rejection rate towards in vivo and VR exposure was analyzed. In a sample of 150 subjects with specific phobia, 27% refused in vivo exposure and only 3% refused VR exposure.

VR allows people to have an exposure experience in a protected environment and then a transition to in vivo exposure with a lower drop-out rate.

Finally, VR would also produce significant behavioral changes in real life. According to a meta-analysis (Morina et al., 2015), patients submitted to VRET for specific phobias achieved significant results after treatment and comparable to those obtained through in vivo exposure also on real-life behavioral changes.

## FUTURE DIRECTIONS

What will be the future of VR? The various uses of this technology already range from the possibility of creating virtual prototypes to be tested digitally to training and simulation programs for pilots and surgeons. In 2018, according to some forecasts made by IDC research,[4] huge investments that will exceed 13 billion euros by 2022, will go for VR and AR.

Beyond the limitations discussed above (weight of the visor, cybersickness, etc.) which will probably be resolved in whole or in part, hypothetically the only limit to the use of VR in any field (from education to clinical and wellness) is imagination. Below are some more recent practical examples that might indicate where and how VR can be used.

Because of the emergence of COVID-19, distance learning systems are increasingly using VR technology in education and training. The Engage platform,[5] for example, is being used by companies such as Facebook, HTC, and the European Commission for distance learning.

In sport psychology, in particular, the use of VR provides an opportunity to train the mind while learning to better manage the emotions associated with the tensest moments for the athlete. Through immersion in specific environments with high emotional activation, such as simulating large crowds or taking a penalty kick, the athlete can focus on identifying the most functional cognitive strategies (recognizing dysfunctional thoughts) and focus on useful techniques to improve performance and well-being.

A study conducted by Michalski and colleagues examined how the performance learned in table tennis training with VR can be transferred to a real-world environment. Compared to the control group without VR training, the study showed that the sports skills of players trained with VR are improved in terms of quality and quantity (Michalski et al., 2019).

Managing emotions more effectively also implies a better regulation of the arousal and consequently a better state of flow (Csikszentmihalyi, 1975; Lazzeri & Porzia, 2021). In clinical psychology it will be possible, thanks to haptic devices such as Teslasuit[6] or the magic glove under development at the Meta[7] company, to integrate therapies such as mindfulness-based cognitive therapy (MBCT) together with sylvan therapy in virtual settings. The Silvotherapy (from the Latin word silva, meaning forest) is a practice, also known as the Anglo-Saxon name "tree hugging," which argues that a new contact with nature can lead people to recharge their batteries with positive energy and better cope with daily stress. This makes it possible to maintain contact with nature even for those who have no opportunities for reasons of cost, distance, or movement (e.g., some physical disability).

As explained above, research on VR in psychology has focused a lot on the treatment of phobias but other directions are possible as in the example below.

There are few studies or investigations to date on the use of VR for the treatment of depression. In a 2019 article, Lindner and colleagues explored how VR can be used for CBT interventions. In the article they refer to the use of VR for immersive psychoeducation and to develop problem solving, behavioral activation, and also cognitive restructuring. Compared to other studies that have also verified the effectiveness of using VR for the treatment of certain disorders, this article provides some suggestions on how it could potentially be employed for the treatment of depression.

Finally, imagine the possibility of being able to assist patients while wearing a visor, such as the Quest 2, in a metaverse similar to Sansar. Furthermore, again thanks to visors, meeting patients in their virtual offices in realities like Second Life will no longer be a simple utopia. Already in 2006, the work done by American colleague D. Craig Kerley anticipated this "unusual" scenario. The psychotherapist was the first to open the Center for Positive Mental Health on Second Life, an online virtual world now in version 5.0 and launched in 2003 by the American company Linden Lab, to practice avatar therapy. Known by the nickname of Craig Kamenev, the colleague impersonated by his avatar holds therapy sessions booked and paid for by the patient on a regular basis, with a duration of 50-minutes each (Lazzeri, 2020).

This would make it possible to go beyond the current distance therapies via webcam or chat. The possibility of having a virtual "body" and meeting one's therapist virtually thanks to the strong sense of presence that VR offers for those who for some reason find it difficult to move and physically reach a mental health professional.

Whatever will be the future of VR in the psychological or clinical fields, it is important to pay attention and to analyze the possible impacts that this powerful tool can generate and therefore the encouragement is to always hold a scientific and objective perspective while maintaining an attitude of healthy curiosity.

As reported in the paragraph on potential risk, there are still limited studies that have extensively investigated the possible negative effects of the use of VR in the psychological field. This should be a signal of attention to the use of VR although numerous studies have verified the many potential benefits.

## NOTES

1. Jarome Lanier is an American computer scientist, composer, and essayist. He founded the Virtual Programming Lab (VPL Research) in 1984.
2. Microsoft HoloLens, originally called "Project Baraboo" is a device developed since 2010 by Microsoft to exploit the potential of the Windows MR system.
3. "Gorilla arm" is when someone who is using an upright or standing touchscreen experiences arm fatigue due to the awkward and unergonomic positioning required.
4. According to idcitalia.com, IDC (the International Data Corporation) is the world's leading company specialized in market research, consulting services, and event organization in the ICT and digital innovation sectors.

5. Ideal communication platform for collaboration, education, simulated training, and virtual events https://engagevr.io/
6. Teslasuit, the haptic suit that transmits tactile sensations, heat, and even pain https://teslasuit.io/
7. Founded in 2004 by Mark Zuckerberg, Meta Platforms, Inc. is the U.S. company that controls the Facebook and Instagram social networking services WhatsApp and Messenger and develops the Oculus Rift VR visors.

## REFERENCES

Aardema, F., O'Connor, K., Côté, S., & Taillon, A. (2010). Virtual reality induces dissociation and lowers sense of presence in objective reality. *Cyberpsychology, Behavior, and Social Networking, 13*(4), 429–435. https://doi.org/10.1089/cyber.2009.0164

Ahmadpour, N., Randall, H., Choksi, H., Gao, A., Vaughan, C., & Poronnik, P. (2019). Virtual reality interventions for acute and chronic pain management. *The International Journal of Biochemistry & Cell Biology, 114*, 105568. https://doi.org/10.1016/j.biocel.2019.105568

Akhtar, S., Justice, L. V., Loveday, C., & Conway, M. A. (2017). Switching memory perspective. *Consciousness and Cognition: An International Journal, 56*, 50–57. https://doi.org/10.1016/j.concog.2017.10.006

Azuma, R. (1997). A survey of augmented reality. *Presence: Teleoperators and Virtual Environments, 6*(4), 355–385. https://doi.org/10.1162/pres.1997.6.4.355

Breton-Lopez, J., Tortella-Feliu, M., Riera del Amo, A., Banos, R., Llabres, J., Gelabert, J. M., & Botella, C. (2015). Participants' preferences regarding three computer-based exposure treatments for fear of flying. *Behavioral Psychology, 23*(2), 265–285. https://www.behavioralpsycho.com/wp-content/uploads/2018/10/04.Breton_23-2rEn.pdf

Catalan, M., Guðmundsdóttir, R. A., Kristoffersen, M. B., Zepeda-Echavarria, A., Caine-Winterberger, K., Kulbacka-Ortiz, K., & Hermansson, L. (2016). Phantom motor execution facilitated by machine learning and augmented reality as treatment for phantom limb pain: a single group, clinical trial in patients with chronic intractable phantom limb pain. *The Lancet, 388*(10062), 2885–2894.

Cesa, G. L., Manzoni, G. M., Bacchetta, M., Castelnuovo, G., Conti, S., Gaggioli, A., Mantovani, F., Molinari, E., Cardenas-Lopez, G., & Riva, G. (2013). Virtual reality for enhancing the cognitive behavioral treatment of obesity with binge eating disorder: Randomized controlled study with one-year follow-up. *Journal of Medical Internet Research, 15*(6), e113. https://doi.org/10.2196/jmir.2441

Chan, E., Foster, S., Sambell, R., & Leong, P. (2018). Clinical efficacy of virtual reality for acute procedural pain management: A systematic review and meta-analysis. *PLoS One, 13*(7), e0200987. https://doi.org/10.1371/journal.pone.0200987

Choy, Y., Fyer, A. J., & Lipsitz, J. D. (2007). Treatment of specific phobia in adults. *Clinical Psychology Review, 27*(3), 266–826. https://doi.org/10.1016/j.cpr.2006.10.002

Cruz-Neira, C., Sandin, D. J., DeFanti, T. A., Kenyon, R. V., & Hart, J. C. (1992). The CAVE: Audio visual experience automatic virtual environment. *Communications of the ACM, 35*(6), 64–72. https://doi.org/10.1145/129888.129892

Csikszentmihalyi, M. (1975). *Beyond boredom and anxiety*. Jossey-Bass Publishers.

Garcia-Palacios, A., Botella, C., Hoffman, H., Fabregat, S. (2007). Comparing acceptance and refusal rates of virtual reality exposure therapy vs in vivo exposure by patients with specific phobias. *Cyberpsychology & Behavior,* 10(5), 722–724. https://doi.org/10.1089/cpb.2007.9962

Ghanouni, P., Jarus, T., Zwicker, J. G., Lucyshyn, J., Mow, K., Ledingham, A. (2019). Social stories for children with autism spectrum disorder: Validating the content of a virtual reality program. *Journal of Autism and Developmental Disorders, 49,* 660–668. https://doi.org/10.1007/s10803-018-3737-0

Girdhar, A. (2022). *The limitations of virtual reality*. Retrieved 10.12.2022 to https://www.appypie.com/virtual-reality-limitations

Hoffman, H. G., Chambers, G. T., Meyer, W. J., Arceneaux, L. L., Russell, W. J., Seibel, E. J., Richards, T. L., Sharar, S. R., & Patterson, D. R. (2011). Virtual reality as an adjunctive non-pharmacologic analgesic for acute burn pain during medical procedures. *Annals of Behavioral Medicine, 41*(2), 183–191. https://doi.org/10.1007/s12160-010-9248-7

Hoffman, H. G., Richards, T. L., Bills, A. R., Van Oostrom, T., Magula, J., Seibel, E. J., & Sharar, S. R. (2006). Using fMRI to study the neural correlates of virtual reality analgesia. *CNS Spectrums, 11*(1), 45–51. https://doi.org/10.1017/s1092852900024202

Kaimara, P., Oikonomou, A., & Deliyannis, I. (2022). Could virtual reality applications pose real risks to children and adolescents? A systematic review of ethical issues and concerns. *Virtual Reality, 26,* 697–735. https://doi.org/10.1007/s10055-021-00563-w

Lavoie, R., Main, K., King, C., & King, D. (2021). Virtual experience, real consequences: The potential negative emotional consequences of virtual reality gameplay. *Virtual Reality, 25,* 69–81. https://doi.org/10.1007/s10055-020-00440-y

Law, C., & Boisseau, C. L. (2019). Exposure and response prevention in the treatment of obsessive-compulsive disorder: Current perspectives. *Psychology Research and Behavior Management, 12,* 1167–1174. https://doi.org/10.2147/PRBM.S211117

Lazzeri, M. (2011). La realtà virtuale in psicologia clinica [Master's thesis]. In F. Del Corno & M. Lang (Eds.), "Terapie senza diretto intervento del terapeuta"—Elementi de Psicologia Clinica, Franco Angeli: Milano, 2013.

Lazzeri, M. (2017a, February 13). *Beyond the playful: Pokemon go among captology, positive technology and emotional intelligence*. Retrieved 08.11.2021 from https://www.stateofmind.it/2017/02/pokemon-go-emotional-intelligence/

Lazzeri, M. (2017b, April 20). *Le controindicazioni attuale e future all'utilizzo della realtà virtuale* [Current and future contraindications to the use of virtual reality]. Retrieved 12.12.2022 from https://www.stateofmind.it/2017/04/realta-virtuale-controindicazoni/

Lazzeri, M. (2020). *Intelligenza artificiale e psicologia: quale futuro?* [Artificial intelligence and psychology: What future?]. COADPT. Retrieved from 06.11.2021 from https://www.co-adapt.it/intelligenza-artificiale-e-psicologia-quale-futuro/

Lazzeri, M., & Porzia, Z. (2021). *Il mondo degli exergames: tra potenzialità e ambiti di intervento?* [The world of exergames: Between potential and areas of intervention?]. Retrieved 04.11.2021 from https://www.stateofmind.it/2021/06/exergames-potenzialita-intervento/

Lindner, P., Hamilton, W., Miloff, A., & Carlbring, P. (2019). How to treat depression with low-intensity virtual reality interventions: Perspectives on translating cognitive behavioral techniques into the virtual reality modality and how to make antidepressive use of virtual reality—Unique experiences. *Frontiers in Psychiatry, 10,* 792. https://doi.org/10.3389/fpsyt.2019.00792

Lorenzo, G., Lledó, A., Arráez-Vera, G., & Lorenzo-Lledó, A. (2019). The application of immersive virtual reality for students with ASD: A review between 1990–2017. *Education and Information Technologies, 24*(1), 127–151. https://doi.org/10.1007/s10639-018-9766-7

Malbos, E., Burgess, G. H., & Lançon, C. (2020). Virtual reality and fear of shark attack: A case study for the treatment of squalophobia. *Clinical Case Studies, 19*(2), 153465012094001. https://doi.org/10.1177/1534650120940014

Manzoni, G. M., Cesa, G. L., Bacchetta, M., Castelnuovo, G., Conti, S., Gaggioli, A., Mantovani, F., Molinari, E., Cardenas-Lopez, G., & Riva, G. (2016). Virtual reality-enhanced cognitive-behavioral therapy for Morbid obesity: A randomized controlled study with 1 Year follow-up. *Cyberpsychology, Behavior, and Social Networking, 19*(2), 134–140. https://doi.org/10.1089/cyber.2015.0208

Maples-Keller, J. L., Bunnel, B. E., Kim, S. J., & Rothbaum, B. O. (2017). The use of virtual reality technology in the treatment of anxiety and other psychiatric disorders. *Harvard Review of Psychiatry, 25*(3), 103–113. https://doi.org/10.1097/HRP.0000000000000138

McCauley, M. E., & Sharkey, T. J. (1992). Cybersickness: Perception of self-motion in virtual environments. *Presence: Teleoperators and Virtual Environments, 1*(3), 311–318. https://doi.org/10.1162/pres.1992.1.3.311

Michalski, S. C., Szpak, A., Saredakis, D., Ross, T. J., Billinghurst, M., & Loetscher, T. (2019). Getting your game on: Using virtual reality to improve real table tennis skills. *PLoS ONE, 14*(9, e0222351. https://doi.org/10.1371/journal.pone.0222351

Moon, J., & Ke, F. (2019). Exploring the treatment integrity of virtual reality-based social skills training for children with high-functioning autism. *Interactive Learning Environments, 29*(2), 1–15. https://doi.org/10.1080/10494820.2019.1613665

Morina, N., Ijntema, H., Meyerbröker, K., & Emmelkamp, P. M. (2015). Can virtual reality exposure therapy gains be generalized to real-life? A meta-analysis of studies applying behavioral assessments. *Behaviour Research and Therapy, 74,* 18–24. https://doi.org/10.1016/j.brat.2015.08.010

Osimo, S. A., Pizarro, R., Spanlang, B., & Slater, M. (2015). Conversations between self and self as Sigmund Freud—A virtual body ownership paradigm for self counselling. *Scientific Reports, 5,* 13899. https://doi.org/10.1038/srep13899

Ougrin, D. (2011). Efficacy of exposure versus cognitive therapy in anxiety disorders: Systematic review and meta-analysis. *BMC Psychiatry, 11,* 200. https://doi.org/10.1186/1471-244X-11-200

Penumudi, S. A., Kuppam, V. A., Kim, J. H., & Hwang, J. (2020). The effects of target location on musculoskeletal load, task performance, and subjective discomfort during virtual reality interactions. *Applied Ergonomics, 84,* 103010 https://doi.org/10.1016/j.apergo.2019.103010

Rheingold, H. (1991). *Virtual reality.* Seeker & Warburg.

Riva, G. (2020). Virtual reality in clinical psychology. *Comprehensive clinical psychology (2nd ed), 10,* 91–105. https://doi.org/10.1016/B978-0-12-818697-8.00006-6

Riva, G., Waterworth, J. A., Waterworth, E. L., & Mantovani, F. (2011). From intention to action: The role of presence. *New Ideas in Psychology, 29*(1), 24–37. https://doi.org/10.1016/j.newideapsych.2009.11.002

Rothbaum, B. O., Hodges, L. F., Kooper, R., Opdyke, D., Williford, J. S., & North, M. (1995). Effectiveness of computer-generated (virtual reality) graded exposure in the treatment of acrophobia. *The American Journal of Psychiatry, 152*(4), 626–628. https://doi.org/10.1176/ajp.152.4.626

Schmalstieg, D., & Hollerer, T. (2016). *Augmented reality: Principles and practice.* Pearson Education.

Segawa, T., Baudry, T., Bourla, A., Blanc, J. V., Peretti, C. S., Mouchabac, S., & Ferreri, F. (2019). Virtual reality (VR) in assessment and treatment of addictive disorders: A systematic review. *Frontiers in Neuroscience, 13.* https://doi.org/10.3389/fnins.2019.01409

Segovia, K. Y., & Bailenson, J. N. (2009). Virtually true: Children's acquisition of false memories in virtual reality. *Media Psychology, 12*(4), 371–393. https://doi.org/10.1080/15213260903287267

Stanney, K., Fidopiastis, C., & Foster, L. (2020a). Virtual reality is sexist: But it does not have to be. *Frontiers in Robotics and AI, 7,* 4. https://doi.org/10.3389/frobt.2020.00004

Stanney, K., Lawson, B. D., Rokers, B., Dennison, M., Fidopiastis, C., Stoffregen, T., Weech, S., & Fulvio, J. M. (2020b). Identifying causes of and solutions for cybersickness in immersive technology: Reformulation of a research and development agenda. *International Journal of Human–Computer Interaction, 36*(19), 1783–1803. https://doi.org/10.1080/10447318.2020.1828535

Steuer, J. (1992). Defining virtual reality: Dimensions determining telepresence. *Journal of Communication, 42*(4), 73–93. https://doi.org/10.1111/j.1460-2466.1992.tb00812.x

Strickland, D., Mesibov, G. B., & Hogan, K. (1996). Two case studies using virtual reality as a learning tool for autistic children. *Journal of Autism and Developmental Disorders, 26*(6), 651–659. https://doi.org/10.1007/BF02172354

Torkington, J., Smith, S. G., Rees, B., & Darzi, A. (2001). Skill transfer from virtual reality to a real laparoscopic task. *Surgical Endoscopy, 15,* 1076–1079. https://doi.org/10.1007/s004640000233

Van Heugten-van der Kloet, D., Cosgrave, J., van Rheede, J., & Hicks, S. (2018). Out-of-body experience in virtual reality induces acute dissociation. *Psychology of Consciousness: Theory, Research, and Practice, 5*(4), 346–357. https://doi.org/10.1037/cns0000172

CHAPTER 7

# VIRTUAL REALITY, BETWEEN APPLICATIONS AND SOFTWARE FOR USE BY MENTAL HEALTH PROFESSIONALS

**Luca Bernardelli**
***BECOME Srl***

*Jeremy Bailenson,* director of Stanford University's Virtual Human Interaction Lab, one of the global most eminent neuroscientists, said that virtual reality (VR) is psychologically more powerful than any medium ever invented and is poised to radically transform our lives (Bailenson, 2018, p. 89).

VR is a digitally reproduced reality, a three-dimensional environment built on a computer that can be explored and interacted with using devices such as headsets, gloves, overalls, and other objects that immerse the wearers in virtual environments.

Why is this technology psychologically so interesting? VR activates the *sense of presence,* the feeling of being and acting within a simulated reality as if it

*Digital Developments,* pages 101–111

were an authentic reality (Coelho et al., 2006). In this way, it is possible to be in a place without having to physically reach it. VR is able to generate a multisensory amplification, above all, when other immersive tools are added, involving all learning systems: cognitive, emotional, experiential, and behavioral. In fact, the most effective learning occurs when the experiential system is strongly engaged and in sync with the other systems (Bonasio, 2018). VR is able to provide users with the ability to navigate within realistic or fantastic scenarios, often triggering such a level of engagement as to stimulate a flow in those who try it (Hassan et al., 2020). VR can even reproduce paradoxical situations that would be impossible in reality, which alter the rules of logic and the laws of nature, helping to stimulate people's imagination and creativity, modify habitual thought patterns and give new meaning to human experiences (Chirico & Gaggioli, 2021). Moreover, VR can activate the embodiment, the feeling to be in another body, perception that allows people to acquire a healthier body image, or to assume another identity, in order to improve new skills and abilities and develop empathy (Bertrand et al., 2018). All these features make VR an ideal psychological tool. From the reproduction of safe situations in which it's possible to experience anxieties to the development of imaginary worlds that can stimulate creativity and lateral thinking, everything is preparatory to patient engagement and learning.

VR can be considered a "psychotechnology" because it can emulate, extend, or amplify the powers of our minds (De Kerckhove, 1999). VR can amplify individuals' perceptual, somatic, imaginative, emotional, cognitive, and metacognitive experience, in order to extract valuable material on which a mental health professional (psychologist and/or psychotherapist) can work towards psychological well-being and positive change, because of the VR ability to bring people inside "healing worlds" with high-level of experientiality and transformative potential (Gaggioli, 2016).

## VIRTUAL REALITY BRIEF HISTORY OF THE SYSTEMS

VR technology was born as early as 1957 thanks to Morton Heilig's "Sensorama" project, not originally intended for use in a clinical setting, of course. The binomial "VR" was subsequently coined by the computer scientist Jaron Lanier, who, in 1984, founded "VPL Research," one of the first companies to develop and commercialize it.

VR in the clinical field was born in 1992 thanks to the cave automatic virtual environment (CAVE) project, a cube-shaped room studded with video projectors that reproduce three-dimensional images on the walls and ceiling. It is a voluminous and very expensive instrument, normally used by hospitals, clinics, and large research institutions for specific interventions, therefore obviously not designed for mass diffusion.

The first real revolution from the point of view of a wider use of VR by consumers comes from the company Oculus VR, born in 2012 on a prototype of a viewer mainly conceived for gamers and for mass use. Two years after its establishment, this startup has been acquired by Facebook.

In 2015, Samsung, in collaboration with Facebook, released the Gear VR plastic viewer, hosting a Samsung smartphone that, thanks to specific apps, turns into a VR device.

Other smartphone viewers worth mentioning are Google's Cardboards (actually cardboard items born as a joke to make fun of Facebook), that have received high media attention and excellent sales success, which initiate the development of a series of plastic imitations, and the more advanced Daydream, quickly withdrawn from trade.

In 2016, Facebook delivered to the world an amazing VR headset called Oculus Rift, after which other powerful viewers arrived: HTC Vive and Sony Playstation VR, which have further raised the prevalence of VR in the world and the quality threshold of these objects.

From May 2018, VR for everyone takes a leap forward with the Oculus GO, one of the most interesting products for the quality/price ratio, which works independently, without the need for a connected smartphone or personal computer. From the following year, the Pico proved to be a viable, albeit more costly, alternative.

In 2019, again Facebook, marketed a new generation of standalone VR helmets, more performing than the previous GOs, and with a greater level of interactivity: the Oculus Quest—and in 2020 the Quest 2 and in 2023 Quest 3—at that time considered the most interesting VR headsets on the market for the cost–benefit ratio.

Since 2016, Apple has carried out numerous acquisitions of entire companies (e.g., NextVR and Spaces in 2020) or specific work groups focused on extended realities, continuing to postpone the release of its own device, currently scheduled for 2023 and probably supported with both VR + augmented reality (AR).

Together with these increasingly advanced viewers, we find a plethora of sensory devices that complement or enhance the virtual human experience. Today it is possible to wear haptic gloves to "touch" objects that are not actually present, or olfactory masks to feel odors that can activate memory and elicit emotions, and even to physically move or fly in virtual environments while remaining in the same point. All these perceptual-sensory extensions will ensure that people can amplify their experience in digital worlds afferent, for instance, to psychological well-being.

In recent years, VR technology has multiplied its use cases and could definitely take hold thanks to the advent of the 5G network and new-concept headsets plus immersive experiences capable of minimizing *cybersickness*, the annoying discomfort represented by a cluster of symptoms that happen in the virtual world in the absence of physical motion (as it happens with traditional motion sickness).

## VIRTUAL REALITY APPLICATIONS AND SOFTWARES

### Virtual Reality as a Simulative Technology

VR environments could replicate any potential anxiety or traumatic experience, allowing to treat almost every kind of phobias: claustrophobia (the fear of confined spaces), acrophobia (the fear of heights), zoophobia (the fear of an animal), agoraphobia (the fear to be in the open space), amaxophobia (the fear of driving), glossophobia (the fear of public speaking), social phobia (the fear to be in public), belonephobia (fear of needles), acluophobia or nictophobia (fear of the dark), and more. A similar intervention is designed for the large number of war veterans experiencing post-traumatic stress disorder. Again, patients are immersed in a virtual environment to relive the stressful experience under controlled circumstances, helping them rework the trauma and alleviate the symptoms of this specific disorder. An analogous intervention also helps people suffering from obsessive-compulsive disorder. Here too, for example, mental health professionals can administer a VR scenario that activates a patient's trigger, for example, linked to dirt or clutter in domestic environments, with the aim of diagnosing and then treating the compulsion. In the case of addictions, VR simulations support therapy by producing realistic conditions in virtual environments in which patients are triggered by their bad habits, such as alcohol, drugs, or gambling, in order to help them gradually develop new responses, with the help of a professional. In virtual environments, the joint work between professional and patient can help to learn to implement new adaptive strategies, in order to cope with real-life situations.

Most known software vendors in this specific simulative VR field are Virtually Better in the United States (for phobias, addictions, and post-traumatic stress disorder), OxfordVR in the United Kingdom (for psychosis), Amelia (ex Psious) in Spain (for phobias and eating disorders), C2Care in France (for phobias, addictions, and eating disorders), Psylaris in Netherlands (for phobias), and Idego in Italy (for phobias). These players offer to mental health professionals different immersive scenarios at different prices for different clinical conditions, typically proposing a web-based system accessible from tablets/laptops able to lead the patient session in VR mode.

### Virtual Reality as Relaxing Technology

Through VR it is possible to recreate natural relaxing visual and sound settings, able to act as a relaxation booster.

Not everyone has easy access to natural environments and this widespread condition is a public health concern for several reasons. In fact, most of the population lives in cities and may have little access to safe green spaces, most hospital windows face gray settings rather than green areas, more than 9 million adults in the United States and Europe live in care facilities that have limited nature nearby and physically disabled people may find it difficult to get outside.

So, immersive technologies can represent the best alternative option to access to nature, because the related feeling of connection does not necessarily depend on the physical place. Some VR scenarios have proved to be valid nature substitutes (Browning et al., 2020). Examples include the The Secret Garden VR experience, part of the CovidFeelGood project, aimed at reducing the psychological burden of confinement and long Covid (Riva et al., 2020).

## Virtual Reality as an Embodied Technology

VR can allow us to enter someone else's body, for different reasons: from eating disorders treatment to skills development.

In the first case, VR can become part of an integrated, structured, and multidisciplinary intervention for anorexia, obesity, and binge eating. In fact, virtual embodiment is useful for patients who have an inaccurate perception of their bodies. For instance, the embodiment illusion (Riva et al., 2019) in a healthy body, could allow anorexic people to experience the perception of a different body and to learn to structure a new body representation and reduce emotional stress related to weight gain. These environments offer the opportunity to address with patients the distortion of their own image, which they can now observe objectively through their actual silhouette. Moreover, bulimic and/or obese people can work to contain the "emotional eating," in which the trigger for the binge does not derive from hunger, but from internal conditions such as stress, sadness or loneliness, or as a need of a reward able to soothe and distract from the real underlying problem. In this way, it's possible to gradually reduce the dysfunctional thoughts and feelings that cause the eating disorder, always working with a mental health professional.

Software vendors in this field are, again, C2Care and Amelia Virtual Care.

## Virtual Reality as an Empathetic Technology

VR can also help to develop new skills or improve existing ones. Some research has testified that temporarily living the identity of Einstein, Freud, or Superman improved some specific soft skills of an individual. For this use case, software vendors are mainly located in the United States like Embodied Labs, STRIVR, and Axon. Other studies on diversity topics have shown how impersonating civilians confined in war areas, homeless, clinical patients, or colleagues discriminated in the society or in a workplace, increased empathy and compassion abilities, enough to make VR deserve the appellation of the "ultimate empathy machine" with the aim to challenge prejudices and stereotypes.

In a 2020 study by Riva et al., patient interaction skills were significantly better in healthcare professionals who trained with virtual patients than in those who only received traditional lectures and assigned readings. Another good example of this is Project Empathy, a VR film series that explores the U.S. prison system, inviting audiences to walk in someone else's shoes, in order to better understand mass incarceration in America.

## Virtual Reality as a Psychodiagnostics Technology

VR is progressively becoming a diagnostic tool for mental health disorders, since it offers the possibility of experiencing realistic situations that can be repeated many times with different patients.

In fact, different studies are confirming that VR offers a chance to assess behaviors in real-time in realistic environments reproducing daily activities (Van Bennekom et al., 2017).

An example in this field is the Spanish-Italian company Nesplora, with its platform that provides a range of neuropsychological assessment tests in VR. Designed for children aged from 6 to 16, this set of tools supports the diagnosis of the five subtypes of attention deficit hyperactivity disorder and specific learning disorders, offering various certified products, which assess attentional, executive, and memory functions.

## Virtual Reality as a Transformative Technology

When virtual immersive experiences are conceived with particular attention to all foundational aspects—technological, psychological, narrative, and artistic (visual and musical)—they can aspire to become true potentially transformative experiences. The emergence of the *transformative immersive storytelling* concept introduces the possibility of using VR in mental health from a different rationale than the mere VR-based exposure therapy (Gaggioli, 2016). In this case, VR-based metaphoric narratives, lived from a first-person perspective, can provide the patients/users the opportunity of eliciting new meanings related to personal world views, generating an unlimited number of possible selves and possible worlds. This paradigm can be integrated in any psychological support model and almost all kinds of psychotherapeutic epistemologies. The psychological effects of these methods can be many, like modifying cognitive schemes, stimulating intuitions, activating exploratory thinking, generating new emotions, either basic or complex, such as, for example, "awe," which has been proved as a potential precursor of transformative change (Chirico et al., 2018). Unusual VR experiences can also put individuals in situations of disorientation that could promote new opportunities for personal growth, always in the context of a therapeutic project. In this arena, there are companies like Become (of which the author is the CEO), that build Augmented Psychology® method, building transformative tridimensional journeys administered through specific clinical protocols. In a nutshell, a patient is immersed in metaphorical stories lasting about 10 minutes, which stimulate insights and abreactions, valuable material for a psychological path with a mental health professional.

## Virtual Reality as a Rehab Technology

Treatment of cognitive functions is not just associated with head trauma, stroke, or dementia, but also to psychiatric pathologies or certain psychopathological conditions. VR has recently proved to be even more effective than classic rehabilitation methodologies, demonstrating greater endurance, stability, and speed in patients undergoing this treatment (Wang et al., 2019). Companies like Neuro Rehab VR, starting from the assumption that an immersive three-dimensional environment involves more the senses than a two-dimensional scenario, made this type of therapies more experiential, integrating VR apps with engaging exercises, biosensors to monitor in real-time body parameters, and automatic learning algorithms to get to know the patient better, offering them, session after session, personalized paths that are increasingly effective.

## Virtual Reality as a Therapeutic Technology

In the psychiatric field, specific VR applications validated as digital therapies could become essential complements of—or perhaps alternatives to—some psychotropic medicines. *Digital therapeutics* (DTx) are a new category of medicine, delivering medical interventions directly to patients using evidence-based, clinically evaluated software to treat, manage, and prevent a broad spectrum of (mental) diseases and disorders (Digital Therapeutics Alliance, n.d.). DTx products are held to the same standards of evidence and regulatory oversight as traditional medical treatments and must adhere to the core principles to demonstrate product safety, efficacy, quality, patient centricity, privacy, and ongoing clinical impact. There are many companies getting funds to develop DTx for mental health in VR. One of the most notable recent partnerships is the one between Sumitomo Dainippon Pharma in Japan and U.S.-based behavioral health firm BehaVR who have signed in 2021 an agreement to develop and market well-being software and DTx for the treatment of the major mental health disorders, like the generalized anxiety disorder and the major depressive disorder. Other companies like the U.K.-based OxfordVR are pioneers in therapeutic VR, working on disorders like the anxious social avoidance and even resistant disorders such as psychosis, thanks to engaging multisession treatments.

## IS THE METAVERSE AN OPPORTUNITY FOR MENTAL HEALTH?

In the new 2020s, we are going to see a real revolution in our lives caused by "extended realities" or "synthetic realities" media (VR, augmented reality, mixed reality). In fact, part of the most important digital giants is spending billions in the construction of parallel realities, called *metaverses* that will allow people to digitally immerse into them to learn and do things, meet and interact with people, live a real life to all intents and purposes, in an alternative world through special VR headsets and custom avatars.

Moreover, the VR industry is encouraging consumers to adopt this medium, thanks to the release of increasingly comfortable and less invasive viewers. In fact, to the degree of the success of the metaverse's vision, the ergonomics of the hardware must increase dramatically, and reduce the costs in the same measure.

Facebook is the company investing first and most in an interoperable metaverse, so much so that it has changed its name to Meta. Other corporates are financing these new social arenas, like Microsoft with Mesh for business users, Unreal (by Epic Games, known for *Fortnite*) and Niantic (who developed *Pokemon GO*) for gaming purposes, just to name a few of the many.

Also known as Web 3, this new embodied Internet will have the capability to transform more and more the reality in virtual simulations, digitally extending the social experiences, but reducing them on a physical reality point of view. But this new kind of interaction will unlock economic, social and . . . psychological opportunities.

What will be the impact from a sociopsychological point of view? How will human–human interactions change?

In a world where we are just now discovering the real and consistent dangers to the mental health of young people caused by the smartphone and social media abuse, we are not yet ready to address the new metaversal version of these risks, so it is critical that parents, teachers, politicians, and . . . mental health professionals are increasingly aware of how to properly channel these extraordinary technological potentials into psyche-healthy modes of use.

## PSYCHOLOGICAL PROFESSIONALS AS BUILDERS OF THERAPEUTIC EXPERIENCES

In this changing scenario, it is interesting to note that figures such as the psychologist and the psychotherapist can become central in the construction of virtual immersive experiences with the purpose of well-being and positive change.

From basic relaxation to therapeutic scopes, mental health professionals can effectively participate in the development process of new generation apps. The contamination of skills—development and design, psychological and artistic—should lead to a future in which every professional figure involved in the development of new digital worlds could finally work structurally and methodologically on the inclusion of benefits to collective mental health.

In a "perfect world," this should be the main prerequisite of all the metaverses that will gradually appear in our lives and that should be properly configured to avoid becoming places of widespread psychological malaise. The hope is that the world of neuroscientific research and the new corporate roles like *impact managers* can increasingly contribute also to Big Tech companies' strategic orientation, in order to seize the opportunity to conceive digital worlds based on the principles of health. The mental health professional field is preparing to experience an epochal change, directed towards a greater contamination between psychological and medical, technological and artistic aspects intended to converge in working groups that will build the digital therapies of the future, through tools such as VR, which certainly has the potential to become crucial in the coming years. Moreover, the public and private investments that have characterized the new digital mental health sector during the pandemic years is a very significant indicator of the imminent transformation of services related to the promotion of psychological and behavioral well-being that awaits us. Projects belonging to the medical and psychological variant of the metaverse—named *mediverse*—are emerging (see Emirates Health Services in Dubai, Sheba Medical Center in Israel, Latus Health in the United Kingdom), so it is really necessary for mental health professionals to be prepared for this earlier future.

## REFERENCES

Bailenson, J. (2018). *Experience on demand: What virtual reality is, how it works, and what it can do*. W. W. Norton & Company.

Bertrand, P., Guegan, J., Robieux, L., McCall, C. A., & Zenasni, F. (2018). Learning empathy through virtual reality: Multiple strategies for training empathy-related abilities using body ownership illusions in embodied virtual reality. *Frontiers in Robotics and AI, 5.* https://doi.org/10.3389/frobt.2018.00026

Bonasio, A. (2018). *Immersive learning: A neuroscience perspective* [Report]. Medium. https://medium.com/edtech-trends/report-immersive-learning-a-neuroscience-perspective-46c62a45b25b

Browning, M., Mimnaugh, K. J., Van Riper, C. J., Laurent, H. K., & LaValle, S. M. (2020). Can simulated nature support mental health? Comparing short, single-doses of 360-degree nature videos in virtual reality with the outdoors. *Frontiers in Psychology, 10.* https://doi.org/10.3389/fpsyg.2019.02667

Chirico, A., Ferrise, F., Cordella, L., & Gaggioli, A. (2018). Designing awe in virtual reality: An experimental study. *Frontiers in Psychology, 8,* 2351. https://doi.org/10.3389/fpsyg.2017.02351

Chirico, A., & Gaggioli, G. (2021). Toward a science of complex experiences. *Frontiers in Psychology, 12,* 775149. https://doi.org/10.3389/fpsyg.2021.775149

Coelho, C., Tichon, J., Hine, T. J., Wallis, G., & Riva, G. (2006). Media presence and inner presence: The sense of presence in virtual reality technologies. In G. Riva, M. T. Anguera, B. K. Wiederhold, & F. Mantovani (Eds.), *From communication to presence: Cognition, emotions and culture towards the ultimate communicative experience* (pp. 25–45). IOS Press. https://psycnet.apa.org/record/2009-20644-002

De Kerckhove, D. (1999). *Virtual reality for collective cognitive processing: EHR guide for your practice.* https://docplayer.net/150721660-Virtual-reality-for-collective-cognitive-processing-derrick-de-kerckhove.html

Digital Therapeutics Alliance. (n.d.). *Understanding DTx: A new category of medicine.* https://dtxalliance.org/understanding-dtx

Gaggioli, A. (2016). Transformative experience design. In A. Gaggioli (Ed.), *Human computer confluence: Transforming human experience through symbiotic technologies* (pp. 97–122). De Gruyter Open Poland. https://doi.org/10.1515/9783110471137-006

Hassan, L., Jylhä, H., Sjöblom, M., & Hamari, J. (2020). *Flow in VR: A study on the relationships between preconditions, experience and continued use.* https://aisel.aisnet.org/hicss-53/da/gamification/2/

Riva, G., Bernardelli, L., Browning, M. H. E. M., Castelnuovo, G., Cavedoni, S., Chirico, A., Cipresso, P., Bengel de Paula, D. M., Di Lernia, D., Fernández-Álvarez, J., Figueras-Puigderrajols, N., Fuji, K., Gaggioli, A., Gutiérrez-Maldonado, J., Hong, U., Mancuso, V., Mzaaeo, M., Molinari, E., Moretti, L. F., . . . Wiederhold, B. K. (2020). COVID feel good—An easy self-help virtual reality protocol to overcome the psychological burden of coronavirus. *Frontiers in Psychiatry, 11.* https://www.frontiersin.org/articles/10.3389/fpsyt.2020.563319/full

Riva, G., Wiederhold, B. K., & Mantovani, F. (2019). Neuroscience of virtual reality: From virtual exposure to embodied medicine. *Cyberpsychology, Behavior, and Social Networking, 22*(1), 82–96. https://www.ncbi.nlm.nih.gov/pmc/articles/PMC6354552/

Van Bennekom, M. J., de Koning, P. P., & Denys, D. (2017). Virtual reality objectifies the diagnosis of psychiatric disorders: A literature review. *Frontiers in Psychiatry, 8*, 163. https://doi.org/10.3389/fpsyt.2017.00163

Wang, B., Shen, M., Wang, Y. X., He, Z. W., Chi, S. Q., & Yang, Z. H. (2019). Effect of virtual reality on balance and gait ability in patients with Parkinson's disease: A systematic review and meta-analysis. *Clinical Rehabilitation, 33*(7), 1130–1138. https://journals.sagepub.com/doi/abs/10.1177/0269215519843174

# SECTION IV

## ROBOTICS AND ARTIFICIAL INTELLIGENCE

CHAPTER 8

# ROBOTICS AND ARTIFICIAL INTELLIGENCE IN CLINICAL PSYCHOLOGY

**Lorenzo Desideri**
***Sigmund Freud University, Milan***

## STATE OF THE ART

Human beings have long dreamt of creating machines that can imitate intelligent behavior (Cohen, 1966). Today, advancements in artificial intelligence and engineering have brought the fulfillment of this dream closer than ever. From self-driving cars and drones to automated factories and houses, to smartphones and thermostats, we are increasingly exposed to a variety of information technologies that are able to independently sense the environment in order to achieve programmed goals. Although different in shape, complexity, and context of application, these technologies—usually referred to as "artificially intelligent machines" or "robots"—all share the capability to perform tasks by themselves without constant human guidance. By means of their "intelligence" and autonomy, robots are already redefining the way we work, learn, move, perform tasks in daily life, and interact with our living environments and the people around us, with the consequence that such

*Digital Developments*, pages 115–126

intelligent machines are soon expected to be the drivers of the next scientific, industrial, and social changes. For instance, the Perseverance rover that landed on Mars in 2021 is capable of autonomously exploring the planet's surface by finding the safest path to follow. Likewise, companies are using robots in place of human workers to automate production processes. Many digital gadgets available on the market are robots designed to simplify our daily lives by taking over most of the mundane tasks in which we are usually engaged: robot vacuum cleaners can drive themself around the house to clean the floor; autonomous delivery robots can bring hot coffee from the cafeteria to our offices; smartphones can detect their owner's face to unlock the screen (and thus relieve us of the "affliction" of using our hands).

## ROBOTS LIKE US

The term *robot* (derived from *robota,* meaning "forced labor" in Slavic languages) was first coined in the play *R.U.R.* by the Czech writer Karel Čapek (1920) to identify human-like machines that were exploited as factory slaves by their human makers. A few decades later, Isaac Asimov (1941) introduced the term "robotics" in his short story *Liar!* (p. 43), which features a robot that deliberately decides to lie to its creators to not upset them. Since then, science fiction has created a variety of robotic characters that have contributed to forming our expectations of robots. As noted by Broadbent (2017), fictional robots often have human or animal likeness. In most movies, for instance, not only robots are used as tools, but they are also endowed with the ability to socially interact with their human creators in a manner that closely resembles that of other humans or animals: they move, communicate, or even *feel* like real living entities.

Inspired by science fiction, robots are now being developed in the real world with a view to emulating humans' or animals' appearance as well as their social and affective capacities. The primary aim of these robots, known as "social robots," is to engage humans in social interaction. They are built based on the notion that people generally tend to anthropomorphize the things around them, from seeing "faces" in the clouds to yelling at a computer when it accidentally deletes a file (Epley et al., 2007). Crucially, when people anthropomorphize an object, they also tend to treat it as if the object were a social agent. In other words, people adopt behaviors towards an anthropomorphized object that they would adopt towards other living entities (e.g., engaging in conversation, feeling emotional attachment).

## EXAMPLES OF SOCIAL ROBOTS

Following the anthropomorphism principle, social robots are designed with certain human-like or animal-like features, such as appearance, verbal and nonverbal behaviors, or certain social cues (e.g., via eyes or hands) to induce people to perceive the robots as social agents. The minimalist social robot Keepon (Robots/IEEE, n.d.-a), for instance, needs only two eyes to involve the perceiver in social interaction (e.g., by mimicking a direct gaze). More sophisticated robots have animal-like appearances that are supposed to strengthen our tendency to interact with them as if they had social abilities. For instance, after a short interaction, children showed emotional attachment with the dog-like robot AIBO (Weiss et al., 2009; Robots/IEEE, n.d.-b). Evidence shows that our tendency to anthropomorphize (and thus to engage in social behaviors) increases with the human-likeness of a robot (Broadbent, 2017). Human-like (or "humanoid") robots such as NAO (Figure 8.1) are thought to further elicit social interaction. NAO, for example, has a human body and can move its head towards a person speaking close to it in order to denote attention and social engagement. In a similar vein, the social robot named "Sophia" (Robots/IEEE, n.d.-c) is referred to as an *android.* An android is a robot that closely resembles humans in both appearance and behavior, such as the robots in the film *Blade Runner* (Scott, 1982) or, more recently, in the TV series *Westworld* (Abrams et al., 2016–2022). Unlike robots in the movies, however, current androids such as Sophia are far from being capable of displaying the range of social competences needed to

**Figure 8.1** The humanoid robot "NAO."

engage people in long-lasting and satisfying interactions as one would expect from a robot whose appearance so closely resembles that of a human. As recently noted by Henschel and colleagues (2021), "The still-limited social repertoire of even the most advanced embodied robots calls into question the proclaimed 'rise of the social robots'" (p. 373). Since the field of social robotics is still in its infancy, more research is needed to understand how to design robots that can create credible social interactions. Despite the limitations of today's social robots, current evidence nonetheless suggests that people are generally well disposed towards these artificial social agents and interested in engaging with them (Prescott & Robillard, 2021).

## INTERACTING WITH SOCIAL ROBOTS

Social robots can be considered "relational artifacts" (Turkle et al., 2006) that differ from other information technologies (e.g., smartphones, smart speakers) since they can physically interact with real-world objects and people through verbal, nonverbal, or affective modalities (Breazeal et al., 2016). When people interact with such robots, two main questions may arise (especially if you are a psychologist): "What are the neurocognitive mechanisms at play when people encounter a social robot?" and "What are the consequences for our behavior of perceiving a robot as a social agent?"

## NEUROCOGNITIVE BASES OF HUMAN–ROBOT INTERACTION

Following Cross and Ramsey (2021), disentangling the neurocognitive processes associated with social robot perception and categorization is challenging for at least three reasons. First, there is currently no agreed definition of what a social robot is. Second, research has documented that people can spontaneously form socio-emotional bonds even with those robots that are not specifically designed to elicit social behavior, such as the robot vacuum cleaner (Sung et al., 2007). Third, neurocognitive processes during human–robot interaction are influenced by a variety of factors, such as an individual's age, expectations (e.g., shaped by media or culture), previous experience with robots (e.g., toys), or amount of time previously spent engaging with the specific robot.

Despite these and other challenges, research is advancing at a fast pace to shed light on the neurocognitive mechanisms engaged when people interact with robots. Traditionally, research has used the lens of social cognition to compare brain and behavioral responses when people interact or perceive robots versus humans. In this regard, the evidence so far has documented that perceiving a social robot or a real person may activate partially overlapping neurocognitive mechanisms (Henschel et al., 2020). For instance, the action observation network has been reported as responding both to watching humans grasp and manipulate objects, as well as to an industrial robot arm performing these same actions (Gazzola et al., 2007). In addition, more recent studies have observed an engagement of the person perception network when the onlooker observes emotional expressions as shown by robots and in interactions between robots and other humans (Hortensius et al., 2018). In contrast, activity within the theory-of-mind network seems to be reduced when people perceive an artificial social agent compared to a real person (Henschel et al., 2020).

Mind perception has received notable interest in understanding the mechanisms that elicit a person's attribution of socialness towards robots (Desideri et al., 2021). Mind perception is the process by which an agent is thought to be capable of having internal states such as intentions or emotions. By attributing a mind to an agent, we adopt what Dennett (1987) has termed the "intentional stance," which is to say we treat this agent by assuming that beliefs and desires underlie its behavioral outcomes. Accumulating converging evidence shows that the mere belief that an agent has a mind (i.e., when an observer adopts the intentional stance) increases the likelihood of people engaging in interaction in a social way compared to when the agent is believed to be just a machine (Wiese et al., 2017). Factors that induce mind perception in agents include human appearance, and behavior that is perceived as predictable, reliable, or generated by a human (Wykowska et al., 2016). For instance, neuroimaging data has repeatedly shown increased activation in brain regions related to mentalizing when individuals interact with a robotic avatar that they believe is controlled by a person, compared to when they interact with this same avatar but believe that its actions are preprogrammed (Schellen & Wykowska, 2019). In turn, activation of mentalizing-related brain structures directly correlates with performance in tasks involving social cognitive processes (Wykowska et al., 2014).

Overall, these findings suggest that robots that appear and behave like humans can be perceived and categorized as social entities by partially recruiting the same neurocognitive mechanisms that are engaged in human–human interactions (Henschel et al., 2020).

## PEOPLE'S REACTIONS TO SOCIAL ROBOTS

When people perceive a robot as a social agent, they usually apply social rules, stereotypes, and prejudices as they would do during any other social encounter (Aylett & Vargas, 2021). For example, German students rated a robot with a German name as warmer and as having a better design than an identical robot with a Turkish name (Eyssel & Kuchenbrandt, 2012). Men in a museum were more likely to donate money to a robot with a female voice than to the same robot with a male voice (Siegel et al., 2009). Other studies have further documented that people may display behaviors ranging from emotional attachment to bullying when interacting with a social robot (Aylett & Vargas, 2021).

An important aspect that should be considered when focusing on human–robot interactions is that the interest and the behaviors displayed by people towards a robot in the short term (i.e., over a few hours) may largely differ from their interest and behaviors in the long term (i.e., over a few weeks). Researchers call this the *novelty effect*, whereby during the first moments of interaction with a social robot "people are interested in almost anything the robot does, are willing to forgive its faults, and make few demands on it for practically useful functionality" (Aylett & Vargas, 2021, p. 182). In the long term, by contrast, people seem to lose interest and the robot may eventually annoy. A desired strategy to avoid such an effect could include equipping robots with enough intelligence to make them capable of flexibly adapting their behaviors to the variability of social interactions. Another and simpler strategy might be to lower people's expectations of the robot. For instance, an animal-like robot rather than a humanoid one would not be expected to engage in a conversation when interacting with humans.

But what if our expectations of a robot are too high? In 1981, Mori et al. (2012) theorized a positive relationship between robots' human-likeness and our feeling of comfort with them. In other words, as a robot looks more human, we like it better because it looks like us. However, when a robot looks almost but not perfectly like a human, as in the case of the Sophia android robot mentioned earlier, the sense of comfort rapidly decreases, and we may feel discomfort and unease towards it. This dip in the otherwise linear relationship between human-likeness and the positive feeling experienced by a robot's perceivers has been called "uncanny valley" and is thought to occur when there is something fundamentally inhuman about a robot despite an otherwise close resemblance, as if we were interacting with a dead body (e.g., a zombie; Broadbent, 2017).

To summarize, aiming to avoid the novelty effect and the uncanny valley stands as one of the main challenges that roboticists should tackle in designing robots capable of engaging people in long-lasting and meaningful social interactions.

## POTENTIAL BENEFITS

Healthcare is a prominent domain of application for social robotics. One subset of social robots is defined as "socially assistive" in that their main purpose is to provide "the appropriate emotional, cognitive, and social cues to encourage development, learning, or therapy for an individual" (Matarić & Scassellati, 2016, p. 1974). In this view, a socially assistive robot is a system that employs social interaction strategies such as speech, communicative gestures, and facial expressions to provide assistance in relation to a specific assistive context. Although research into the benefits of socially assistive robotics is still at a preliminary stage, encouraging evidence suggests that robots may be useful as companions for older adults, to improve psychosocial outcomes, to prevent cognitive decline, and to improve the effectiveness of interventions targeting children with neurodevelopmental disorders (Rabbitt et al., 2015). This section provides an overview of application examples of socially assistive robots for an adult population. Chapter 9 will review uses of socially assistive robots for children.

## Socially Assistive Robots for Older Adults

Almost every country in the world is experiencing growth in the number and proportion of older adults in its population. While population aging can be seen as one of the biggest achievements of modern medicine and public health measures, an aging society also poses important challenges for the sustainability of healthcare systems. In this view, socially assistive robots have been used as companions to help older adults overcome a feeling of loneliness and social isolation. For instance, Banks and colleagues (2008) found that the robotic dog AIBO was as effective as a real dog in reducing perceived loneliness. Other investigations have documented that a social robot could facilitate communication among older people (Ostrowski et al., 2019).

## Socially Assistive Robots for Dementia Rehabilitation and Care

An aging population is associated with an increase in people with dementia, one of the leading causes of disability. Socially assistive robots in this area have been used, for example, to slow down cognitive decline by engaging people in cognitive training activities to strengthen abilities such as working memory and executive functions (Abdi et al., 2018). More advanced robots have been used to provide both in-home assistance in daily tasks (e.g., by bringing fluids and food, detecting falls, or offering communication via video conference) and cognitive support (e.g., by reminding individuals to take medications; Moyle, 2019). The animal-like Paro was used in a seminal study in Japan involving residents at a nursing home and was found to produce significant improvements in mood scores (Kang et al., 2020).

### Socially Assistive Robots to Promote Mental Health, Well-Being, and Behavior Change

Based on the assumption that social robots are generally perceived as more helpful than their non-embodied intelligent counterparts such as virtual avatars and conversational agents, research was undertaken to document the usefulness of socially assistive robots to cover a wide range of psychology-related interventions. Robots were used, for instance, to involve older adults with mild-to-moderate depression in cognitive behavioral therapy interventions (Dino et al., 2019). Preliminary evidence is also available on the usefulness of social robots endowed with conversational abilities to promote self-disclosure and reduce anger. In addition, socially assistive robots resulted as further promising when used for health-behavior change interventions, such as motivating older adults to engage in physical exercises, giving reminders to drink water, assisting in the tracking of calories intake, reducing consumption of high-calorie foods and drinks, coaching physical exercise sessions, and managing diabetes (Robinson et al., 2020).

## POTENTIAL RISKS

Despite the promise of social robotics to promote well-being and reduce social isolation for individuals, the use of artificially intelligent machines in healthcare should be carefully balanced against its potential risks. Prescott and Robillard (2021), for instance, stress the risk related to a loss of human contact because of robot use. As a consequence, the use of robots as carers or companions to older adults could produce psychological damage as well as reduce human dignity. Further risks may include overdependence on robots, addiction, and loss of control, loss of personal freedom, and loss of privacy. Emotional deception is an additional risk that may arise when using robots in healthcare settings. This occurs when the user (e.g., an older adult with early-stage dementia) believes the robot can *experience* "emotions, thus leading to unrealistic expectations that can possibly result in the user prioritizing the robot's well-being over other people's or their own well-being" (Van Maris et al., 2020, p. 2).

## FUTURE DIRECTIONS

As soon as robots become capable of understanding and communicating in a life-like way, they are expected to pervasively enter our everyday environments and become social agents with which people will socially engage for a variety of purposes, "from love to war" (Royakkers & van Est, 2015).

Considering that the variety of (social) robots will increase in the near future, along with the contexts in which they will be implemented, recent accounts in the field of cognitive science and human–robot interaction stress the importance of recognizing their unique and multifaceted nature: social robots indeed differ from other living entities (e.g., humans, animals) in that they are *both* objects and social agents. This implies that, since we will increasingly interact with artificially intelligent machines, our cognitive system should be flexible enough to deal with a new ontological category at the intersection between living and nonliving entities (Cross & Ramsey, 2021). Very likely, these new technologies will not replace humans' skills, but will supplement them, especially in healthcare settings, that is, the sector in which demographic changes are causing the most dramatic effects for society. In this view, the key challenge for psychologists is to recognize the added value of social robots for their practice and ultimately adapt or develop intervention strategies that include assistive tools (i.e., robots) that may cause social as well as emotional reactions in their users.

## REFERENCES

Abdi, J., Al-Hindawi, A., Ng, T., & Vizcaychipi, M. P. (2018). Scoping review on the use of socially assistive robot technology in elderly care. *BMJ Open, 8*(2), e018815. https://doi.org/10.1136/bmjopen-2017-018815

Abrams, J. J., Nolan, J., Joy, L., Weintraub, J., Burk, B., Lewis, R. J., Patino, R., Wickha, A., Stephenson, B., & Thé, D. (2016–2022). *Westworld* [TV series]. Kilter Films; Bad Robot Productions; Jerry Weintraub Productions; Warner Bros. Television.

Asimov, I (1941). Liar! In J. W. Campbell (Ed.). *Astounding science fiction* (pp. 43–55). Available online at: https://archive.org/details/Astounding_v27n03_1941-05/page/n41/mode/2up?view=theater

Aylett, R., & Vargas, P. A. (2021). *Living with robots: What every anxious human needs to know.* MIT Press.

Banks, M. R., Willoughby, L. M., & Banks, W. A. (2008). Animal-assisted therapy and loneliness in nursing homes: Use of robotic versus living dogs. *Journal of the American Medical Directors Association, 9*(3), 173–177. https://doi.org/10.1016/j.jamda.2007.11.007

Breazeal, C., Dautenhahn, K., & Kanda, T. (2016). Social robotics. In B. Sicilano & O. Khatib (Eds.), *Springer handbook of robotics* (pp. 1935–1972). Springer.

Broadbent, E. (2017). Interactions with robots: The truths we reveal about ourselves. *Annual Review of Psychology, 68,* 627–652. https://doi.org/10.1146/annurev-psych-010416-043958

Čapek, K. (1920). *R. U. R.: Rossum's universal robots.* Penguin Books.

Cohen, J. (1966). *Human robots in myth and science.* A. S. Barnes.

Cross, E. S., & Ramsey, R. (2021). Mind meets machine: Towards a cognitive science of human–machine interactions. *Trends in Cognitive Sciences, 25*(3), 200–212. https://doi.org/10.1016/j.tics.2020.11.009

Dennett, D. C. (1987). *The intentional stance.* MIT Press.

Desideri, L., Bonifacci, P., Croati, G., Dalena, A., Gesualdo, M., Molinario, G., Gherardini, A., Cesario, L., & Ottaviani, C. (2021). The mind in the machine: Mind perception modulates gaze aversion during child–robot interaction. *International Journal of Social Robotics, 13*(4), 599–614. https://doi.org/10.1007/s12369-020-00656-7

Dino, F., Zandie, R., Abdollahi, H., Schoeder, S., & Mahoor, M. H. (2019, November). Delivering cognitive behavioral therapy using a conversational social robot. In *2019 IEEE/RSJ International Conference on Intelligent Robots and Systems* (pp. 2089–2095). IEEE.

Epley, N., Waytz, A., & Cacioppo, J. T. (2007). On seeing human: A three-factor theory of anthropomorphism. *Psychological Review, 114*(4), 864. https://doi.org/10.1037/0033-295X.114.4.864

Eyssel, F., & Kuchenbrandt, D. (2012). Social categorization of social robots: Anthropomorphism as a function of robot group membership. *British Journal of Social Psychology, 51*(4), 724–731. https://doi.org/10.1111/j.2044-8309.2011.02082.x

Gazzola, V., Rizzolatti, G., Wicker, B., & Keysers, C. (2007). The anthropomorphic brain: The mirror neuron system responds to human and robotic actions. *Neuroimage, 35*(4), 1674–1684. https://doi.org/10.1016/j.neuroimage.2007.02.003

Henschel, A., Hortensius, R., & Cross, E. S. (2020). Social cognition in the age of human–robot interaction. *Trends in Neurosciences, 43*(6), 373–384. https://doi.org/10.1016/j.tins.2020.03.013

Henschel, A., Laban, G., & Cross, E. S. (2021). What makes a robot social? A review of social robots from science fiction to a home or hospital near you. *Current Robotics Reports, 2*(1), 9–19. https://doi.org/10.1007/s43154-020-00035-0

Hortensius, R., Hekele, F., & Cross, E. S. (2018). The perception of emotion in artificial agents. *IEEE Transactions on Cognitive and Developmental Systems, 10*(4), 852–864. https://doi.org/10.1109/TCDS.2018.2826921

Kang, H. S., Makimoto, K., Konno, R., & Koh, I. S. (2020). Review of outcome measures in PARO robot intervention studies for dementia care. *Geriatric Nursing, 41*(3), 207–214. https://doi.org/10.1016/j.gerinurse.2019.09.003

Matarić, M. J., & Scassellati, B. (2016). Socially assistive robotics. In B. Sicilano & O. Khatib (Eds.), *Springer handbook of robotics* (pp. 1973–1994). Springer.

Mori, M., MacDorman, K. F., & Kageki, N. (2012). The uncanny valley [from the field]. *IEEE Robotics & automation magazine, 19*(2), 98–100. https://doi.org/10.1109/MRA.2012.2192811

Moyle, W. (2019). The promise of technology in the future of dementia care. *Nature Reviews Neurology, 15*(6), 353–359. https://doi.org/10.1038/s41582-019-0188-y

Ostrowski, A. K., DiPaola, D., Partridge, E., Park, H. W., & Breazeal, C. (2019). Older adults living with social robots: Promoting social connectedness in long-term communities. *IEEE Robotics Automation Magazine, 26*, 59–70. https://doi.org/10.1109/MRA.2019.2905234

Prescott, T. J., & Robillard, J. M. (2021). Are friends electric? The benefits and risks of human–robot relationships. *Iscience, 24*(1), 101993. https://doi.org/10.1016/j.isci.2020.101993

Rabbitt, S. M., Kazdin, A. E., & Scassellati, B. (2015). Integrating socially assistive robotics into mental healthcare interventions: Applications and recommendations for expanded use. *Clinical Psychology Review, 35*, 35–46. https://doi.org/10.1016/j.cpr.2014.07.001

Robinson, N. L., Connolly, J., Hides, L., & Kavanagh, D. J. (2020). Social robots as treatment agents: Pilot randomized controlled trial to deliver a behavior change intervention. *Internet Interventions, 21*, 100320. https://doi.org/10.1016/j.invent.2020.100320

Robots/IEEE. (n.d.-a). *Keepon.* Robots. https://robots.ieee.org/robots/keepon/ [accessed 14th April 2023].

Robots/IEEE. (n.d.-b). *Aibo (1999).* Robots. https://robots.ieee.org/robots/aibo/ [accessed 14th April 2023].

Robots/IEEE. (n.d.-c). *Sophia.* Robots. https://robots.ieee.org/robots/sophia/ [accessed 14th April 2023].

Royakkers, L., & van Est, R. (2015). A literature review on new robotics: Automation from love to war. *International Journal of Social Robotics, 7*(5), 549–570. https://doi.org/10.1007/s12369-015-0295-x

Schellen, E., & Wykowska, A. (2019). Intentional mindset toward robots—Open questions and methodological challenges. *Frontiers in Robotics and AI*, 5, 139. https://doi.org/10.3389/frobt.2018.00139

Scott, R. (Director). (1982). *Blade Runner* [Film]. The Ladd Company; Shaw Brothers; Tandem Productions.

Siegel, M., Breazeal, C., & Norton, M. I. (2009). Persuasive robotics: The influence of robot gender on human behavior. In *2009 IEEE/RSJ International Conference on Intelligent Robots and Systems* (pp. 2563–2568). IEEE.

Sung, J.-Y., Guo, L., Grinter, R. E., & Christensen, H. I. (2007). "My Roomba is Rambo": Intimate home appliances. In J. Krumm, G. D. Abowd, A. Seneviratne, & T. Strang (Eds.), *UbiComp 2007: Ubiquitous computing* (pp. 145–162). Springer.

Turkle, S., Taggart, W., Kidd, C. D., & Dasté, O. (2006). Relational artifacts with children and elders: The complexities of cybercompanionship. *Connection Science, 18*(4), 347–361. https://doi.org/10.1080/09540090600868912

Van Maris, A., Zook, N., Caleb-Solly, P., Studley, M., Winfield, A., & Dogramadzi, S. (2020). Designing ethical social robots—A longitudinal field study with older adults. *Frontiers in Robotics and AI, 7.* https://doi.org/10.3389/frobt.2020.00001

Weiss, A., Wurhofer, D., & Tscheligi, M. (2009). "I love this dog"—Children's emotional attachment to the robotic dog AIBO. *International Journal of Social Robotics*, 1, 243–248. https://doi.org/10.1007/s12369-009-0024-4

Wiese, E., Metta, G., & Wykowska, A. (2017). Robots as intentional agents: Using neuroscientific methods to make robots appear more social. *Frontiers in Psychology, 8*, 1663. https://doi.org/10.3389/fpsyg.2017.01663

Wykowska, A., Wiese, E., Prosser, A., & Müller, H. J. (2014). Beliefs about the minds of others influence how we process sensory information. *PloS One, 9*(4), e94339. https://doi.org/10.1371/journal.pone.0094339

CHAPTER 9

# ROBOTICS AND ARTIFICIAL INTELLIGENCE IN DEVELOPMENTAL PSYCHOLOGY

**Lorenzo Desideri**
***Sigmund Freud University, Milan***

## STATE OF THE ART

Children and youths are growing up in a world in which most of their life experiences are mediated by digital devices. They use mobile technologies to play, read, and learn, or to watch online videos for several hours a day (UNICEF, 2017). Nature is mostly experienced through documentaries or pictorial displays, rather than directly (Kahn et al., 2009). Ubiquitous connectivity has redefined social interactions and peer relationships by creating virtual spaces in which children can connect to one another at any time using multiple identities. The containment measures to cope with the COVID-19 pandemic have further accelerated the increase of virtual child–child interactions and relationships, with significant impact on children's education as well as on traditional family dynamics.

*Digital Developments*, pages 127–134

On the grounds of such socio-technological transformations, current advancements in robotics and artificial intelligence are further determining important changes in children's social lives. Most notably, with the advent of intelligent technologies capable of engaging people in social interactions, children can not only interact through technologies but also with technologies.

Social robots (see Chapter 8), in particular, are attracting notable attention from researchers, educators, and mental health professionals for their potential to engage children in innovative educational and rehabilitation scenarios. The aim of this chapter is to highlight some of the most promising applications of social robotics for children, with a view to providing the reader with an understanding of the benefits of these emerging technologies for clinical and educational practice, while also underscoring some of the main risks associated with introducing an artificial agent in the life of a developing child.

## DEVELOPMENTAL PERSPECTIVES IN CHILD–ROBOT INTERACTION

How children conceptualize objects (e.g., toys, tools) and distinguish them from living entities has been a subject of research for decades. Computerized toys in the 1970s and 1980s, then digital pets such as Tamagotchi and Furby in the 1990s, have given developmental researchers the opportunity to understand the extent to which children recognize digital technologies as artefacts, as well as whether children could form emotional, social, and even moral, relationships with objects that behave similarly to living entities. Seminal research in this area has indeed documented that children, although aware that a computer is an inanimate object, may perceive it as endowed with psychological attributes (e.g., intelligence, emotions; Turkle, 2012).

Focusing on social robots, available literature on how children understand and engage with such technologies has flourished in the last 2 decades and is rapidly accumulating. Evidence suggests that age seems to be a strong determinant of robot acceptance in children. Specifically, while children in general seem to be more attracted by social robots than adults, younger children (4 to 8 years old) are more willing to engage with (social) robots compared to older children (9 to 13 years old; Burdett et al., 2022). Younger children, in particular, are capable of distinguishing between robotic and non-robotic toys and behave accordingly. For instance, it has been observed that 3-year-old children prefer to learn information from social robots that give accurate (rather than inaccurate) information over inanimate toys that give either accurate or inaccurate information (Brink & Wellman, 2020).

A fundamental tenet in the area of child–robot interaction is the notion for which young children may conceptualize social robots at the intersection of animate and inanimate objects, with important consequences for their interaction, behavior, and understanding. This has been clearly documented by Kahn and colleagues, who let preschool children (34–74 months old) interact both with a robotic dog and a stuffed dog (Kahn et al., 2006). When asked to verbally report their views on the two artefacts at the end of the interaction, the children accorded similar animacy, mental states, social rapport, and moral standing to the robotic dog and the stuffed dog. However, when the researchers analyzed the videos recorded during the interactions, it resulted that the children—contrary to their verbal responses—behaved differently with the two dogs, in that they only treated the robotic dog as if it were a real dog. For instance, while approximately half of the children stated that the two dogs could feel pain, the children mistreated the robotic dog far less than the stuffed one.

The study by Kahn, together with similar converging evidence, further supports the idea that as robotic technologies become more intelligent and socially responsive, it is possible that children will increasingly treat social robots as having life, mental states, emotions, sociality, and moral worth (Severson & Carlson, 2010). Such children's attitudes towards robots might in turn enable the creation of innovative interaction scenarios in which children accept to interact with robots as social partners or companions.

## POTENTIAL BENEFITS

Thanks to their capacity to engage children in socially relevant interactions and to elicit social responses, social robots have been employed in a variety of contexts, most notably for entertainment purposes. Of relevance for psychologists, however, are the benefits that social robots may produce in the healthcare and education domains.

### Benefits for Healthcare

Perhaps one of the most promising (and researched) application domains of social robots is as support in treatment interventions for children with neurodevelopmental disorders (Samaddar et al., 2022). Most research in this application domain has been carried out with children with autism spectrum disorder (ASD) to foster the development of their communication and interaction skills as well as joint attention (Pennisi et al., 2016). Recent literature has indeed highlighted that children with ASD appear to have a special interest in computerized activities, and has identified the advantages that computers provide with regard to the core deficits of ASD (Grynszpan et al., 2014). These include consistency in a clearly defined task and a usually specific focus of attention due to reduced distractions from unnecessary sensory stimuli. This seemingly positive attitude by most (but not all) children with ASD towards computerized devices has encouraged researchers to introduce different robotic devices (e.g., human-like, animal-like) into treatment interventions targeting children with ASD to open promising new scenarios for their treatment (Kouroupa et al., 2022). In a recent randomized controlled study (van den Berk-Smeekens et al., 2022), for instance, the researchers adapted the intervention: based on the principles of applied behavior analysis, it was carried out with the presence of a humanoid robot that delivered prompts and support to teach social-communicative skills to children with ASD. At the 3-month follow up, the robot-assisted intervention produced larger gains compared to the usual treatment, providing credible support to the idea that social robots may contribute to treatment efficacy for ASD children.

Social robots have been further used to help children with a variety of health conditions in healthcare settings (e.g., hospitals) with a view to coping with healthcare demands and to enhancing care (Dawe et al., 2019). In this view, robots have been mostly used with the aim to provide comfort, reduce anxiety, pain and distress, express empathy and increase motivation, as well as stimulate joy. For instance, one study documented that the presence of a social robot programmed to use cognitive-behavioral strategies reduced children's pain and distress during flu vaccination (Beran et al., 2013). Social robots have also been used as a telepresence system to provide hospitalized children with a means to participate in social contexts (e.g., classroom) from a remote location (i.e., hospital).

## Benefits for Education

Traditionally, teachers have used robots as an extension for computer programming with a view to teach robotics and STEM (science, technology, engineering, and mathematics) subjects. In this view, robots can be conceptualized as tools which may be used to foster students' coding skills.

Recent applications of robotics in education have instead focused on the use of robots as social agents with which students (usually primary school pupils) can interact in order to improve learning achievement. Compared to screen-based technologies such as tablets, social robots have been shown to promote more learning gains and to evoke more expression of emotion through the creation of personalized learning ecosystems. In this view, social robots may take on a variety of different roles in educational settings (Alnajjar et al., 2021).

In most cases, the social robots have been used as tutors. In this role, the robot usually supports a student in a one-to-one (or a one-to-few) interaction to perform an academic task by providing feedback, keeping the student motivated through social reinforcement, or helping the student stay focused on the task. Robot-based tutoring has been effective, for instance, in helping preschool children to learn a second language by involving them in conversation (Vogt et al., 2019).

Social robots have also been applied in education as peers to act as co-learners. In this case, a robot that incorporates some degree of interactivity (e.g., speaking) can be used in a collaborative peer learning scenario helping students to work through a task or to encourage discovery.

Interestingly, social robots have also been used as students. Through a "learning by teaching" approach, the human student is invited to take the role of the teacher to help a robot acquire new skills or knowledge. For instance, children were asked to help a robot improve its handwriting skills (Lemaignan et al., 2016). The robot wrote on a tablet with its fingers and the child was asked to correct its writing. The results indicated that this activity helped the children with poor handwriting skills to reflect on their handwriting and to draw consistent shapes in a repeated manner.

A further important role that a robot can take on in a classroom is that of being a mediator. In this case, for instance, the robot can be used to alleviate children's social anxiety when they are involved in a group activity with their peers (e.g., in the case of students with ASD).

## POTENTIAL RISKS

In the short story *Robbie*, Isaac Asimov (1950) imagines a future in which a child, Gloria, is cared for by a humanoid robot (nicknamed Robbie). Even if the robot is unable to speak, it understands what Gloria says and soon becomes her best friend. After 2 years, during which Gloria interacted and played with Robbie on a daily basis, Gloria's parents decided to return the robot to the factory, concerned that their daughter seems to be more interested in playing with Robbie than with the other children. However, due to her emotional attachment to the robot, as soon as Gloria discovers that Robbie will not be returning home, she starts losing all interest in playing, refuses to take care of their puppy dog, and appears melancholic and inconsolable. Pushed into a corner, Gloria's parents bring the robot back home.

As is clearly shown by Gloria's behavior in Asimov's short story, engaging children in social interactions with deceptively intelligent robots may generate important ethical concerns (Boada et al., 2021), primarily because children can form emotional bonds with devices that have artificial emotions. This in turn may raise concerns about children's psychological and social development. For instance, it has been suggested that regular interactions with these types of artificial social agents may lead certain individuals to become less prone to engage in real social interactions (Kahn et al., 2013).

A further matter of concern is related to the consequences for the cognitive, social, and emotional development of the most vulnerable children who interact with a companion that is not irritable, has limited social behaviors, and is highly predictable. For instance, the idea that children with ASD prefer robots over humans has been criticized, as has been the use of autonomous robots that replace a human caregiver in therapy sessions. Such criticism does not point at eliminating robots from the lives of children with autism, but highlights that research and clinical practice need to be aware of the multifaceted and complex nature of this condition, in order to avoid reductionist approaches that see the autistic mind as more similar to that of a robot (i.e., lacking empathy and emotions; McBride, 2020). To overcome such challenges, it has recently been stressed that a more cross-disciplinary perspective on robotic applications is necessary (van den Heuvel et al., 2022). User-centered codesign methods should be followed. Therapists, parents, and other key stakeholders should play a central role in developing scenarios where robots may be useful tools in achieving child-centered goals.

## FUTURE DIRECTIONS

Despite the encouraging results from application of robot-based activities in healthcare and educational settings, it should be recognized that research in this area is still in its infancy. With reference to applying social robots in healthcare, more evidence is needed not only on the effectiveness of robot-based intervention protocols in low-resourced settings such as primary care, but also on demonstrating their transferability from one context to another in order to address cross-country variables (e.g., cultural, policy-based; Van Den Heuvel et al., 2022).

With reference to applying social robots in education, translating evidence into real educational practice is challenging due to the lack of accessible indications and best practice examples on how teachers can use commercially available robots in their day-to-day activities. Therefore, the decision by teachers to use robots in their classrooms is—in many cases—driven by availability (and affordability) of ready-to-use robot-enhanced pedagogical activities rather than by pedagogically sound considerations. It is thus not surprising that teachers' interest in adopting potentially useful robotic applications is hindered by the difficulties they face in understanding the pedagogical value of robots as well as in integrating such innovative solutions within their settings (Samaddar et al., 2022). Furthermore, despite research having demonstrated promising applications of robots in school settings, teachers' attitudes towards robots are still mixed, as they are not yet considered usable outside highly controlled settings or isolated structured interactions.

## REFERENCES

Alnajjar, F., Bartneck, C., Baxter, P., Belpaeme, T., Cappuccio, M., Di Dio, C., Eyssel, F., Handle, J., Mubin, O., Obaid, M., & Reich-Stiebert, N. (Eds.). (2021). *Robots in education: An introduction to high-tech social agents, intelligent tutors, and curricular tools.* Routledge.

Asimov, I. (1950). *I, Robot.* Doubleday & Company.

Beran, T. N., Ramirez-Serrano, A., Vanderkooi, O. G., & Kuhn, S. (2013). Reducing children's pain and distress towards flu vaccinations: A novel and effective application of humanoid robotics. *Vaccine, 31*(25), 2772–2777. https://doi.org/10.1016/j.vaccine.2013.03.056

Boada, J. P., Maestre, B. R., & Genís, C. T. (2021). The ethical issues of social assistive robotics: A critical literature review. *Technology in Society, 67,* 101726. https://doi.org/10.1016/j.techsoc.2021.101726

Brink, K. A., & Wellman, H. M. (2020). Robot teachers for children? Young children trust robots depending on their perceived accuracy and agency. *Developmental Psychology, 56*(7), 1268. https://doi.org/10.1037/dev0000884

Burdett, E. R., Ikari, S., & Nakawake, Y. (2022). British children's and adults' perceptions of robots. *Human Behavior and Emerging Technologies.* https://doi.org/10.1155/2022/3813820

Dawe, J., Sutherland, C., Barco, A., & Broadbent, E. (2019). Can social robots help children in healthcare contexts? A scoping review. *BMJ Paediatrics Open, 3*(1). https://doi.org/10.1136/bmjpo-2018-000371

Grynszpan, O., Weiss, P. L. T., Perez-Diaz, F., & Gal, E. (2014). Innovative technology-based interventions for autism spectrum disorders: a meta-analysis. *Autism, 18*(4), 346–361. https://doi.org/10.1177/1362361313476767

Kahn, P. H., Friedman, B., Perez-Granados, D. R., & Freier, N. G. (2006). Robotic pets in the lives of preschool children. *Interaction Studies,* 7(3), 405–436. https://doi.org/10.1075/is.7.3.13kah

Kahn, P. H., Gary, H. E., & Shen, S. (2013). Children's social relationships with current and near-future robots. *Child Developmental Perspectives,* 7(1), 32–37. https://doi.org/10.1111/cdep.12011

Kahn, P. H., Severson, R. L., & Ruckert, J. H. (2009). The human relation with nature and technological nature. *Current Directions in Psychological Science, 18*(1), 37–42. https://doi.org/10.1111/j.1467-8721.2009.01602.x

Kouroupa, A., Laws, K. R., Irvine, K., Mengoni, S. E., Baird, A., & Sharma, S. (2022). The use of social robots with children and young people on the autism spectrum: A systematic review and meta-analysis. *PloS One, 17*(6), e0269800. https://doi.org/10.1371/journal.pone.0269800

Lemaignan, S., Jacq, A., Hood, D., Garcia, F., Paiva, A., & Dillenbourg, P. (2016). Learning by teaching a robot: The case of handwriting. *IEEE Robotics & Automation Magazine, 23*(2), 56–66. https://doi.org/10.1109/MRA.2016.2546700

McBride, N. (2020). Robot enhanced therapy for autistic children: An ethical analysis. *IEEE Technology and Society Magazine, 39*(1), 51–60. https://doi.org/10.1109/MTS.2020.2967493

Pennisi, P., Tonacci, A., Tartarisco, G., Billeci, L., Ruta, L., Gangemi, S., & Pioggia, G. (2016). Autism and social robotics: A systematic review. *Autism Research, 9*(2), 165–183. https://doi.org/10.1002/aur.1527

Samaddar, S., Desideri, L., Encarnação, P., Gollasch, D., Petrie, H., & Weber, G. (2022). Robotic and virtual reality technologies for children with disabilities and older adults. In K. Miesenberger, G. Kouroupetroglou, K. Mavrou, R. Manduchi, M. Cavarrubias Rodriguez, & P. Penáz (Eds.), *International conference on computers helping people with special needs* (pp. 203–210). Springer. https://link.springer.com/book/10.1007/978-3-031-08645-8

Severson, R. L., & Carlson, S. M. (2010). Behaving as or behaving as if? Children's conceptions of personified robots and the emergence of a new ontological category. *Neural Networks, 23*(8–9), 1099–1103. https://doi.org/10.1016/j.neunet.2010.08.014

Turkle, S. (2012). *Alone together: Why we expect more from technology and less from each other.* Basic Books.

UNICEF. (2017). *State of the world's children 2017: Children in a digital world.* https://www.unicef.org/reports/state-worlds-children-2017

van den Berk-Smeekens, I., de Korte, M. W., van Dongen-Boomsma, M., Oosterling, I. J., den Boer, J. C., Barakova, E. I., Lourens, T., Glennon, J. C., Staal, W. G., & Buitelaar, J. K. (2022). Pivotal response treatment with and without robot-assistance for children with autism: A randomized controlled trial. *European Child & Adolescent Psychiatry, 31*(12), 1871–1883. https://doi.org/10.1007/s00787-021-01804-8

Van Den Heuvel, R., Jansens, R., Littler, B., Huijnen, C., Di Nuovo, A., Bonarini, A., Desideri, L., Encarnação, P., Lekova, A., & De Witte, L. (2022). The potential of robotics for the development and wellbeing of children with disabilities as we see it. *Technology and Disability, 34*(1), 25–33. https://doi.org/10.3233/TAD-210346

Vogt, P., van den Berghe, R., De Haas, M., Hoffman, L., Kanero, J., Mamus, E., Montanier, J-M., Oranç, C., Oudgenoeg-Paz, O., García, D. H., Papadopoulos, F., Schodde, T., Verhagen, J., Wallbridgell, C. D., Willemsen, B., de Wit, J., Belpaeme, T., Göksun, T., Kopp, S., Krahmer, E., . . . Pandey, A. K. (2019). Second language tutoring using social robots: a large-scale study. In 2019 14th ACM/IEEE International Conference on Human-Robot Interaction (HRI) (pp. 497–505). IEEE. https://doi.org/10.1109/HRI.2019.8673077

CHAPTER 10

# SOCIAL COGNITION AND HUMAN–ROBOT INTERACTION

**Davide Ghiglino**
***Istituto Italiano di Tecnologia, Genoa***

**Agnieszka Wykowska**
***Istituto Italiano di Tecnologia, Genoa***

## STATE OF THE ART

### Artificial Agents and Mind Attribution

The diffusion of new technologies and smart devices is giving researchers new tools for scientific inquiry in the areas of experimental psychology and cognitive sciences (Wykowska, 2021). Nowadays, even "pocket technologies" seem to display a certain degree of "artificial thinking," which might remind us of human mental processes (Ghiglino & Wykowska, 2020). This similarity could affect the human tendency to attribute anthropomorphic traits to technologies, evoking social cognition mechanisms that are typical

*Digital Developments*, pages 135–148

of human–human interaction. However, it is still an open question whether it is possible (or even desirable) to ascribe a "mind" to artificial agents. Several authors claimed that attributing mental states might help individuals in predicting and explaining the behavior of artificial agents, which, in turn, should positively affect collaborative scenarios (de Graaf & Malle, 2019; Imamura et al., 2015; Levin et al., 2013; Thellman et al., 2017). Addressing this issue seems to be pivotal for fundamental sciences as well as for the design and development of artificial agents that are supposed to assist humans in the everyday life of the future. Indeed, this question has been approached already in the 1970s, when the philosopher Daniel Dennett proposed a model to explain how humans process the behavior displayed by agents of a different nature (Dennett, 1971). Dennett (1971) hypothesized that humans adopt spontaneously different strategies when interacting with inert objects, complex artifacts, and biological systems. For example, when humans need to explain and predict the behavior of a simple object, such as a ball rolling on an inclined plane, they tend to rely on physical laws guiding the behavior itself (i.e., gravity pull, attrition, etc.). Thus, under such circumstances, humans tend to adopt what Dennett calls the "design stance" (p. 88). However, if the object displaying the behavior is more unfamiliar and complex than a rolling ball, such as a car approaching a crossing, this stance might not be adequate to provide the perceiver with reliable explanations and predictions. In these cases, humans need to rely on more complex representations and refer to the design and functionality of the artifact displaying the behavior, adopting what the Dennett calls the *design stance.* Indeed, the fact that the car is moving is not explicable solely in terms of inertial motion, but it becomes clearer as soon as we start thinking about the design of the motor or the brake. However, there are entities whose behavior can be summarized neither as a mere effect of physical laws nor as a consequence of their design, as in the case of biological agents. Indeed, if we talk with a person that is cooking, and they repetitively move their head in the direction of the oven, we need to include in our predictive model a representation of the agent's internal states (in this case, the inference that the person wants or needs to check if the food in the oven is at the right temperature) adopting what Dennett (1971) calls the "intentional stance" (p. 90). This means that we need to treat the action as motivated by the agent's mental states (i.e., beliefs, desires, feelings, and intentions). In other words, the intentional stance consists of treating the behavior as a consequence of mental operations, which are directed towards a goal. Importantly, the adoption of the intentional stance does not imply the ascription of a mind to the agent that is displaying the behavior (Dennett, 1981). On the contrary, its function is limited to providing the most accurate strategy available to approach an agent whose behavior is ambiguous, even when the agent is artificial (Marchesi et al., 2019). This implies that under certain circumstances, humans might adopt the intentional stance even when interacting with complex artificial agents. It has been found, for example, that humans often describe complex artificial agents (i.e., robots) using a mentalistic vocabulary, referring to their intentions or will, while also denying that they have a mind (Banks, 2020). Indeed, the ambiguity of an agent's behavior, especially if the agent is human-like, might recall cognitive processes that are normally recruited during the interaction between biological agents. We can even argue that the tendency to attribute human traits to artificial agents might extend to social cognition mechanisms in general, which can be evoked spontaneously when interacting with technologies that resemble human beings. Indeed, social cognition strategies are flexible, adaptable, and depend upon the knowledge, experience, and representation that an individual develops around a certain agent and/or context (Wykowska, 2020). Fifty years after Dennett's first model, the scientific debate on social cognition mechanisms that are evoked during the interaction between humans and artificial agents is still heated. In particular, robotic technologies are of great interest, because of their embodiment and their physical presence, which allow them to actively interact with their environment. Furthermore, the possibility to manipulate objects, jointly with humans, makes such platforms suitable to investigate social cognition mechanisms in naturalistic scenarios (Moreno & Etxeberria, 2005). Yet, artificial agents can still be programmed to behave exactly as designed, offering excellent experimental control for research paradigms. In recent years, human–robot interaction (HRI) has become an interdisciplinary trend, attracting social scientists as well as engineers, interested in understanding whether the behavior of robots can be perceived by human partners as a reflection of mental operations (Frith & Frith, 2008). Such diversity requires inter- and transdisciplinary discussions to define research methods that are suitable to investigate social cognition applied to HRI (Thellman et al., 2021). In the following sections of the chapter, we will present some key concepts of HRI research, trying to define a common ground for practitioners. We will first explore the concept and definition(s) of embodiment, as it may be considered one of the crucial aspects of contemporary HRI, offering researchers the possibility to experiment with the second-person neuroscience approach[1] (see Schilbach et al., 2013). Then, we will briefly present the most common methodologies applied to HRI, highlighting the complementarity of different approaches. Eventually, we will present some of the practical implications of multidisciplinary HRI.

## FUTURE DIRECTIONS

### Practical Implications for the Investigation of Social Cognition in Human–Robot Interaction

The need for smooth communication among HRI practitioners is not limited to the understanding of different methodologies. It is becoming more and more crucial to build a common knowledge that can serve the future directions of the discipline, taking into account fundamental research as well as practical applications of HRI. Indeed, robots embedded with social abilities can be used to test the flexibility of human social cognition (Wykowska, 2020), but, at the same time, they are designed to assist humans in daily routines. To smoothen the interaction and maximize the support that such technologies can provide, robots should be embedded with enough "social intelligence" to understand the needs of the user and provide appropriate behavior, which is a huge technical challenge (Złotowski et al., 2015). Tailoring the behavior of an artificial agent to the requests and needs of the human interacting with it demands a deep knowledge of social cognition mechanisms that are put in place by humans during HRI scenarios, as well as appropriate technical solutions that can grant smooth communication and interaction. Previous literature suggested that performance during HRI may be boosted when the human socially attunes to the artificial agent, treating it as if it possessed mental states and anthropomorphic traits (see, e.g., Wiese et al., 2017). For example, recent literature supports the idea that artificial agents that are able to behave like human beings facilitate the spontaneity and naturalness of interaction (Wiese et al., 2017). Thus, providing artificial agents with human-like behaviors may positively affect the quality of the interaction (Thepsoonthorn et al., 2018). In particular, when the physical aspect and the behavioral repertoire of artificial agents resemble one of the human beings, individuals tend to spontaneously attribute to the agent anthropomorphic traits, including mental states and intentional agency (Martini et al., 2015). We can speculate that embedding artificial agents with human-like behaviors could boost social attunement towards them, and this aspect could be particularly crucial for deploying social robots in environments where social interaction is desirable (e.g., assistive robotics; Leite et al., 2013). Indeed, treating artificial agents as if they were anthropomorphic entities with a synthetic "mind" may help individuals during natural interactions, as these processes allow us to predict and explain the behaviors displayed by other individuals in everyday interactions with our conspecifics (Barresi & Moore, 1996). Even the acceptance of robots as social companions might depend on their ability to adequately elicit such social cognitive processes during the interaction. For many decades, researchers of social cognition focused on understanding how the human mind works during interaction with other agents, and now researchers can move even forward thanks to the spreading of robotic technologies.

However, this topic is extremely complex, as social cognitive mechanisms displayed by humans during HRI scenarios could be influenced also by individual differences, such as personality traits, demographic characteristics, cultural belonging, and previous experience with artificial agents. Indeed, the same interaction with the same robot could be perceived as smooth or stressful, depending on the user's biases and prior beliefs. The complex interplay between individual factors and artificial agents' behaviors requires further systematic investigation. In particular, it is still unclear whether priors and biases towards social robots could be modulated by exposing individuals to direct HRI (Ghiglino et al., 2020a, 2020b). Conversely, some individuals' dispositions towards artificial agents, including knowledge and experience with robotics, might override empirical evidence provided by the robot behavior and might modulate the attitude displayed during the interaction (Ciardo et al., 2020). Previous studies reported in this chapter (see, as examples, Wiese et al., 2017; Ghiglino & Wykowska, 2020) suggest the need for combining the neuroscientific and engineering methods, to better understand which individual factors and which features of robots' behavior affect HRI. This includes the adoption of assessment tools that are typical of psychological and neuroscientific research, to define whether the factors that affect human–human interaction may influence HRI as well. At the same time, limiting research to extremely well-controlled experiments might deprive HRI of the possibility to understand how individuals behave in naturalistic environments when the interaction is more spontaneous. Conversely, it will be not sufficient to investigate HRI solely by relying on the assessment of individuals' dispositions and explicit measures of human-likeness attribution. Instead, HRI researchers should try to combine the investigation of individuals' automatic (and, often, implicit) reactions during interactive scenarios, finding a balance between the (usually) extremely controlled in-lab experiments and the "into-wild" approach of interactive research. Indeed, the adoption of implicit measures able to discriminate whether individuals engage and attune with artificial agents could be crucial to understand the factors that maximize the communication between natural and artificial agents. Still, the nature of artificial agents allows for exerting a strong control on their behavior, allowing for the experimental rigor that is typical for the neuroscientific approach. Hopefully, in the near future, social robots will be equipped with enough artificial intelligence (AI) to understand users' needs, feelings, and intentions, and to adapt their skills and behaviors accordingly (Leite et al., 2013). This will allow for the design of more and more interactive scenarios and experiments, and further exploration of social cognition mechanisms underlying human behavior. This is the reason why it is of the utmost importance to grant a constant interchange between fundamental and applicative sciences in HRI if the final aim is to expand our knowledge about the human mind, as well as to provide humans with novel technologies that can assist them during everyday life.

## A MATTER OF "EMBODIMENT": 4E COGNITION

In the previous paragraphs, we referred to a concept that has been extensively debated for decades in the HRI literature: the concept of *embodiment*. This term took different meanings throughout the history of this discipline, stemming from discussions on AI. Nowadays, many AI researchers consider embodiment as a condition *sine qua non* for any form of natural or artificial cognition. According to a provocative statement by Pfeifer and Scheier (2001), cognition cannot exist in the form of abstract algorithms but requires physical instantiation. A few years after the work of Pfeifer and Scheier (1999), Ziemke (2003) identified six different notions of embodiment that are commonly used in research: (a) structural coupling, (b) historical embodiment, (c) physical embodiment, (d) organized embodiment, (e) organismic embodiment, and (f) social embodiment. The notion of structural coupling is probably the broadest, defining embodiment as the property of a system that can perturb the environment where it exists (Dautenhahn et al., 2002; Franklin, 1997). However, this notion is still ambiguous, as systems can affect the surrounding environment without necessarily having a body (e.g., a thermostat regulating the temperature of a room) or cognitive capabilities (e.g., ocean waves shaping coastal landforms). For this reason, some authors tried to expand the definition of embodiment taking into account the history of structural coupling and mutual specifications between agent and environment (Riegler, 2002; Ziemke, 1999). Thus, historical embodiment was proposed as an evolutionary take on this concept, putting the accent on the development of the system in a certain environment, and the level of competence derived from this development. Still, this definition lacked specificity, as it could be applied to most living beings (e.g., a virus growing and adapting to the environment), and did not exclude non-bodily systems. From an AI perspective, a more restrictive version of the structural coupling notion is the one proposed by Brooks (1990). The author referred to the concept of physical grounding, adding to the interaction between the system and the physical world the need for a psychical connection, which happens via sensors and actuators. The requirement of such an instantiation of the system within the environment excludes software agents, but even the notion of physical embodiment could not overcome the problem that arose from inert systems (e.g., a pressure cooker is a physical system that can communicate with the environment through a valve, but it cannot be considered a system with cognitive capabilities). One of the first attempts to provide a definition that excludes inert systems is the notion of organized embodiment. According to this notion, there are types of organism-like cognition that are limited to organism-like bodies (i.e., systems with sensory-motor capacities; Lakoff, 1988; Dreyfus, 1996). In this context, the embodiment is defined almost as a prerequisite for cognition, and not only for physical interaction with the environment. This definition in particular is extremely important for cognitive sciences applied to HRI as robots (and humanoids in particular) fall under the category of "organismoids." Such a take on embodiment assumes that there might be similarities between living organisms and complex artifacts in terms of their ability to interact with the environment. In other words, under certain circumstances, natural and artificial agents might display a similar level of embodiment. This might lead individuals interacting with such artificial agents to approach them as if their behavior reflects cognitive processes. The hypothesis is in line with the concepts we discussed previously: robots might occupy an ontological niche between cognitive and noncognitive agents, which might affect the strategies humans adopt to predict and explain their behavior. However, according to some authors, embodiment should be considered an ontogenetic characteristic of living beings and limited to biological organisms (Maturana & Varela, 1987; von Uexküll, 1982). According to this account, biological beings are autonomous and autopoietic, while artificial beings are heteronomous and allopoietic (Sharkey & Ziemke, 2001; Ziemke & Sharkey, 2001). This definition, also called organismic embodiment, takes into account the phylogenetic and ontogenetic history of interactions that living beings developed with their environment(s). Indeed, through experience, living beings develop adaptability to environmental changes that are still unmatched by artificial agents. Furthermore, this theory does not leave room for AI improvements, which would grant artificial agents a higher level of autonomy and autopoiesis only artificially. That is, autonomy cannot be provided to a system that does not already possess it, as it is viewed as an ontogenetic characteristic. In line with the notions of the embodiment presented so far, the organismic account attempts to define what type of "body" is required for certain types of cognition. Orthogonal to these accounts, the notion of social embodiment moves the focus on the interactive aspect of embodiment. According to Barsalou et al. (2003), for example, embodiment should be considered as a state of a system that arises during social interaction and affects social information processing. Indeed, the authors define cognition as a process that involves, at the same time, sensory, motor, and introspective states, and that is influenced by the environment. This notion could even be considered as an extension of the organismoid embodiment, as it refers to systems that can interact with their environment socially, regardless of their biology. The crucial aspect of this notion is that both the system and the environment are recognized to play a fundamental role in cognitive processes. Even though the requirement of a physical body for cognitive processes is not at all generally accepted, the definition of the social embodiment is in line with the recent philosophical theories of distributed cognition (i.e., 4E cognition, see Newen et al., 2018). Indeed, according to proponents of active externalism (see Clark & Chalmers, 1998), cognition is not an abstract process that happens solely in the brain but is rather dependent on, and distributed across, an agent's brain, body, and the surrounding environment (natural, technological, social). This means that cognition can be considered an active process that requires a system to interact with its environment. This hypothesis holds even if we consider the development of social cognition in humans: according to Vygotskij, for example, individuals acquire social cognition competencies through repetitive interactions with their (social) environment (see Bruner, 1984). In this view, the environment scaffolds the development of individuals, shaping their cognitive abilities. This interdependence between agents and their environment seems to apply to biological agents, but it is less clear what happens when artificial agents are added to this interplay. This makes it fundamental to investigate the role played by the (social) embodiment in HRI scenarios, where humans are interacting with embodied artificial agents. In particular, it is fundamental to understand whether the embodiment affects social cognition mechanisms adopted by humans during HRI, and which are the main features of artificial agents that could modulate it.

## IMPLICATIONS OF SOCIAL COGNITION IN RESEARCH

Robots embedded with social abilities are designed to assist humans in daily routines. Social robots are supposed to interact and support humans in several contexts, from the domestic to the healthcare environments. In order to smoothen the interaction and maximize the support that such technologies can provide, robots should be embedded with enough "social intelligence" to understand the needs of the user and provide appropriate behavior. Tailoring the behavior of an artificial agent to the requests and needs of the human interacting with it is a huge challenge for social robotics. Aside from the development of appropriate technical solutions, it is crucial to understand, from a cognitive point of view, how humans interact with artificial agents. Indeed, the success of HRI depends not only on the technical capabilities and behavioral repertoire of the artificial agent but also on the ease with which humans attune and coordinate with it. Previous literature suggested that performance during HRI might be boosted when the human socially attunes with the artificial agent, treating it as if it possessed mental states and anthropomorphic traits (see, e.g., Wiese et al., 2017). However, personality traits, demographic characteristics, cultural belonging, and previous experience could influence social cognitive mechanisms displayed by humans during HRI scenarios. Indeed, the same interaction with the same robot could be perceived as smooth or stressful, depending on the user's biases and prior beliefs (Hinz et al., 2019; Lyons et al., 2020). Several individual differences might concur in the attribution of mental states and intentional agency towards artificial agents (Perez-Osorio et al., 2020). Still, the complex interplay between individual differences and artificial agents' behaviors requires further systematic investigation. For example, it is still unclear whether exposing individuals to direct HRI (i.e., making participants interact in first person with embodied artificial agents) could modulate priors and biases towards social robots. Recent literature suggests that exposing individuals to direct HRI might not be sufficient to modulate priors and biases (Ghiglino et al., 2020a). Conversely, some individuals' dispositions towards artificial agents, including knowledge and experience with robotics, might override empirical evidence provided by the robot behavior and might modulate the attitude displayed during the interaction (Ciardo et al., 2020). This may suggest the need for assessing such differences more in-depth, to better understand which personality traits and individual factors affect HRI. This includes the adoption of assessment tools that are typical of psychological and neuroscientific research, to define whether the factors that affect human–human interaction influence HRI as well. Therefore, it will be not sufficient to investigate HRI solely relying on the assessment of individuals' dispositions and explicit measures of human-likeness attribution. HRI research should focus also on the investigation of individuals' automatic (and, often, implicit) reactions during interactive scenarios. The adoption of implicit measures able to discriminate whether an individual engages and attunes with an artificial agent is crucial for maximizing the communication between the two agents (Ghiglino et al., 2020b).

Indeed, we are exposed to seemingly smart devices on a daily basis. This makes the interaction with technology increasingly smooth and dynamic (Gonzáles et al., 2012), and literature supports the idea that artificial agents able to behave like human beings facilitate the spontaneity and naturalness of interaction (Wiese et al., 2017). Providing artificial agents with human-like behavior positively affects the quality of the interaction (Thepsoonthor et al., 2018). In particular, when the physical aspect and the behavioral repertoire of artificial agents resemble one of the human beings, individuals tend to attribute to the agent anthropomorphic traits, including mental states and intentional agency (Martini et al., 2015). We can even speculate that not only the attribution of human-like traits towards an artificial agent but also spontaneous attentional engagement can be modulated by the behavior it displays (see, e.g., Ghiglino et al., 2021). Facilitating attentional engagement would cause, as a cascade effect, the improvement of the communication with artificial agents. Thus, embedding artificial agents with human-like behaviors might boost social attunement towards them, and this aspect could be particularly crucial for deploying social robots in environments where social interaction is desirable (e.g., assistive robotics; Leite et al., 2013). Indeed, treating artificial agents as if they were anthropomorphic entities with a synthetic "mind" may help individuals during natural interactions, as these processes allow us to predict and explain the behaviors displayed by other individuals in every-day interactions with our conspecifics (Leite et al., 2013). Previous research showed that similar mechanisms might be activated in interaction with artificial agents (Krach et al., 2008), and vary depending upon individual differences and available contextual information (Hinz et al., 2019). Still, it is important to highlight the complex interplay between individual differences, explicit attribution of anthropomorphic traits, mind-ascription, and attentional engagement. For example, in a series of studies, Ghiglino et al. (2020a, 2020b, 2021) showed that individual differences do not affect the implicit processing (i.e., visual processing) and attentional engagement, which might rely on more low-level components of social-cognition. Conversely, attentional engagement seems to be driven mainly by the behavior of the artificial agent, rather than by the individual's dispositions towards the agent itself. This provides useful insight that could be used for the development of artificial agents that will interact, in the future, with human users on a daily basis. The acceptance of robots as social companions might actually depend on their ability to adequately elicit such social cognitive processes during the interaction, even at an implicit level (Ghiglino et al., 2020a, 2020b). At the same time, social robots need to be able to understand the users' needs, feelings, and intentions in order to adapt their skills and behaviors accordingly (Leite et al., 2013).

Previous studies investigated how attitudes and biases towards robotics could affect the interaction with artificial agents (Perez-Osorio et al., 2020), along with personality traits and cultural differences (Weiss & Evers, 2011). However, such systematic investigation of individual differences has been scarce so far. Most of the past research relies solely on the administration of questionnaires and online surveys. Nevertheless, biases and attitudes towards social robots could be modulated during HRI scenarios, through the accumulation of empirical shreds of evidence (Cross et al., 2019). It is also still unclear whether eliciting mind ascription and human-like traits towards social robots during the interaction could reduce negative attitudes and biases towards robots.

Considerable progress has been made in recent years in terms of the technical realization of artificial agents. However, further interdisciplinary research is required to complement technical solutions with the understanding of social cognitive processes that are uniquely adopted during the interaction with social robots (Dautenhahn, 2007; Schellen & Wykowska, 2019). Indeed, the ability of robots to interact socially and intuitively with the users is still limited, and future research on the psychological underpinning of HRI could improve both the design of artificial agents and our understanding of social cognitive mechanisms in humans. The investigation of social cognition mechanisms elicited in HRI scenarios needs to comprise the collection of explicit and implicit measures, assessing individual's differences/attitudes towards robots as well as attentional engagement during interaction with artificial agents. In particular, the combination of surveys and questionnaires (more typical of HRI) with more implicit measures (more typical of psychological investigation) might allow for a better understanding of spontaneous social mechanisms elicited by the interaction with artificial agents.

## NOTE

1. The concept refers to the need for investigating social cognition adopting real-time interaction paradigms, which is a more naturalistic approach than studying social cognition using observational paradigms.

## REFERENCES

Banks, J. (2020). Theory of mind in social robots: Replication of five established human tests. *International Journal of Social Robotics, 12*(2), 403–414. https://doi.org/10.1007/s12369-019-00588-x

Barresi, J., & Moore, C. (1996). Intentional relations and social understanding. *Behavioral and Brain Sciences, 19*(1), 107–122. https://doi.org/10.1017/S0140525X00041790

Barsalou, L. W., Niedenthal, P. M., Barbey, A. K., & Ruppert, J. A. (2003). Social embodiment. In B. H. Ross (Ed.), *The psychology of learning and motivation: Advances in research and theory* (Vol. 43, pp. 43–92). Elsevier Science.

Brooks, R. (1990). Elephants don't play chess. *Robotics and Autonomous Systems, 6*(1–2), 3–15. https://doi.org/10.1016/S0921-8890(05)80025-9

Bruner, J. (1984). Vygotsky's zone of proximal development: The hidden agenda. *New Directions for Child Development, 1984*(23), 93–97. https://doi.org/10.1002/cd.23219842309

Ciardo, F., Ghiglino, D., Roselli, C., & Wykowska, A. (2020). The effect of individual differences and repetitive interactions on explicit and implicit attitudes towards robots. In A. R. Wagner, D. Feil-Seifer, K. S. Haring, S. Rossi, T. Williams, H. He, & S. S. Ge (Eds.), *Social robotics: 12th international conference,*

*ICSR 2020, Golden, CO, USA, November 14–18, 2020, proceedings* (pp. 466–477). Springer.

Clark A., & Chalmers D. (1998). The extended mind. *Analysis, 58*(1), 7–19. https://doi.org/10.1093/analys/58.1.7

Cross, E. S., Hortensius, R., & Wykowska, A. (2019). From social brains to social robots: Applying neurocognitive insights to human–robot interaction. *Philosophical Transactions of the Royal Society B, 374*(1771), 20180024. https://doi.org/10.1098/rstb.2018.0024

Dautenhahn, K. (2007). Methodology & themes of human–robot interaction: A growing research field. *International Journal of Advanced Robotic Systems, 4*(1), 15. https://doi.org/10.5772/5702

Dautenhahn, K., Ogden, B., & Quick, T. (2002). From embodied to socially embedded agents—Implications for interaction-aware robots. *Cognitive Systems Research, 3*(3), 397–428. https://doi.org/10.1016/S1389-0417(02)00050-5

De Graaf, M. M., & Malle, B. F. (2019, March). People's explanations of robot behavior subtly reveal mental state inferences. In *2019 14th ACM/IEEE International Conference on Human-Robot Interaction (HRI)* (pp. 239–248). IEEE. https://doi.org/10.1109/HRI.2019.8673308

Dennett, D. C. (1971). Intentional systems. *The Journal of Philosophy, 68*(4), 87–106. https://doi.org/10.2307/2025382

Dennett, D. C. (1981). *True believers: The intentional strategy and why it works.* https://philarchive.org/archive/DENTB

Dreyfus, H. (1996). The current relevance of Merleau-Ponty's phenomenology of embodiment. *The Electronic Journal of Analytic Philosophy,* 4. https://ejap.louisiana.edu/ejap/1996.spring/dreyfus.1996.spring.html

Franklin, S. (1997) Autonomous agents as embodied AI. *Cybernetics and Systems, 25*(8), 499–520. https://ccrg.cs.memphis.edu/assets/papers/Autonomous%20Agents%20as%20Embodied%20AI.htm

Frith, C. D., & Frith, U. (2008). Implicit and explicit processes in social cognition. *Neuron, 60*(3), 503–510. https://doi.org/10.1016/j.neuron.2008.10.032

Ghiglino, D., & Wykowska, A. (2020). When robots (pretend to) think. In B. P. Goecke & A. M. Rosenthal-von de Pütten (Eds.), *Artificial intelligence* (pp. 49–74). mentis.

Ghiglino, D., De Tommaso, D., Willemse, C., Marchesi, S., & Wykowska, A. (2020a, May 11). *Can I get your (robot) attention? Human sensitivity to subtle hints of human-likeness in a humanoid robot's behavior.* https://doi.org/10.31234/osf.io/kfy4g

Ghiglino, D., Willemse, C., De Tommaso, D., Bossi, F., & Wykowska, A. (2020b). At first sight: robots' subtle eye movement parameters affect human attentional engagement, spontaneous attunement and perceived human-likeness. *Paladyn, Journal of Behavioral Robotics, 11*(1), 31–39. https://doi.org/10.1515/pjbr-2020-0004

Ghiglino, D., Willemse, C., De Tommaso, D., & Wykowska, A. (2021). Mind the eyes: Artificial agents' eye movements modulate attentional engagement and anthropomorphic attribution. *Frontiers in Robotics and AI, 8.* https://doi.org/10.3389/frobt.2021.642796

González, A., Ramírez, M. P., & Viadel, V. (2012). Attitudes of the elderly toward information and communications technologies. *Educational Gerontology, 38*(9), 585–594. https://doi.org/10.1080/03601277.2011.595314

Hinz, N. A., Ciardo, F., & Wykowska, A. (2019, November). Individual differences in attitude toward robots predict behavior in human–robot interaction. In M. A. Salichs, S. S. Ge, E. I. Barakova, J.-J. Cabibihan, A. R. Wagner, Á. Castro-González, & H. He (Eds.), *Social robotics: 11th international conference, ICSR 2019, Madrid, Spain, November 26–29, 2019, Proceedings* (pp. 64–73). Springer.

Imamura, Y., Terada, K., & Takahashi, H. (2015, October). Effects of behavioral complexity on intention attribution to robots. In *HAI'15: Proceedings of the 3rd international conference on human-agent interaction* (pp. 65–72). Association for Computing Machinery. https://doi.org/10.1145/2814940.2814949

Krach, S., Hegel, F., Wrede, B., Sagerer, G., Binkofski, F., & Kircher, T. (2008). Can machines think? Interaction and perspective taking with robots investigated via fMRI. *PLoS ONE, 3*(7), e2597. https://doi.org/10.1371/journal.pone.0002597

Lakoff, G. (1988). Cognitive semantics. In U. Eco (Ed.), *Meaning and mental representations* (pp. 119–154). Indiana University Press.

Leite, I., Martinho, C., & Paiva, A. (2013). Social robots for long-term interaction: A survey. *International Journal of Social Robotics, 5*(2), 291–308. https://doi.org/10.1007/s12369-013-0178-y

Levin, D. T., Killingsworth, S. S., Saylor, M. M., Gordon, S. M., & Kawamura, K. (2013). Tests of concepts about different kinds of minds: Predictions about the behavior of computers, robots, and people. *Human–Computer Interaction, 28*(2), 161–191. https://psycnet.apa.org/record/2013-01935-003

Lyons, J. B., Nam, C. S., Jessup, S. A., Vo, T. Q., & Wynne, K. T. (2020, September). The role of individual differences as predictors of trust in autonomous security robots. In *2020 IEEE International Conference on Human-Machine Systems (ICHMS)* (pp. 1–5). IEEE. https://doi.org/10.1109/ICHMS49158.2020.9209544

Marchesi, S., Ghiglino, D., Ciardo, F., Perez-Osorio, J., Baykara, E., & Wykowska, A. (2019). Do we adopt the intentional stance toward humanoid robots? *Frontiers in Psychology, 10.* https://doi.org/10.3389/fpsyg.2019.00450

Martini, M. C., Buzzell, G. A., & Wiese, E. (2015, October). Agent appearance modulates mind attribution and social attention in human-robot interaction. In *Social robotics: International conference on social robotics* (pp. 431–439). Springer.

Maturana, H., & Varela, F. (1987). *The tree of knowledge.* Shambhala.

Moreno, A., & Etxeberria, A. (2005). Agency in natural and artificial systems. Artificial Life, *11*(1–2), 161–175. https://doi.org/10.1162/1064546053278919

Newen, A., De Bruin, L., & Gallagher, S. (Eds.). (2018). *The Oxford handbook of 4E cognition.* Oxford University Press.

Perez-Osorio, J., Marchesi, S., Ghiglino, D., Ince, M., & Wykowska, A. (2020). Correction to: More than you expect: Priors influence on the adoption of intentional stance toward humanoid robots. In M. A. Salichs, S. S. Ge, E. I. Barakova, J.-J. Cabibihan, A. R. Wagner, Á. Castro-González, & H. He (Eds.), *Social robotics: 11th international conference, ICSR 2019, Madrid, Spain, November 26–29, 2019, Proceedings* (pp. C1–C1). Springer.

Pfeifer, R., & Scheier, C. (2001). *Understanding intelligence.* MIT Press.

Riegler, A. (2002). When is a cognitive system embodied? *Cognitive Systems Research, 3*(3), 339–348. https://doi.org/10.1016/S1389-0417(02)00046-3

Schellen, E., & Wykowska, A. (2019). Intentional mindset toward robots—Open questions and methodological challenges. *Frontiers in Robotics and AI, 5.* https://doi.org/10.3389/frobt.2018.00139

Schilbach, L., Timmermans, B., Reddy, V., Costall, A., Bente, G., Schlicht, T., & Vogeley, K. (2013). Toward a second-person neuroscience 1. *Behavioral and Brain Sciences, 36*(4), 393–414. https://doi.org/10.1017/S0140525X12000660

Sharkey, N., & Ziemke, T. (2001). Mechanistic vs. phenomenal embodiment–Can robot embodiment lead to strong AI? *Cognitive Systems Research, 2*(4), 251–262. https://doi.org/10.1016/S1389-0417(01)00036-5

Thellman, S., de Graaf, M., & Ziemke, T. (2021). *Mental state attribution to robots: A systematic review of conceptions, methods, and findings.* http://urn.kb.se/resolve?urn=urn:nbn:se:liu:diva-178805

Thellman, S., Silvervarg, A., & Ziemke, T. (2017). Folk-psychological interpretation of human vs. humanoid robot behavior: Exploring the intentional stance toward robots. *Frontiers in Psychology, 8.* https://doi.org/10.3389/fpsyg.2017.01962

Thepsoonthorn, C., Ogawa, K. I., & Miyake, Y. (2018). The relationship between robot's nonverbal behaviour and human's likability based on human's personality. *Scientific Reports, 8*(1), 1–11. https://doi.org/10.1038/s41598-018-25314-x

von Uexküll, J. (1982). The theory of meaning. *Semiotica, 42*(1), 25–82. https://monoskop.org/images/4/4a/Uexkull_Jakob_von_1982_The_Theory_of_Meaning.pdf

Weiss, A., & Evers, V. (2011). Exploring cultural factors in human-robot interaction: A matter of personality. In *International Workshop on Comparative Informatics* (IWCI-2011), Copenhagen, Denmark (Vol. 700).

Wiese, E., Metta, G., & Wykowska, A. (2017). Robots as intentional agents: Using neuroscientific methods to make robots appear more social. *Frontiers in Psychology, 8.* https://doi.org/10.3389/fpsyg.2017.01663

Wykowska, A. (2020). Social robots to test flexibility of human social cognition. *International Journal of Social Robotics, 12*(6), 1203–1211. https://doi.org/10.1007/s12369-020-00674-5

Wykowska, A. (2021). Robots as mirrors of the human mind. *Current Directions in Psychological Science, 30*(1), 34–40. https://doi.org/10.1177/0963721420978609

Ziemke, T. (1999). Rethinking grounding. In A. Riegler et al. (Eds.), *Understanding representation in the cognitive sciences* (pp. 177–190). Plenum Press.

Ziemke, T. (2003). What's that thing called embodiment? In *Proceedings of the annual meeting of the cognitive science society, 25*(25), 1305–1310. https://escholarship.org/uc/item/60w6v9jz

Ziemke, T., & Sharkey, N. E. (2001). A stroll through the worlds of robots and animals: Applying Jakob von Uexkülls theory of meaning to adaptive robots and artificial life. *Semiotica, 134*(1–4), 701–746. https://doi.org/10.1515/semi.2001.050

Złotowski, J., Proudfoot, D., Yogeeswaran, K., & Bartneck, C. (2015). Anthropomorphism: Opportunities and challenges in human–robot interaction. *International Journal of Social Robotics,* 7(3), 347–360. https://doi.org/10.1007/s12369-014-0267-6

# SECTION V

## SOCIAL MEDIA

CHAPTER 11

# A CLINICAL PERSPECTIVE ON SOCIAL MEDIA

## Opportunities and Risks for Users, Patients, and Psychologists

**Federica Sibilla**
***University of Parma***

**Tiziana Mancini**
***University of Parma***

## STATE OF THE ART

When we talk of social media, we are talking about online platforms that allow users to create and share content with virtual communities and networks, facilitating a two-way interaction with the virtual audience. In fact, "social media" is an umbrella term that includes a variety of platforms such as social network sites (e.g., Facebook), microblogs (e.g., Twitter), blogs (e.g., LiveJournal), content-sharing sites (e.g., YouTube), virtual communities (e.g., Second Life), and many others, which constitute different social media sub-genres (Stoycheff et al., 2017; Wong et al., 2021).

*Digital Developments,* pages 151–165

The current world of social media is quite large and rich. After all, humans are social animals, and "throughout much of human history, we've developed technologies that make it easier for us to communicate with each other" (Carton, 2009, para. 10). Nowadays, there is an uncountable number of social media, the estimated number of social media users worldwide is 4.55 billion—which is more than half of the world population—and this number is expected to grow year after year. These users spend a mean number of about 2.5 hours each day using social media, and they use them for very different reasons: from filling up spare time to doing work-related activities, from staying in touch with family and friends to knowing new people and creating new relationships, but also to reading the news, staying up-to-date, entertaining themselves, shopping, and so on (DataReportal, n.d.). In other words, thanks to their great development and to the increase in their features, social media are currently used for both social and individual purposes, they have entered many areas of human existence changing how they are experienced, and they have become an integral part of our lives. This can open up some opportunities, lead to some risks, and, in any case, this implies changes, as it will be discussed by the following.

The great diffusion and pervasiveness of the phenomenon has obviously attracted the interest of several areas of psychology—from clinical to social, from developmental to marketing—which have extensively reflected on various aspects and processes associated with social media usage. In the specific field of clinical psychology, a great amount of studies focused on the positive and negative implications of social media use, investigating how it associates with or impacts on variables such as self needs, distress, psychopathology, well-being, and so on (e.g., Bashir & Bhat, 2017; Best et al., 2014). Many studies also focus on problematic social media use, trying to define this condition, identifying its antecedents and consequences, as well as creating appropriate measures to assess it (e.g., Marino et al., 2020; Sun & Zhang, 2021; Van den Eijnden et al., 2016). Other studies investigate the association between social media and personal variables such as personality traits or attachment style, wondering what elements guide the way in which people use social media (e.g., D'Arienzo et al., 2019; Gil de Zúñiga et al., 2017). Some other scholars focus on the clinical practice itself and therefore investigate the implications of the more or less conscious use of social media within the clinical setting (e.g., Creaner, 2015; Snowdy et al., 2016).

In this chapter we will focus on the potential benefits and risks of social media use in the field of clinical psychology and clinical practice.

## POTENTIAL BENEFITS

Literature showed that there are many benefits that can be associated with the use of social media in general. For example, using social media can be beneficial for the identity of the person, since the creation, management, and presentation of one's virtual identity can promote identity exploration and self-clarity (Reid & Weigle, 2014; Uhls et al., 2017). Using social media can also be useful for maintaining and strengthening pre-existing social relationships, it allows us to create new relationships and to do it more easily than in offline contexts, and it can increase the sense of social connection and social support, reducing loneliness (Burke et al., 2011; Reid & Weigle, 2014; Uhls et al., 2017). But there are some benefits that are even more closely related to clinical psychology. In fact, if social media are widely and increasingly used by the general population, it has been observed that they are increasingly used also by people with mental health conditions, as well as by psychologists and psychotherapists, for reasons that are strictly related to mental health (Lustgarten & Elhai, 2018; Naslund et al., 2020; Smailhodzic et al., 2016).

It is important to consider that people with psychological difficulties may prefer computer-mediated-communication over face-to-face communication. In fact, the lack of face-to-face interaction, the reduced social cues, the reduced nonverbal communication, the visual anonymity, and the greater control the user has on the interaction, make computer-mediated-communication more sustainable and empowering for people who have difficulties in social interaction (e.g., social anxiety issues) or for those who are afraid of stigma and rejection (Naslund et al., 2016, Naslund et al., 2020). In this sense, for people with psychological difficulties, social media is often a preferential and relevant tool. That said, the specific health-related reasons why they use them, and the consequent benefits, can be different.

For example, Internet is currently the first source of health information (Eckler et al., 2010; Hesse et al., 2010), and it has been observed that especially people with stigmatized problems rely on the Web to search for health information, comforted by the lack of face-to-face interaction. In this sense, social media can be a means by which to increase the knowledge and awareness on one's health and on treatment options, which can facilitate the access to health systems (Berger et al., 2005).

People with mental health conditions often use social media also to connect and interact with people with their same or with similar psychological problems. This process occurs spontaneously and leads to the creation of online communities whose members share the same difficulties (Naslund et al., 2016). In this sense, social media often serve as places to freely express (pleasant and unpleasant) emotions and to share experiences with people who probably have similar ones, to find help, to learn from others, and to support each other (De Martino et al., 2017; Naslund et al., 2016; Smailhodzic et al., 2016).

The expressive and relational possibilities that social media offer are useful for anyone, but they seem to be particularly important especially for people with mental health conditions. In fact, it has been observed that, compared to people without mental disorders, this population is more likely to express their thoughts and emotions through blogging, to connect online with people who have similar interests, and to establish significant relationships through social media (Gowen et al., 2012). After all, as early as the 1990s it was known that connecting with similar others has a great relevance for people with mental issues, favoring social integration, recovery, and well-being (Davidson et al., 1999). First, meeting and being connected with people who share the same characteristics, difficulties, or experiences, allow us to feel less different and less alone, and to increase the feelings of social connectedness and group belonging (Naslund et al., 2016). Furthermore, the possibility to express one's emotions, experiences, and thoughts—and especially doing it with people that live something that is similar—can help release and regulate one's disturbing and difficult emotions. Many people also use social media to make social comparisons with other people with their same problem: in particular, they read the testimonies of others in an attempt to understand and compare the experiences, the severity of the conditions as well as the effectiveness of the treatments. Reading other people's testimonials can help raise awareness and the ability to cope with mental health problems. In fact, reading success stories can increase confidence in improving or resolving one's condition, and reading stories about the difficulties others encountered can make the person more aware and ready for the path ahead (Smailhodzic et al., 2016). People who share their experiences can also act as a model and inspiration for those who suffer, and, in general, can contribute to raise awareness in mental health and to fight against stigma (Naslund et al., 2016). Finally, and generally speaking, other people on social media can be seen as an important source of social support: We speak of "online peer-to-peer support," which can be information support, esteem support, emotional support, or network support (Naslund et al., 2016; Smailhodzic et al., 2016).

In conclusion, the use of social media by people with mental health conditions can have multiple benefits, at the informative, relational, and affective level. Taken together, these benefits contribute to the person's empowerment, that is "the discovery and development of one's inherent capacity to be responsible for one's own life. Patients are thus empowered when they are in possession of the knowledge, skills, and self-awareness necessary to identify and attain their own goals" (Wentzera & Bygholm, 2013, p. e387). Empowerment is crucial, as it involves increased self-efficacy and motivation, which favor the active participation in one's health and the trust in care, elements that can facilitate the access to health systems and/or an increased adherence to therapy, and thus, finally, favoring subjective and psychological well-being (Smailhodzic et al., 2016). Furthermore, as empirically observed, these benefits can be experienced by all users regardless of their specific ways of using social media (Chung, 2014; Mo & Coulson, 2010; van Uden-Kraan et al., 2008).

Social media use can also lead to a change in the relationship between the patient and the psychologist or psychotherapist. For example, the patient–clinician communication could become easier and more equal, and the patient could be more able to understand their condition as well as more confident in the therapeutic process, in which he/she could take a more active role (Smailhodzic et al., 2016). In this regard, it is important to underline that social media is not only a means that facilitates the connection with peers but also with professionals. In fact, as already mentioned, social media are increasingly used also by psychologists and psychotherapists for reasons that are strictly related to their profession, and this use can have several benefits (Naslund et al., 2020; Smailhodzic et al., 2016).

Clinicians could use social media to communicate with patients. In this case, social media can be an additional communication tool, useful both for "service communications"—for example, to reschedule an appointment—and for timely support in everyday situations—for example, to counsel in difficult moments occurring between one session and another (Barnett, 2018). These communication possibilities are obviously very helpful to the patient and could increase their engagement and compliance with the therapy. The clinical service can also be entirely delivered through social media (e.g., video call apps). In this case, social media do not constitute additional communication tools, but the means through which the therapeutic relationship and treatment take place. This possibility has some benefits, for example it often allows us to overcome practical limits such as geographical distances and it thus increases the accessibility to care (Kolmes, 2012; Naslund et al., 2016, Naslund et al., 2020).

Given that social media gives the opportunity to communicate one-to-many, clinicians can also use them to easily communicate with general population and potential patients, and to do so, using modes—for example, images or videos—that are more user-friendly, emotionally engaging, and effective than static text (Soetens et al., 2014). In this case, social media can be used to educate people about mental health, disseminating informative and psychoeducational material, and illustrate treatment options, favoring people's awareness as well as encouraging the access to health systems (Tutelman et al., 2018). Professionals can also use social media for marketing reasons, that is, to inform the population about the services they offer, to advertise their private activity, and to encourage potential clients to contact them (Kolmes, 2012). The opportunity to easily communicate one-to-many is often used by clinicians also with the purpose of recruiting research participants. In fact, compared to offline recruitment, online recruitment allows us to reach a greater number of participants spending significantly less time and less energy (Tutelman et al., 2018). Furthermore, some studies have shown that data collected through online recruitment are equally valid than those collected through in-person recruitment (Casler et al., 2013).

Social media are also used as screening tools. In fact, users leave on social media a huge amount of footprints about their moods, tendencies, behaviors, and experiences (Guntuku et al., 2017; Kern et al., 2016), and the analysis of social media language and activities ("social media monitoring") can be used to evaluate personality traits, to monitor mood, or to identify bullying behaviors or suicidal risk (Fleury & Dowdy, 2022). This opens up possibilities for screening, reporting, prevention, and research, but it also raises ethical issues (e.g., Liu et al., 2021).

Finally, social media is often used for communication between clinicians, thus becoming a tool for creating and strengthening the network between colleagues, for presenting themselves as a professional reference, for sharing information on the profession, for discussing clinical issues, and for updating each other on evidence-based care. In this sense, social media helps the clinician in their work, supporting an improvement in the quality of the treatments and therefore in the health outcomes for patients (Tutelman et al., 2018; Ventola, 2014).

## POTENTIAL RISKS

Like all tools, social media includes both benefits and potential risks, and the latter are primarily associated with the excessive or inadequate use of social media.

In general, some of the potential risks are the problematic social media use and the consequent impairment in functioning, or possible sleep changes and disturbances, which could contribute to various issues including depression (Lemola et al., 2015). The term "Facebook depression" has also been coined, but the potential of social media to cause depression has not been confirmed to date (Rafla et al., 2014). Social media also exposes us to idealized content that can reinforce impossible body standards and disfavor self-esteem (Common Sense Media, 2015). They also can expose us to dysfunctional contexts such as "pro-eating disorder" or "pro-self harm" online groups, which could encourage risky behaviors (Reid & Weigle, 2014). Online interactions that take place through social media could also favor offline social isolation (Best et al., 2014). Finally, using social media increases the risk of encountering inadequate relational dynamics—for example, online harassment (Pew Research Center, 2021) or hate speech (e.g., European Commission, n.d.).

Also in this case, the use of social media by people with mental health issues, patients, or psychologists and psychotherapists for mental health reasons entails some specific risks (Naslund et al., 2020; Snowdy et al., 2016).

For example, although people usually use social media as a complement to the professional services they receive (Colineau & Paris, 2010), we have also seen that people can use social media as a source of health information or to find comfort in peers: this exposes us to the risk that potential patients use social media to avoid resorting professional health services (Househ et al., 2014). In addition, when it comes to the use of social media for health reasons, it is important to talk about the quality of the information that users encounter on these platforms. Many elements lead to questioning the quality of social media information. First, on social media anyone has the opportunity to publish material on a certain topic (e.g., mental health), regardless of the level of competence and reliability they have on that topic (Agarwal & Yiliyasi, 2010; Smailhodzic et al., 2016). Furthermore, the authors of this material may be anonymous or difficult to identify (Househ et al., 2014). Second, in order to be engaging and to become popular, the material published on social media must be simple, immediate, and easily usable. For this reason, on social media, all the information (including information regarding mental health) is often conveyed in a colloquial, approximate, and anecdotal way, without providing references, and (unrealistically) suggesting quick and simple solutions (Agarwal & Yiliyasi, 2010; Househ et al., 2014). Moreover, social media allows the exchange of short and fast messages, which prevents from appropriately discussing complex issues such as those concerning mental health (Pirraglia & Kravitz, 2012; Rossotti et al., 2012). Finally, the dynamic nature of social media makes it very difficult to control and guarantee the quality of the published material (De Martino et al., 2017). All these elements cause health information posted on social media often lacking in quality, reliability, and credibility (Moorhead et al., 2013). This means that there is a big risk of misinformation and disinformation, which can be harmful both for people's health and safety and for the credibility of the health professions and professionals (De Martino et al., 2017; Househ et al., 2014).

As we have seen, people who have mental health issues can use social media to connect with peers. These connections can be a source of social support, which is extremely useful and beneficial and which can contribute to the resolution of the problems experienced. Nevertheless, the online social connections also involve some potential risks. In this sense, the decision of who to reach out to is a critical factor that can have repercussions on the path to well-being (Naslund et al., 2016). As already mentioned, a first risk is that the advice received online is not reliable and that the trustworthiness of their authors is not evaluated or evaluable (Entwistle et al., 2011). In addition, the advice and experiences read online may not be applicable to the user's condition (Armstrong & Powell, 2009; Schrank et al., 2010) or may generate unrealistic expectations, social comparison pressure, and anxiety or confusion (Rideout & Fox, 2018). Online social contexts can also provide the exact opposite of social support: As already said, they can expose to hostile comments from others or to dynamics such as harassment or bullying (Naslund et al., 2016), and they can promote or reinforce dysfunctional and pathological behaviors (Ziebland & Wyke, 2012). Finally, online relationships can also become a "refuge," favoring the avoidance of offline relationships and social withdrawal (Lawlor & Kirakowski, 2014). In general, these various risks may contribute to an increase in symptoms (e.g., depressed mood or anxiety), or to a worsening of the pre-existing psychopathological symptoms (Naslund et al., 2020). However, literature shows that the benefits of online peer support outweigh the possible risks (Naslund et al., 2016).

Using social media also presents ethical issues related to privacy and confidentiality. For example, the personal information that people with mental health conditions disclose on social media could be shared, without consent, to other people (Lober & Flowers, 2011). Also in the clinical professional context, patient data entrusted to social media (such as video calling apps) may be subjected to privacy breaches due to human error (e.g., accidentally pressing a key) or malicious acts (e.g., hacker attacks on servers). In addition, the professional should investigate how the privacy of data is ensured by the IT companies and services they rely on (Drummond et al., 2015). Similarly, in social media monitoring and social media screening, the protection of collected data must be considered with particular care (Fleury & Dowdy, 2022; Liu et al., 2021).

When it comes to the relationship between patients and psychotherapists, an additional risk related to the use of social media concerns the unintentional disclosure of personal information. In fact, many psychotherapists and patients make personal use of social media, revealing information about themselves and disseminating online traces. In this sense, psychotherapists and patients can, unintentionally or not, access reciprocal information online, which can disturb the therapeutic relationship and work (Baier, 2019). For the therapists it could be complex, both professionally and ethically, to understand how to manage certain patient information acquired through social media without the awareness of the patient. For example, through social media they might become aware of certain unhealthy lifestyles of the patient (Tunick et al., 2011). Access to such information may be involuntary—for example, the patient is represented in a photo that a mutual friend uploaded online—or voluntary—for example, through the so-called "patient-targeted Googling" (Farnan et al., 2013) or through searches on social networks sites. A 2010 study found that 28% of psychotherapists involuntarily found online information about their current patients, while 48% intentionally sought this information (Kolmes & Taube, 2010). On the other hand, the therapist's sharing of personal information—that is, self-disclosure—is a well-known therapeutic tool. But if such disclosure is not conscious and controlled, and does not fit within a clear rationale, then it risks to alter the professional boundaries, to irreversibly change the therapeutic relationship, to damage the therapeutic alliance, and thereby to impair the effectiveness of the treatment (Tunick et al., 2011). This is even more true when this information relates to issues dealt within the therapy: let's imagine, for example, if a patient who is being treated for an alcohol use disorder finds on social media a photo depicting their therapist consuming alcohol. Again, personal information about the therapist can be acquired online either unintentionally or intentionally. In the latter case, patients are often motivated by curiosity (Kolmes & Taube, 2016) but they can feel shame, discomfort, and embarrassment for the search they carried out, also fearing that revealing it to the therapist would involve a judgment or rejection (Kolmes & Taube, 2011). Finally, for both therapists and patients, the therapeutic risks of unintentional disclosure of personal information are even higher if a "friendship" connection is established between the two on social networks sites (Tunick et al., 2011). Usually, in fact, this condition greatly increases the number of information that is shared and, consistently, this can be a significantly embarrassing or challenging condition for patients (Dombo et al., 2014).

## FUTURE DIRECTIONS/NEW SOLUTIONS

Nowadays, for literally "more than half the world," life takes place both offline and online, in an "interreality" in which it is increasingly difficult to distinguish the border between real and virtual world (Riva, 2017). The huge space occupied by social media in daily life inevitably involves clinical psychology, both because the use of social media can have important implications on the psychological well-being of the general population, and because their use directly involves patients, clinicians, the relationship between them, and the clinical practice itself.

As regards (potential) patients, clinical psychologists, and clinical practice, we have observed that the use of social media offers both benefits and risks. Nevertheless, fortunately, literature seems to suggest that the former exceed the latter (Househ et al., 2014). In light of this, the future direction should (and probably will) be to continue to let social media be used by (potential) patients and clinicians, and let them be part of the therapeutic work, so as to continue enjoying the benefits they bring. At the same time, however, the risks that social media use entails for people with mental health issues and for clinicians must be managed. In this way, social media can reach its maximum potential as a tool to support mental health and clinical practice.

In order to achieve this goal, it is necessary to work on three main fronts in the coming years. First, many risks associated with the use of social media for mental health reasons have already been highlighted by the research;

nevertheless, there is still and there will be much to know about what (current and future) social media use implies. In this sense, the first action to take is scientific research, which must keep pace with the development of both social media platforms and usage practices. So, the attention of researchers and research centered on these issues needs to be maintained and increased, and institutions need to support the research on this topic. Second, theoretical knowledge on the topic should not remain separate from practice. In this sense, a second action to be taken is greater education of the general population, patients, and clinical psychologists, to make them more aware of the processes associated with the use of these tools and, therefore, to improve their social media usage. In this sense, the implementation and diffusion of digital education courses can be useful. Finally, a third fundamental action to take concerns the drafting of precise ethical and practical standards, indications, or guidelines—which are currently missing (Drude & Messer-Engel, 2021; Lustgarten & Elhai, 2018)—to which clinical psychologists can refer in their use of social media. In this sense, the professional associations could help in a very valuable way, by providing indications that are scientifically and clinically grounded. It is also advisable to better regulate the contents that are conveyed on social media, for example by developing more stringent policies, enhancing the activity of moderators, and countering the spread of false information.

## REFERENCES

Agarwal, N., & Yiliyasi, Y. (2010). Information quality challenges in social media. *Proceedings of the 15th International Conference on Information Quality*, 234–248. http://mitiq.mit.edu/ICIQ/Documents/IQ%20Conference%202010/Papers/3A1_IQChallengesInSocialMedia.pdf

Armstrong, N., & Powell, J. (2009). Patient perspectives on health advice posted on Internet discussion boards: A qualitative study. *Health Expectations*, *12*(3), 313–320. https://doi.org/10.1111/j.1369-7625.2009.00543.x

Baier, A. (2019). The ethical implications of social media: Issues and recommendations for clinical practice. *Ethics & Behavior*, *29*(5), 341–351. https://doi.org/10.1080/10508422.2018.1516148

Barnett, J. E. (2018). Integrating technological advances into clinical training and practice: The future is now! *Clinical Psychology: Science and Practice*, *25*(2), e12233. https://doi.org/10.1111/cpsp.12233

Bashir, H., & Bhat, S. A. (2017). Effects of social media on mental health: A review. *The International Journal of Indian Psychology*, *4*(3), 125–131. https://doi.org/10.25215/0403.134

Berger, M., Wagner, T. H., & Baker, L. C. (2005). Internet use and stigmatized illness. *Social Science and Medicine*, *61*(8), 1821–1827. https://doi.org/10.1016/j.socscimed.2005.03.025

Best, P., Manktelow, R., & Taylor, B. (2014). Online communication, social media and adolescent wellbeing: A systematic narrative review. *Children and Youth Services Review, 41*, 27–36. https://doi.org/10.1016/j.childyouth.2014.03.001

Burke, M., Kraut, R., & Marlow, C. (2011). Social capital on Facebook: Differentiating uses and users. In *CHI '11: Proceedings of the SIGCHI Conference on Human Factors in Computing Systems* (pp. 571_580). https://doi.org/10.1145/1978942.1979023

Carton, S. (2009, July 20). *Defining social media.* https://www.clickz.com/defining-social-media-2/72139/

Casler, K., Bickel, L., & Hackett, E. (2013). Separate but equal? A comparison of participants and data gathered via Amazon's MTurk, social media, and face-to-face behavioral testing. *Computers in Human Behavior, 29*(6), 2156–2160. https://doi.org/10.1016/j.chb.2013.05.009

Chung, J. E. (2014). Social networking in online support groups for health: How online social networking benefits patients. *Journal of Health Communication, 19*(6), 639–659. https://doi.org/10.1080/10810730.2012.757396

Colineau, N., & Paris, C. (2010). Talking about your health to strangers: Understanding the use of online social networks by patients. *New Review of Hypermedia and Multimedia, 16*(1–2), 141–160. https://doi.org/10.1080/13614568.2010.496131

Common Sense Media. (2015). *Children, teens, media, and body image: A common sense media research brief.* https://www.commonsensemedia.org/sites/default/files/research/report/csm-body-image-report-012615-interactive.pdf

Creaner, M. (2015). The role of social media in counselling and psychotherapy. In R. Tribe & J. Morrissey (Eds.), *Handbook of professional and ethical practice for psychologists, counsellors and psychotherapists* (pp. 158–169). Routledge.

D'Arienzo, M. C., Boursier, V., & Griffiths, M. D. (2019). Addiction to social media and attachment styles: A systematic literature review. *International Journal of Mental Health and Addiction, 17*, 1094–1118. https://doi.org/10.1007/s11469-019-00082-5

DataReportal. (n.d.). *Global social media statistics.* https://datareportal.com/social-media-users

Davidson, L., Chinman, M., Kloos, B., Weingarten, R., Stayner, D., & Tebes, J. K. (1999). Peer support among individuals with severe mental illness: A review of the evidence. *Clinical Psychology: Science and Practice, 6*(2), 165–187. https://doi.org/10.1093/clipsy.6.2.165

De Martino, I., D'Apolito, R., McLawhorn, A. S., Fehring, K. A., Sculco, P. K., & Gasparini, G. (2017). Social media for patients: Benefits and drawbacks. *Current Reviews in Musculoskeletal Medicine, 10*(1), 141–145. https://doi.org/10.1007/s12178-017-9394-7

Dombo, E. A., Kays, L., & Weller, K. (2014). Clinical social work practice and technology: Personal, practical, regulatory, and ethical considerations for the twenty-first century. *Social Work in Health Care, 53*(9), 900–919. https://doi.org/10.1080/00981389.2014.948585

Drude, K., & Messer-Engel, K. (2021). The development of social media guidelines for psychologists and for regulatory use. *Journal of Technology in Behavioral Science, 6*, 388–396. https://doi.org/10.1007/s41347-020-00176-1

Drummond, A., Cromarty, P., & Battersby, M. (2015). Privacy in the digital age: Implications for clinical practice. *Clinical Psychology: Science and Practice, 22*(3), 227–237. https://doi.org/10.1111/cpsp.12105

Eckler, P., Worsowicz, G., & Rayburn, J. W. (2010). Social media and health care: An overview. *PM&R: The Journal of Injury, Function, and Rehabilitation, 2*(11), 1046–1050. https://doi.org/10.1016/j.pmrj.2010.09.005

Entwistle, V. A., France, E. F., Wyke, S., Jepson, R., Hunt, K., Ziebland, S., & Thompson, A. (2011). How information about other people's personal experiences can help with healthcare decision-making: A qualitative study. *Patient Education and Counseling, 85*(3), e291–e298. https://doi.org/10.1016/j.pec.2011.05.014

European Commission. (n.d.). *The EU code of conduct on countering illegal hate speech online.* https://ec.europa.eu/info/policies/justice-and-fundamental-rights/combatting-discrimination/racism-and-xenophobia/eu-code-conduct-countering-illegal-hate-speech-online_en

Farnan, J. M., Snyder Sulmasy, L., Worster, B., Chaudhry, H. J., Rhyne, J. A., & Arora, V. M. (2013). Online medical professionalism: Patient and public relationships: Policy statement from the American college of physicians and the federation of state medical boards. *Annals of Internal Medicine, 158*(8), 620–627. https://doi.org/10.7326/0003-4819-158-8-201304160-00100

Fleury, I., & Dowdy, E. (2022). Social media monitoring of students for harm and threat prevention: Ethical considerations for school psychologists. *Contemporary School Psychology, 26*(3), 299–308. https://doi.org/10.1007/s40688-020-00311-y

Gil de Zúñiga, H., Diehl, T., Huber, B., & Liu, J. (2017). Personality traits and social media use in 20 countries: How personality relates to frequency of social media use, social media news use, and social media use for social interaction. *Cyberpsychology, Behavior, and Social Networking, 20*(9), 540–552. https://doi.org/10.1089/cyber.2017.0295

Gowen, K., Deschaine, M., Gruttadara, D., & Markey, D. (2012). Young adults with mental health conditions and social networking websites: Seeking tools to build community. *Psychiatric Rehabilitation Journal, 35*(3), 245–250. https://doi.org/10.2975/35.3.2012.245.250

Guntuku, S. C., Yaden, D. B., Kern, M. L., Ungar, L. H., & Eichstaedt, J. C. (2017). Detecting depression and mental illness on social media: An integrative review. *Current Opinion in Behavioral Sciences, 18*, 43–49. https://doi.org/10.1016/j.cobeha.2017.07.005

Hesse, B. W., Moser, R. P., & Rutten, L. J. (2010). Surveys of physicians and electronic health information. *New England Journal of Medicine, 362*(9), 859–860. https://doi.org/10.1056/NEJMc0909595

Househ, M., Borycki, E., & Kushniruk, A. (2014). Empowering patients through social media: The benefits and challenges. *Health Informatics Journal, 20*(1), 50–58. https://doi.org/10.1177/1460458213476969

Kern, M. L., Park, G., Eichstaedt, J. C., Schwartz, H. A., Sap, M., Smith, L. K., & Ungar, L. H. (2016). Gaining insights from social media language: Methodologies and challenges. *Psychological Methods, 21*(4), 507–525. https://doi.org/10.1037/met0000091

Kolmes, K. (2012). Social media in the future of professional psychology. *Professional Psychology: Research and Practice, 43*(6), 606–612. https://doi.org/10.1037/a0028678

Kolmes, K., & Taube, D. O. (2010). *Findings on therapist-client interactions on the Internet: Boundary considerations in cyberspace.* https://vdocuments.net/findings-on-therapist-client-interactions-on-the-internet-boundary-considerations.html

Kolmes, K., & Taube, D. O. (2011). *Summary of client-therapist encounters on the web: The client experience.* https://drkkolmes.com/research/

Kolmes, K., & Taube, D. O. (2016). Client discovery of psychotherapist personal information online. *Professional Psychology: Research and Practice, 47*(2), 147–154. https://doi.org/10.1037/pro0000065

Lawlor, A., & Kirakowski, J. (2014). Online support groups for mental health: A space for challenging self-stigma or a means of social avoidance? *Computers in Human Behavior, 32,* 152–161. https://doi.org/10.1016/j.chb.2013.11.015

Lemola, S., Perkinson-Gloor, N., Brand, S., Dewald-Kaufmann, J. F., & Grob, A. (2015). Adolescents' electronic media use at night, sleep disturbance, and depressive symptoms in the smartphone age. *Journal of Youth and Adolescence, 44*(2), 405–418. https://doi.org/10.1007/s10964-014-0176-x

Liu, M., Xue, J., Zhao, N., Wang, X., Jiao, D., & Zhu, T. (2021). Using social media to explore the consequences of domestic violence on mental health. *Journal of Interpersonal Violence, 36*(3–4), NP1965-1985NP. https://doi.org/10.1177/0886260518757756

Lober, W. B., & Flowers, J. L. (2011). Consumer empowerment in health care amid the internet and social media. *Seminars in Oncology Nursing, 27*(3), 169–182. https://doi.org/10.1016/j.soncn.2011.04.002

Lustgarten, S. D., & Elhai, J. D. (2018). Technology use in mental health practice and research: Legal and ethical risks. *Clinical Psychology: Science and Practice, 25*(2), e12234. https://doi.org/10.1111/cpsp.12234

Marino, C., Lenzi, M., Canale, N., Pierannunzio, D., Dalmasso, P., Borraccino, A., Cappello, N., Lemma, P., Vieno, A., & the 2018 HBSC-Italia Group. (2020). Problematic social media use: associations with health complaints among adolescents. *Annali Dell'Istituto Superiore Di Sanità, 56*(4), 514–521. https://doi.org/10.4415/ANN_20_04_16

Mo, P. K., & Coulson, N. S. (2010). Empowering processes in online support groups among people living with HIV/AIDS: A comparative analysis of 'lurkers' and 'posters.. *Computers in Human Behavior, 26*(5), 1183–1193. https://doi.org/10.1016/j.chb.2010.03.028

Moorhead, S. A., Hazlett, D. E., Harrison, L., Carroll, J. K., Irwin, A., & Hoving, C. (2013). A new dimension of health care: Systemic review of the uses, benefits, and limitations of social media for health care professionals. *Journal of Medical Internet Research, 15*(4), e85. https://doi.org/10.2196/jmir.1933

Naslund, J. A., Aschbrenner, K. A., Marsch, L. A., & Bartels, S. J. (2016). The future of mental health care: Peer-to-peer support and social media. *Epidemiology and Psychiatric Sciences, 25*(2), 113–122. https://doi.org/10.1017/S2045796015001067

Naslund, J. A., Bondre, A., Torous, J., & Aschbrenner, K. A. (2020). Social media and mental health: Benefits, risks, and opportunities for research and practice. *Journal of Technology in Behavioral Science, 5*, 245–257. https://doi.org/10.1007/s41347-020-00134-x

Pew Research Center. (2021, January 13). *The state of online harassment.* https://www.pewresearch.org/internet/2021/01/13/the-state-of-online-harassment/

Pirraglia, P. A., & Kravitz, R. L. (2012). Social media: New opportunities, new ethical concerns. *Journal of General Internal Medicine, 28*(2), 165–166. https://doi.org/10.1007/s11606-012-2288-x

Rafla, M., Carson, N. J., & DeJong, S. M. (2014). Adolescents and the Internet: What mental health clinicians need to know. *Current Psychiatry Reports, 16*, 472. https://doi.org/10.1007/s11920-014-0472-x

Reid, D., & Weigle, P. (2014). Social media use among adolescents: Benefits and risks. *Adolescent Psychiatry, 4*(2), 73–80. https://doi.org/10.2174/221067660402140709115810

Rideout, V., & Fox, S. (2018). *Digital health practices, social media use, and mental well-being among teens and young adults in the U.S.* https://digitalcommons.psjhealth.org/publications/1093/

Riva, G. (2017). Interrealtà: Reti fisiche, digitali e post-verità [Interreality: Physical, digital and post-truth networks]. *Il Mulino, 2*, 210–217. https://doi.org/10.1402/86030

Rossotti, R., Gabrielli, E., Gervasoni, C., Rosso, R., Sabbatini, F., Uglietti, A., Rosso, V., & Orani, A. (2012). HIV education and counselling using Facebook: A possible new approach. *Journal of Telemedicine and Telecare, 18*(4), 239–240. https://doi.org/10.1258/jtt.2012.120107

Schrank, B., Sibitz, I., Unger, A., & Amering, M. (2010). How patients with schizophrenia use the Internet: Qualitative study. *Journal of Medical Internet Research, 12*(5), e70. https://doi.org/10.2196/jmir.1550

Smailhodzic, E., Hooijsma, W., Boonstra, A., & Langley, D. J. (2016). Social media use in healthcare: A systematic review of effects on patients and on their relationship with healthcare professionals. *BMC Health Services Research, 16*(1), 442. https://doi.org/10.1186/s12913-016-1691-0

Snowdy, C. E., Shoemaker, E. Z., Chan, S., & Hilty, D. M. (2016). Social media and clinical practice: What stays the same, what changes, and how to plan ahead? In D. Mucic & D. M. Hilty (Eds.), *E-mental health* (pp. 151–170). Springer International Publishing. https://doi.org/10.1007/978-3-319-20852-7_8

Soetens, K. C. M., Vandelanotte, C., de Vries, H., & Mummery, K. W. (2014). Using online computer tailoring to promote physical activity: A randomized trial of text, video, and combined intervention delivery modes. *Journal of Health Communication, 19*(12), 1–16. https://doi.org/10.1080/10810730.2014.894597

Stoycheff, E., Liu, J., Wibowo, K. A., & Nanni, D. P. (2017). What have we learned about social media by studying Facebook? A decade in review. *New Media & Society, 19*(6), 968–980. https://doi.org/10.1177/1461444817695745

Sun, Y., & Zhang, Y. (2021). A review of theories and models applied in studies of social media addiction and implications for future research. *Addictive Behaviors, 114*, 106699. https://doi.org/10.1016/j.addbeh.2020.106699

Tunick, R. A., Mednick, L., & Conroy, C. (2011). A snapshot of child psychologists' social media activity: Professional and ethical practice implications and recommendations. *Professional Psychology: Research and Practice, 42*(6), 440–447. https://doi.org/10.1037/a0025040

Tutelman, P. R., Dol, J., Tougas, M. E., & Chambers, C. T. (2018). Navigating your social media presence: Opportunities and challenges. *Clinical Practice in Pediatric Psychology, 6*(3), 289–298. https://doi.org/10.1037/cpp0000228

Uhls, Y. T., Ellison, N. B., & Subrahmanyam, K. (2017). Benefits and costs of social media in adolescence. *Pediatrics, 140*(s2), e20161758. https://doi.org/10.1542/peds.2016-1758E

Van den Eijnden, R. J. J. M., Lemmens, J., & Valkenburg, P. M. (2016). The social media disorder scale: Validity and psychometric properties. *Computers in Human Behavior, 61*, 478–487. https://doi.org/10.1016/j.chb.2016.03.038

van Uden-Kraan, C. F., Drossaert, C. H., Taal, E., Seydel, E. R., & van de Laar, M. A. (2008). Self-reported differences in empowerment between lurkers and posters in online patient support groups. *Journal of Medical Internet Research, 10*(2), e18. https://doi.org/10.2196/jmir.992

Ventola, C. L. (2014). Social media and health care professionals: Benefits, risks, and best practices. *P&T: A Peer-Reviewed Journal for Formulary Management, 39*(7), 491–520. https://www.ncbi.nlm.nih.gov/pmc/articles/PMC4103576/

Wentzera, H. S., & Bygholm, A. (2013). Narratives of empowerment and compliance: Studies of communication in online patient support groups. *International Journal of Medical Informatics, 82*(12), e386–e394. https://doi.org/10.1016/j.ijmedinf.2013.01.008

Wong, A., Ho, S., Olusanya, O., Antonini, M. V., & Lyness, D. (2021). The use of social media and online communications in times of pandemic COVID-19. *Journal of the Intensive Care Society, 22*(3), 255–260. https://doi.org/10.1177/1751143720966280

Ziebland, S., & Wyke, S. (2012). Health and illness in a connected world: How might sharing experiences on the internet affect people's health? *Milbank Quarterly, 90*(2), 219–249. https://doi.org/10.1111/j.1468-0009.2012.00662.x

www.ingramcontent.com/pod-product-compliance
Lightning Source LLC
LaVergne TN
LVHW022044200926
848481LV00003B/776

* 9 7 9 8 8 8 7 3 0 5 9 2 9 *